A HOLY GOD REACHES DOWN

A Devotional

THOMAS R. FELLER

TREE PRESS

A Holy God Reaches Down
A Devotional

By Thomas R. Feller

ISBN 979-8-3304-9082-0

Copyright © 2024 by Thomas R. Feller

The moral right of the author and publisher has been asserted. All rights reserved. No part of this publication may be reproduced or transmitted in any form or by any means, electronic or mechanical, including photocopying, recording, or any information storage or retrieval system, without permission in writing from the author and publisher.

Verses are from New Heart English Bible and are not copyrighted. They have been dedicated to the Public Domain by the editors and translators. You may publish, copy, memorize, translate, quote, and use the New Heart English Bible freely without permission.

Cover and book design by Magdalene Pagratis

Published by Tree Press
2024

CONTENTS

INTRODUCTION 4
THE BEGINNING 7
WELCOME TO FEBRUARY 31
WELCOME TO MARCH 51
WELCOME TO APRIL 77
WELCOME TO MAY 99
WELCOME TO JUNE 124
WELCOME TO JULY 153
WELCOME TO AUGUST 183
WELCOME TO SEPTEMBER 215
WELCOME TO OCTOBER 243
WELCOME TO NOVEMBER 273
WELCOME TO DECEMBER 300
ABOUT THE AUTHOR 331
ENOCH: RECOGNIZING THE EXTRAORDINARY 333

INTRODUCTION

This project, this devotional, is not a vanity project. It is a legacy project.

Let me explain. I never knew my maternal and barely knew my paternal grandparents. As I aged, I began to wonder what these men and women whom I shared DNA with believed about life, and especially about God. Now, in my latter years, there is no one alive that can provide any detail about their lives. For that void, I'm saddened. I want to prevent that same mystery for my posterity, my grandchildren, great grandchildren, and beyond. I don't want to be just a name on a family tree. I want my descendants a hundred years from now to know about me, what I believed about life and especially about God. I want to leave a digital footprint and a physical footprint (book) that will give insight into who I was and what I believed. Hence, this devotional.

Although it will be a published book and will be available for purchase, I'm not necessarily interested in the income stream it may or may not create. My *Tree Book Series* is my commercial endeavor into writing and that, at times, has been a tenuous foray. Even so, my intent in that series was to provide a unique perspective on four key Biblical events that have forever impacted Mankind, the last one culminating in the death, burial, and resurrection of Jesus. My prayer while writing that series was for someone, anyone to understand how God was working through individuals to bring about salvation to a fallen world. Thankfully, I've heard from many readers how their interest in spiritual issues was stirred while reading the books. Some

INTRODUCTION

shared how their faith was strengthened while reading the accounts and for that I'm both grateful and thankful.

This devotional is truly a window into my soul in regard to my personal understanding about my relationship with my Creator, made possible by my Savior, Jesus. That understanding is tethered to my comprehension of the Bible. I'm not suggesting that my understanding is for everyone. It's not. I suspect many will read these devotions and find fault. My intent is not to evangelize but reveal what I believe, and I want that revelation to be brazenly clear. Yes, some entries will challenge the reader to agree or disagree, but their choice is theirs and theirs alone. Nonetheless, I'm reminded what a good friend once told me; "All inerrant theology will be corrected at death." A smile came across my face as I typed those words.

For a brief autobiography, I encourage the reader to consider the "About the Author" section found else ware in this book. It is there the reader will find sufficient information about my background, adventures, successes, and failures. To be sure, they are generalities but when the reader connects the dots they will have a fairly good idea of who I was and how I lived my life. If you are a descendant of mine, perhaps you see something familiar in that autobiography, perhaps even something haunting. Perhaps you see me in you. I suspect some of my ancestry is in me. Could it be that the strengths and weaknesses of our ancestors migrate to future generations? It's worth consideration. If you are wondering, I am seventy-eight years old as I craft this devotional.

Many of the individual devotions in this book were sent to my children, granddaughters, grandsons, and Goddaughter at the time they were written while others have been shared with friends. Some are brief, just the scripture reference with a challenge, some are doctrinal in nature and lengthy, some are multi-day, some scriptures have more than one devotion, some are lighthearted, some are reflective, some are challenging, some are controversial, some are only a reiteration of the facts presented in the passage, but all are meant to engage the reader. You will undoubtedly notice that at the end of many devotions a pertinent prayer is included. At the end of others there is a suggestion to do something I believe will enrich your day. I suspect many of those will be criticized for their frivolity.

Just a few more things. I asked my youngest son, Tom Jr., to collaborate with me on this project. Devotions that are authored by him are designated with an asterisk (*) immediately following the date. Also, at the end of the devotional there is a short story written in the genre of the Tree Books.

THE BEGINNING

January 1

"In the beginning God created the heavens and the earth. Now the earth was formless and empty, and darkness was on the surface of the watery depths. And God's Spirit was hovering over the surface of the waters."
Genesis 1:1, 2

✝ ✝ ✝

There is a beginning to all things, even planet earth. Imagine total darkness and a formless planet. Imagine no greenery, birds, animals, or humans. Imagine no sun, moon, stars, sound, smells, or movement of any kind. Imagine utter silence and stillness. This was the earth before God finished His creative work.

I remember exploring a cave in Missouri with a friend. After crawling on our belly through a long narrow shaft we came into generous room filled with stalagmites and stalactites. It was amazing. We then decided to extinguish our carbon lights and suddenly we were standing in TOTAL darkness and silence. I could not even see my hand in front of my face. It was actually quite frightening and truthfully, I was glad to return to the surface.

Sometimes our life circumstances are analogous to the darkness I experienced in that cave. The strange beauty of the cave and the world at large was still there, I just could not see it. I have been in many pitch black "caves" in my life, but thankfully God has always brought me back to the surface and to the light.

One day He will take His children to a place where the light will always be shining, where there will be no darkness. I suspect, dear reader, that you may, at times, feel like you are in a cave without any light. I can assure you that you have a bright future, a future where there will be no sickness, anxiety, pain, or bad behavior. A future where love will not just be a word, it will be the reality of everyday life. Until that day comes let us be the light for others who may be in the "cave" of unbelief.

Today is the first day of a brand new year. Enjoy it while looking forward to God working out His perfect plan for your life.

January 2

> "Blessed be the God and Father of our Lord Jesus Christ, the Father of mercies and God of all comfort; who comforts us in all our affliction, that we may be able to comfort those who are in any affliction, through the comfort with which we ourselves are comforted by God."
> II Corinthians 1:3, 4

☩ ☩ ☩

These verses help us understand the difficult times in our lives. They have a God given purpose and that purpose is to comfort others who are experiencing similar circumstances. It is so much easier for us to understand the pain others are feeling when we have felt that same pain ourselves. We understand the comfort they need. Is that fair? Perhaps not, but it is a privilege that God has entrusted to the believer!

Be brave in Him today. He loves you more than you can truly understand.

January 3

"Direct me in the path of your commandments, for I delight in them."
Psalms 119:35

Elsewhere in the Bible the Psalmist says that he is led into the PATH of righteousness. Jesus talks about entering through a narrow gate that leads to life. Solomon writes about the various TIMES that we experience in our lives. The point is that our earthly life is a JOURNEY that starts at birth and ends at physical death. But where are we going on that journey? Do we just live day to day knowing that someday our life will end, much like treading water, staying afloat but never going anywhere? Does our journey in this life have a destination? Are we meant to pass over some invisible bridge and enter eternity? And then what?

Jesus told a man being crucified next to Him that the man would be in Paradise that very day. Obviously, this would occur AFTER his physical death. Jesus also warns of an AWFUL place where some people will spend eternity. Yes, we are all on a journey that will lead to one or the other. Think about it: did you ever decide to go on a trip without a destination in mind? But that is exactly what billions of people are doing this very moment. They are living life without ever considering where their journey in this life will culminate.

We can tell them about eternity and how to enter heaven by sharing the Gospel with them. Some will listen and believe the

Gospel while others will reject it. Rejoice with those who accept and pray for those who reject; it is what Jesus would do.

January 4

"But now faith, hope, and love remain—these three. The greatest of these is love."
I Corinthians 13:13

†††

I saw this sign today and it made me chuckle. "Would be a lot easier if my therapist could just shadow me for a day." As humorous as that sounds it is exactly how I feel about God some days. If only He knew what I was experiencing, thinking, and feeling, if only He would shadow me for a day. But then I come to my senses and remember the promise that Jesus makes to believers. He promises to never leave or forsake them and that includes ME.

If a person has been born again, Jesus is present by virtue of the Holy Spirit. The believer may feel lonely, but they are never alone.

Jesus, I pray that you would give me a keen awareness of your presence in my life.

January 5

And Jesus said, "Father, forgive them, for they do not know what they are doing."
Luke 23:34

†††

This is one of seven times that Jesus spoke when nailed to His Cross. It may very well be the first of the seven. Exactly who He is asking to be forgiven is a matter of speculation. Was it the executioners, was it Pilate who authorized the crucifixion, was it the Jewish leaders who plotted His death, or was it everyone who had planned and participated? What we can be sure of is that Jesus considers them to be ignorant of facts surrounding His execution. They really did NOT know what they were doing.

Unfortunately, MY prayer is, "Forgive me, Father, because I DO know what I am doing." It is true that most every sin I ask to be forgiven of is one that I KNOW to be sin. I cannot feign ignorance. It is God's forgiveness that demonstrates the incomparability and magnificence of God's grace, and it is all connected to the death, burial, and resurrection of Jesus. Is it any wonder why millions of people gather to worship Him in every part of the earth? The problem is that millions more do not. They stubbornly refuse to avail themselves of God's grace. Let us be faithful in praying for those who have yet to see the bright light of the Gospel. Jesus wants no one to be left behind and neither should we.

January 6

"The LORD is my shepherd; I lack nothing. He makes me lie down in green pastures; He leads me beside still waters."
Psalms 23:1, 2

† † †

Peace, especially personal peace seems so elusive at times. I am so glad and grateful we have a Heavenly Father who WANTS us to have peace in our lives? He is always leading us in that direction. He gives believers His Holy Spirit, prayer to both talk with and listen to God, the Bible to gain wisdom and knowledge of Him, and fellow believers to help us in life's journey. Think about it: is there any benefit to have disruption or hostility in your earthly family? The same is true for God's family on earth. The problem is we often want to go in another direction, our OWN direction. It's our choice to follow Him or take our own path. I pray you and I will choose to follow Him today. It is the best path.

Watch children play today. It will bring a smile to your heart.

January 7

"The LORD's faithful love does not cease; his compassion does not fail. They are new every morning; great is your faithfulness."
Lamentations 3:22, 23

†††

As this new day unfolds, I pray your spirit will rejoice in what your eyes behold. Perhaps a cloud, a child playing, a bird in flight, or a butterfly flittering. These are all gifts from God. And just like these things are gifts, so, too, are you a gift to the world. Everyone has the potential to bless others, but not everyone chooses to do so.

Father, help me to be a blessing to others today. Help me to be a blessing to You today.

January 8

"Even so, I tell you, there is joy in the presence of the angels of God over one sinner repenting."
Luke 15:10

†††

This is a remarkable claim that could only be made by someone who has actually seen this occur. Elsewhere in the Gospels, Jesus reveals that He came from heaven so this revelation about the activities of angels is not surprising to readers of Matthew, Mark, Luke, or John. After all, Jesus has first person knowledge of such things.

The only question is if we believe Him or not. Do we accept His words as literal, or do we view them as metaphorical? If literal, and it is a claim I believe to be literal, then at the time of my becoming a believer and follower of Jesus there was a celebration among angels, and if a celebration occurred for me, then it is true for every repentant sinner. Take a few minutes to consider how significant this is; angels celebrating individuals on planet earth, angels celebrating YOUR spiritual rebirth. Suddenly heaven on earth is real.

But there is another group of angels, fallen angels expelled from heaven along with their leader, Satan. There was no celebration in that group, only anger and disgust that another soul had been snatched from the eventual fires of hell. So, the next time they come knocking on the door of your heart, pay them no attention. One sure fire way to determine good inspiration from bad is this: does it draw you to the Cross of Jesus or push you away from that Cross? Does it build you up or tear you down? One you run toward and from the other you flee!

January 9

> "If a wise man goes to court with a foolish man, the fool rages or scoffs, and there is no peace."
> Proverbs 29:9

Life is way too short to spend time contending with a fool, be it a man or a woman. Bless them, go on your way and ask God to show them the truth about life. Remember that Jesus died for them just like

He died for you. I recall with precision the day I surrendered my life to Him and trusted His sacrifice to cleanse me from my sins. In that moment I was given NEW life, and I am forever grateful for God's redemption of my soul. I can with authority say that I was once a fool, but God rescued me from unbelief and foolishness. Join me is praying for those who have yet to surrender their foolishness and unbelief to their Creator.

Tell someone you love them today. Better yet, SHOW someone you love them today. It will be well for their soul and yours to do so.

January 10

"Let the words of my mouth and the meditation of my heart be acceptable in your sight always, LORD, my rock and my redeemer."
Psalms 19:14

†††

Today we will speak many words and our hearts will consider many things. I pray those words and thoughts will be pleasing to our Heavenly Father. I pray our words will be encouraging to others, and our thoughts would inspire us to acts of love and mercy toward all that we come in contact with today.

Our body may be frail, but our spirit is bold and always being strengthened by the Creator of all things seen and unseen. He loves us more than we can possibly understand.

Listen to a bird sing today. God has sent that bird especially for you.

January 11

> "But Jesus said, "Leave her alone. Why do you trouble her? She has done a good work for me. For you always have the poor with you, and whenever you want to, you can do them good; but you will not always have me."
> Mark 14:6, 7

† † †

On this occasion Jesus is rebuking people who had criticized a woman for anointing Him with a costly oil. The critics protested that the oil should have been sold and the proceeds given to the poor. In normal circumstances perhaps their claim would have been valid but there is no normality in Jesus. He was, after all, the Son of God, the King of kings and the Lord of lords. Her gesture was most appropriate.

In His response, Jesus points out that they (and us) will ALWAYS have the poor with them and will ALWAYS have opportunity to reach out to them. I wonder how many of them helped a person in need that very day? Of course, that is the challenge for you and I today. Poor people are everywhere, poor in spirit and poor in resources. Let us look for opportunities to minister to the poor while also following this woman's example of worshipping Jesus.

January 12

> "Trust in the LORD with all your heart, and do not lean on your own understanding. In all your ways remember him, and he will make your paths straight. Do not be wise in your own eyes. Fear the LORD, and depart from evil. It will be health to your body, and nourishment to your bones."
> Proverbs 3:5-8

† † †

There are so many things the world offers for us to place our trust in; ourselves, money, the government, and people are just a few. Sadly, these things are not immune from failure and often fail spectacularly when we need them most. There is, however, ONE that will never fail or leave us - Jesus. He has promised to never leave or forsake us (Matt 28:20). Trust Him for this life and the next.

Enjoy the wind today. It is a reminder of the ever-changing nature of life. Someone once said, "Time is like a circus, always packing up and moving away." Enjoy each minute for once they are lived, they are gone forever!

January 13

"One who is greedy stirs up strife; but one who trusts in the LORD will prosper. One who trusts in himself is a fool; but one who walks in wisdom is kept safe."
Proverbs 28:25, 26

† † †

How many times have you heard or said, "trust your heart?" I have seen or heard that sentiment expressed in movies, songs, and literature, but is our heart trustworthy? The Prophet Jeremiah, inspired by God says, "The heart is deceitful above all things, and desperately wicked; who can know it?" That does not sound reliable to me. There will come a time when our heart will be absolutely reliable, but not today. Today it struggles with conflicting influence from the Holy Spirit and the world. Sometimes we are completely in sync on one side or the other while at other times we think we can amalgamate the two. Amalgamating God's principles with the World's principles is a fool's errand.

The point is we need a sure guide to lead us in life. Mariners use the North Star to navigate the world because it is reliable, it is fixed in the sky relative to the movement of the earth. But where will we find a spiritual "North Star" to guide and instruct us? God's precious book, the Bible, can be trusted to lead us in ways that will result in a life well lived. Because God created the North Star as a witness of reliability for the physical world, we can trust His Word to be even more reliable as it transcends the physical by revealing the spiritual. Now that is something to think about!

January 14

"Watch and pray, that you may not enter into temptation. The spirit indeed is willing, but the flesh is weak."
Mark 14:38

Two truths emerge from this verse. First, prayer is a powerful deterrent to temptation. Second, we should put no confidence in the flesh. Knowing this, one would think that we would spend more time in prayer and be aware of the weakness of the flesh, but this is rarely the response. Our flesh wants to dominate our lives, it wants to be in control and often is just that. Is it because it is tangible while our spirit is not? Is it because prayer leads us away from the things of this world, and we are fond or even in love with those things? Is it because we have been disappointed in previous prayer requests and consider them powerless? Is it because we are convinced that we have the wherewithal to craft and manage our own lives? Perhaps.

King Solomon once remarked, "There is nothing new under the sun." He was right then, and those words ring true to this very day. The words that Jesus spoke in this verse are as true today as the day they were first uttered. Let us not ignore these truths.

Happy birthday to my daughter today!

January 15

"There is one body, and one Spirit, even as you also were called in one hope of your calling; one God and Father of all, who is over all, and through all, and in all."
Ephesians 4:4, 6

† † †

Notice that are an equal number of the words "one" and "all" in these verses. That indicates something both unique and all-encompassing is being revealed. So how do we synthesize the two? We cannot because they are mutually exclusive, but today, society demands "all" rather than "one" be the priority. Loud voices everywhere proclaim that the oneness of truth is wrong, that truth is somehow subjective or situational. Ironically, they argue for the very thing they oppose—oneness, advocating THEIR oneness being superior to all others.

Their argument is hopelessly flawed. Scientific laws like thermodynamics demand an absolute, an unconditional truth. Gravity is an absolute and undisputed truth, it is singular. Yes, a person could defy it by simply jumping up but, nonetheless, it is a certainty that gravity will prevail. And so it is with God, there is only ONE true God while EVERYTHING else is created and subject to the Creator. When we personally maintain that truth in our mind and hearts, we will always maintain a correct perspective on life, both physical and spiritual.

Father, remind me daily that I am not God.

January 16

"There is gold and abundance of rubies; but the lips of knowledge are a rare jewel."
Proverbs 20:15

✝ ✝ ✝

Gold and precious jewels were most likely the currency of the day when this Proverb was written, but in our economy, it is dollars and cents. Still, the principle holds true. The author of this Proverb realized that knowledge is more precious than money and those who SPEAK wisely are a precious and valued commodity. The reference here is to those who speak with knowledge of God and how our lives relate and are dependent on Him, and not just for life on planet earth but for eternity.

It is always refreshing to be around people who are able to knowledgably speak of God's will for us, and especially refreshing if they are actually fleshing out their words. Jesus did both while with us in His time of ministry on earth. Can people say that about you and me? What do they hear from our lips and what do they see in our behavior. Here's the point; they are listening, and they are watching. Beyond that, so is God

January 17

"Praise the LORD, my soul, and all that is within me, praise his holy name."
Psalms 103:1

† † †

Usually, we ask God to bless us, and it is His good pleasure to do so, but did you know that we can bless Him? It is true, and it can be one of our greatest joys. However, how can we, mere mortals, bless the Creator of all things? How can we who are prone to disobedience and selfishness bless a holy and righteous God? When we BELIEVE and TRUST Him, we bless Him. When we do not call Him a liar. To that end, there is only one way to discover what He has said about us and about Him. We discover those things by reading the Bible. Take time today to read and believe what He has revealed in His precious Word. Be a blessing to Him today.

Eat your FAVORITE meal today. You will not be disappointed in doing so.

January 18

"Great is our Lord, and mighty in power. His understanding is infinite. The LORD upholds the humble. He brings the wicked down to the ground."
Psalms 147:5, 6

† † †

Some people think that God is just a myth, that He exists only in the imagination of believers. The people of Noah's day felt that way as they ignored God's call to abandon their bad behavior and enjoy fellowship with Him. Sadly, all but Noah and his family escaped the judgment of God and perished in the Flood. God is still calling for people to turn from wickedness and come to the Cross of Jesus for forgiveness. He has made a way for us to escape the coming judgment. He has provided that escape because He loves us and wants us to spend eternity with Him. Let's take every opportunity we have to share that good news with others.

Pray that today will be an exceptional day, filled with good health and happy thoughts. Enjoy the many shades of the color green today. They are a gift from your Heavenly Father.

January 19

"Turn my eyes away from looking at worthless things. Revive me in your ways."
Psalms 119:37

† † †

Our eyes will see many things today, some worthwhile and some worthless. Pray that God will give you the ability to discern between the two. What we see often influences our behavior. I pray your eyes will be blessed with worthwhile visions today.

Reading the Bible is a good place to start. Your eyes will see worthwhile things!

January 20

"And if I go and prepare a place for you, I will come again, and will receive you to myself; that where I am, you may be there also." (Jesus speaking)
John 14:3

† † †

At times, I am disappointed and frustrated with events that occur in the world, whether near-by or far away. It seems like bad things continue to recycle themselves over and over again. But then I remember the promise of Jesus, and my heart rejoices that one day I will be free of my bondage to life on planet earth. That is why I continue to tell others that they too can enjoy an eternity in heaven by trusting Jesus for forgiveness and reconciliation to their Creator. Sadly, many reject the offer and choose to live as if there are no consequences to bad behavior. Nonetheless, I continue to present the offer and pray for their souls.

I do not know how this day will unfold for my life today. No one does. But one thing is for certain, our eternity in heaven has been secured by Jesus and no thing or person can change that. Let us pray for those who do not know about Him, that they too will enjoy the peace of knowing where they will spend eternity.

I hope you see a butterfly today. They are remarkable.

January 21

"Rejoice with those who rejoice. Weep with those who weep."
Romans 12:15

† † †

Life, at times, can be overwhelming and complicated, especially when we are stricken with a serious medical condition or personal tragedy. That is the bad news.

Perhaps you are experiencing a crisis, medical or otherwise this very day. But like all things in life, there is more to your story. If you choose to do so, God will use you to share His love with others. You may very well come in contact with people in crisis, people you would never have met except for your own crisis. Doctors, nurses, clinical technicians, and most of all, patients may all in your orbit this very day. God can use you to minister to people who may have no one else in their life to pray for them.

Look for opportunities to both rejoice and weep for others today. They are all around us.

January 22

"I can do all things through him who strengthens me."
Philippians 4:13

Those words, penned by the Apostle Paul, rang true in his life. He faced enormous challenges and hardships as he preached Jesus to the men and women of his time. He understood he was unable to do so in his own strength, he needed something greater than himself. He needed Jesus! You and I, dear reader, have that same need. Let us be sure we look to Him for strength to negotiate this new day. He will surely give us all we need.

As I write this, I hear the birds singing. I hope you hear a bird sing today. It is lovely music.

January 23

"The secret things belong to the LORD our God; but the things that are revealed belong to us and to our children forever, that we may do all the words of this law."
Deuteronomy 29:29

I do not necessarily like secrets. There are, however, some things the Lord keeps to Himself. Because we are finite, there are things we simply are unable to understand. Because our thinking is restricted to time and space, we are puzzled by infinity, by eternity. Because we do not know the future, we are restricted to experiencing the present. Thankfully, God does not have those restrictions. But our restrictions do not prevent God from revealing what is necessary to live a life that reflects His character and will. He has provided everything we need to know about Him and us in His Word, and He has given us His Holy Spirit to correctly discern His Word. I encourage you to take time today to explore this marvelous resource.

Consider the complexity and beauty of a flower and enjoy the miracle of fragrance. Our prayers are a pleasant fragrance to God.

January 24

"Let a bear robbed of her cubs meet a man, rather than a fool in his folly."
Proverbs17:12

†††

At first reading this Proverb may seem humorous. It is not, the message is sobering. Getting between a mother bear and her cubs will likely result in the violent death of the human. The outcome would be tragic. The Biblical definition of a fool is someone who says in their heart "there is no God" (Ps 14:1). Sadly, history is full of men and women who believed there would be no consequence for their outrageous behavior. In some cases that behavior resulted in the death of millions of people. When in the company of a fool be gracious, but be cautious, very cautious, lest you be swayed by the fool's misguided understanding of life. If possible, share Jesus with the person. At the very least, pray for that person's soul, it is precious and redeemable by trusting Jesus for forgiveness.

Today is new, fresh, and filled with possibilities. Let us keep our eyes and ears wide open to see and hear whatever comes into our lives, good or bad. Let us determine to rejoice in the good and mediate the bad.

I saw a bird in flight this morning and marveled at the phenomenon of flight. Perhaps you, too, will see a phenomenon today. If you struggle to identify one, just look in a mirror and you will see a one-of-a-kind phenomenon!

January 25

"But the LORD said to Samuel, "Do not look on his face, or on the height of his stature; because I have rejected him. For man does not see as God sees, for man looks at the outward appearance, but God looks at the heart."
I Samuel 16:7

✝ ✝ ✝

When evaluating a person, the Lord uses a different metric than we do. He looks at our hearts. As our Creator, He, and only He, has the ability to do so. There is only one other that knows my heart, and that person is me. Sometimes I am ashamed of what is in my heart, and it is in those times that I ask forgiveness for things I can only hope will never happen yet are still in my heart. I still desire them. But then I am reminded it is exactly those very thoughts and desires why it was necessary for Jesus to die on my behalf, to take my punishment for a corrupt nature. And when I finally accepted that His death and resurrection was necessary for me personally, I was given new life. Not just another chance, but a brand-new life. Sadly, sometimes the old Tom resurfaces, but always under the auspices and control of the Holy Spirit. Thankfully the old me is no longer in control.

I pray your heart will embrace Godly thoughts and behavior today. I pray you will share the love of Jesus with others today. I pray you will experience a peace that passes all understanding today.

January 26

"And we know that all things work together for good for those who love God, to those who are called according to his purpose."
Romans 8:28

† † †

Sometimes this verse can pose a challenge and even a dilemma for people. Death of a loved one, sickness, chronic illness, loss of employment, an unfaithful spouse, a rebellious son or daughter, war, and so many other life tragedies and crisis' can be devastating. So how can we reconcile this verse to accommodate the oft times complexities of life? We cannot explain away these things - no one can. The answers lie in eternity and until we arrive there we are called to live by faith. Faith that our Heavenly Father has a unique plan for our lives and is always working on our behalf. Whatever this day or tomorrow may bring He has promised to be with us. Trust Him.

Talk with your best friend today. They understand you.

January 27

"I have told you these things, that in me you may have peace. In the world you have oppression; but cheer up. I have overcome the world."
John 16:33

† † †

    I thought of this verse last night while reading a recent note from a sick friend. Jesus was acquainted with sorrow and tribulation. He felt pain, cried at the tomb of a friend, was rejected by men and women, and crucified for telling the truth about who he was. He has the authority and credibility to speak the words of today's verse. He knows of our struggles, doubts, and fears. He really has overcome the world.

    I pray, dear reader, that you will have normality in your life today. I pray that any physical or mental issue will be resolved and that you will have inexplicable joy in your heart and countenance.

    Enjoy sunshine on your face today. Think of it as God's love falling on you.

January 28

"Every way of a man is right in his own eyes, but the LORD weighs the hearts."
Proverbs 21:2

† † †

    Without an absolute we are left to ourselves to decide what is right and what is wrong. We become masters of the universe. Fortunately, the One who created us has given us that absolute, He has revealed absolute truth to us in His Word, the BIBLE. Sadly, many people reject His absolute for their own. They live their lives convinced there will be no eternal consequences. They are wrong and one day will experience frightening consequences.

    But it does not have to be that way. God has provided a Savior in the person of Jesus. When we surrender our lives to Him, we will receive a new heart that will embrace the ABSOLUTES of the Bible. We receive forgiveness and the comfort that our eternity will be in His presence and loving care.

As this new day unfolds, I pray, dear reader, that your heart will be filled with love for your Creator and for people, especially people that you encounter today. Consider the miracle of thought today. Unlike the animals who live by instincts, we have the ability to consider and choose, we have the ability to dream, to write books, create music, draw and paint pictures, plant and harvest crops, and determine how we want to live our lives, and so much more.

January 29

Do you ever wonder what God would say if you had an opportunity to personally visit with Him. What would He say about this or about that? If so, consider what Jesus says in this verse:

> Jesus said to him, "Have I been with you all this time, and still you do not know me, Philip? He who has seen me has seen the Father. How can you say, 'Show us the Father?'
> John 14:9

✝ ✝ ✝

We really do not have to wonder what God would say about the issues of life. In Jesus, He lived a life on earth. He experienced it all, the good and the bad. Like us, He, too, was tempted to be anthropocentric rather than theocentric. All His comments and teachings are recorded in the Gospels. Our responses to His teaching range from "I like and agree with that" to "No way, I don't think so." But that is what makes them a two-edged sword. We will never be able to stand before Him and say that He did not warn us. He will simply point to a teaching of Jesus, and we will have no defense of our bad behavior. We might even claim that we never read that verse. His response, "Who's fault is that?" Let's make it a goal to be familiar with the Gospels and therefore familiar with His Will for our lives. It is a noble goal!

I petted a dog yesterday and it was wonderful. I looked into her eyes and saw a wonderful creation of God. Her eyes were full of life. Perhaps you will have an opportunity to pet an animal today. I think you will appreciate it.

January 30

"And I will also give you a new heart, and I will put a new spirit within you. And I will take away the stony heart out of your flesh, and I will give you a heart of flesh. I will put my Spirit within you, and cause you to walk in my statutes, and you shall keep my ordinances, and do them."
Ezekiel 36:26, 27

† † †

Do you know anyone who needs to hear this promise from God today? If so, do not wait to tell them. Tomorrow may be too late for you or them.

Encourage a stranger today. They could very well be your next friend.

January 31

"Which one of you, if you had one hundred sheep, and lost one of them, would not leave the ninety-nine in the wilderness, and go after the one that was lost, until he found it?
Luke 15:4

†††

In this verse we find our marching orders from God. He never gives up on the lost and expects us to do the same. I am forever grateful that He never gave up on me. Without that tenacity, I would have been doomed to an eternity in hell. Let us do for others what He has done for us by sharing His love to those who are separated from the forgiveness of the Cross of Jesus.

Enjoy the sunset this evening knowing the certainty of its rising tomorrow morning. God's love is more certain than that!

WELCOME TO FEBRUARY

"Come to me, all you who labor and are heavily burdened, and I will give you rest."
Matthew 11:28

February 1

"Blessed is the man who makes the LORD his trust, and doesn't respect the proud, nor such as turn aside to lies."
Psalm 40:4

☦ ☦ ☦

It is a brand-new day! Possibilities abound. How will you and I use it? Let us look for opportunities to share God's love with others today, family, friends, and even strangers. Let us look beyond ourselves and trust Him to show us where the need for love and forgiveness is greatest.

Do you want to be blessed today? Read the verse again to find out how.

February 2

"in hope of everlasting life, which God, who cannot lie, promised before time began"
Titus 1:2

☦ ☦ ☦

One reason we may have difficulty in believing what God says is because we are often skeptical of what PEOPLE say. Who among us has not lied or been the victim of a lie? It is this culture of lies and bending the truth in which we live that has fostered our rightful skepticism. Deception is everywhere. Consequently, we find it extremely difficult or even impossible to believe that someone, even God, cannot lie, but in this verse the Apostle Paul, by inspiration of the Holy Spirit, declares that God CANNOT lie. Nonetheless, we remain skeptical.

Fortunately, there is a SOLUTION to this dilemma; we can be rescued from skepticism by FAITH. When God told Abraham that his descendants would be as numerous as the stars in the sky, by faith Abraham believed God even though he had no children when this exchange took place. Beyond that, who could reasonably expect to have such an outrageous number of descendants? We are called to have that same kind of faith when asked to BELIEVE that a man claiming to be the Son of God dying on a Cross thousands of years ago can determine where we will spend eternity.

Sadly, there is a probability that once again we will lie and be lied to, but NEVER by God. One last thought; because Jesus is God incarnate, He also cannot lie. EVERY word He said is absolute truth. It would be well with our soul if we believed this unconditionally.

February 3

A number of years ago a friend came to me and asked for advice on how he might develop a hunger for God's word, the Bible. I encouraged him to ask God for that desire because only He can give us that desire and furthermore, He WANTS to give us that desire. Still, he sought my advice, so I encouraged my friend to read a chapter of Proverbs every morning along with a Psalm. Proverbs has thirty-one chapters so we can easily read the chapter that corresponds with the date of the month. I shared with my friend that I always start my daily devotions by first reading a chapter of this book of wisdom. Perhaps you too will find value in adding a daily reading of Proverbs to your devotions.

I pray you and your family will experience SHALOM today, peace of mind, body, and soul. I pray you will experience love, both inbound and outbound today.

February 4

"For I am not ashamed of the Good News, for it is the power of God for salvation for everyone who believes . . ."
Romans 1:16

†††

Many times when people consider the power of God, they think only of His ability to create the world, the heavens, or move mountains. To be sure, He is capable of doing such things as evidenced by planet earth and the solar system. The power the Holy Spirit references in this verse, however, is the power to save His most prized creation, *people*. The Good News referred in this verse is the Gospel; the death, burial, and resurrection of Jesus. But what do we need to be saved from, some might ask? The answer is both simple and profound. The answer is eternal separation from a Holy God. Physical death is not the end of a person, as some believe. The spirit and soul of the person is eternal and lives on. The Bible reveals there will come a time when our dead bodies will be reunited with our soul and spirit and stand before God for the final judgement of our life. Faith in the Gospel provides the righteousness that will save us from God banishing us to eternity in hell. That power is greater than any other God possesses. It is the power of love; Jesus, God's Son dying on a Roman Cross to pay the penalty for our sin.

Billions of people will miss out on eternal life in heaven because they rejected the Good News. Do not be one of them!

February 5

"There comes a point in the journey of faith when you become okay not knowing what you're not meant to know. We continually seek to know God more, knowing that He can't be fully known this side of Heaven." -Billy Graham

Because we are restricted to time and space it is impossible to fully understand infinity and eternity. Our minds will not allow for it. Because God has no such limitations, He is able to know the future. He knows the future as certain as we know the present. Because that is true, we can have confidence in His promises about OUR future. God's promises will all be fulfilled, both the sublime and the frightening. Let us be sure we are included in the sublime. He has told us how in the Bible.

February 6

"This is the end of the matter. All has been heard. Fear God, and keep his commandments; for this is the whole duty of man."
Ecclesiastes 12:13

In Ecclesiastes, Solomon gives an accounting of all the pursuits of his life. The man apparently was bent on experiencing it all. I think most of us have similar aspirations, I know I did. It is difficult to corral youthful enthusiasm and lust. In the end, however, Solomon comes to his senses and realizes what will bring him true and lasting satisfaction. Sadly, there are those that will live their entire lives and never realize the joy of knowing their Creator intimately. I am grateful that God is rescuing many of these souls and has given US opportunities to share the "Way" with others. Most importantly, let each of us be certain we embrace the conclusion that Solomon reveals in this verse.

Make a funny face in a mirror today. It will make you laugh.

February 7

"The LORD is my shepherd; I lack nothing"
Psalms 23:1

In this verse the Psalmist reveals one of the great secrets to a joyful life - contentment. Too often our hearts yearn for what we do not have instead of enjoying what is ours at the moment. We ignore the blessings of a relationship with our Creator, family and friends, the beauty of nature, and love. Let us appreciate what we have and not waste time and energy thinking about what we want. Ask God for the things we want and leave that request and desire with Him. He will give us what we need, not necessarily what we want.

Father, help me to be content to be in your will for my life.

February 8

"Hatred stirs up strife, but love covers all wrongs."
Proverbs 10:12

† † †

I am so grateful that our God is not a God of hate but rather a God of love. Hate is easy, love takes effort to rightly accomplish. Love requires commitment, self-sacrifice, and surrender. Because His Spirit now lives in me, I also am called to be a person who shares God's love with others, but not only His love but mine also. I sometimes fail, but, nonetheless, that is my mission.

Father, help me to fulfill my mission today. Give me both the desire and ability to do so.

February 9

Jesus therefore said to those Judeans who had believed him, "If you remain in my word, then you are truly my disciples. You will know the truth, and the truth will make you free."
John 8:31, 32

† † †

In our present culture, we are often told that there is no such thing as absolute TRUTH, what is true for one may not be true for all. We are told that truth can be situational or subjective. Those who advance this notion are calling Jesus a liar. But, just like gravity is true and undisputed for every person on planet earth, God's word, the Bible, reigns supreme as truth. Do not be tempted to abandon truth for the lies of the evil one. Remember, it was Satan who challenged Eve to question the truth of what God prohibited in the Garden of Eden. Bad outcome, to be sure!

Dear reader, let us enjoy this new day, it may be our LAST one on planet earth.

February 10

"Be therefore imitators of God, as beloved children."
Ephesians 5:1

† † †

When we are born again, we become a full-fledged child of God. I remember, as a child, I imagined myself a cowboy or sometimes a soldier. My friends and I would dress appropriately and play the part, imitating our character the best we knew how. It was fun imitating someone I admired.

Now, however, I am called to imitate God, but how do I do that? Because the Bible reveals God's character, and also tells us that His Spirit lives in us to guide us, I have no excuse not to imitate my Heavenly Father. It becomes a choice, my choice. I am not always successful, but it is my goal. Think about the implications of being an imitator of God. It is a huge responsibility and privilege. Some will argue that they just want to be free to be who they want to be. Think how devastating it would be for a child to grow up without any guidance. It is far better to have the guidance of a loving and holy Father to guide and inspire us. Who is better to craft our lives and who is better to imitate?

I pray as this day unfolds you too will imitate God in your thoughts, speech, and actions. It really is a choice.

February 11

"Let no one deceive himself. If anyone thinks that he is wise among you in this age, let him become a fool, that he may become wise. For the wisdom of this world is foolishness with God. For it is written, "He traps the wise in their craftiness."
I Corinthians 3:18, 19

† † †

We live in a postmodern world, meaning truth and reality are now individually determined, not bound by previous cultural beliefs and norms. One out cropping of postmodernism is that our culture is moving away from belief in God, and specifically the gospel (good news) of forgiveness and redemption of the Cross of Jesus. Enlightenment is the mantra of the postmodernist. Human reason and intellect reign supreme in the eyes of many. Faith has been replaced by knowledge.

God, however, views the wisdom of this world as foolishness. Why? Because God is omniscient, meaning He knows everything there is to know about everything there is to know, past, present, and future. God never discovers anything, He already knows. Man is limited to the past and the present, and then only provisionally. Even collectively, we will never know everything that has ever occurred everywhere and will never fully know every motive of every person.

For reasons only God knows, we have been born in this season of Man and live in our American culture. Let us be certain we do not get caught in the net of postmodernism. Further, let us exercise humility as we share the wisdom of God with others. We will be blessed when we do.

I listened to crickets last night and marveled at their chorus. We really do live in a spectacular creation! And it would not be the same without you, dear reader.

Happy birthday to my son today!

February 12

"I have told you these things, that in me you may have peace. In the world you have oppression; but cheer up. I have overcome the world."
John 16:33

The world defines peace as the absence of conflict, but Jesus promises peace in the midst of conflict. How can this be possible? Jesus promises believers eternal life and when we focus on eternity and not on the temporal, suddenly the troubles of this world begin to fade away. When we focus on eternity, we begin to grasp the temporary nature of our lives and consequently begin to see our struggles as temporary. Let us keep our eyes and hearts focused on the longest perspective of life, eternity.

Today I visited friends and once again was reminded how precious, good friends, can be. Like most good things in life, however, we tend to not appreciate them until they are no longer available. It is often in that void when we come to realize how very special was the thing or person that we carelessly took for granted. I hope you realize the precious things and people in your life before they are gone. You, dear reader, are precious and appreciated and are in my prayers.

February 13

"Truly I tell you, among those who are born of women there has not arisen anyone greater than John the Baptist; yet he who is least in the kingdom of heaven is greater than he."
Matthew 11:11

†††

This verse humbles me each time I read it. Why? John the Baptist rightly "earned" his status by obedience, living an austere and dedicated life that ended in a violent death orchestrated by a wicked woman and her daughter. By worldly standards, John deserved the commendation of Jesus.

Conversely, I enjoy my underserved elevated status by living in the shadow of the Cross of Jesus. His violent death was in my stead. It should have been me on that Cross. I enjoy my status because of Grace alone and I am so very grateful to and for a loving Creator, and now, Heavenly Father. How about you?

Enjoy your elevated status today. Consider how much God loves you, and how Jesus took your place on the Cross so you could be forgiven of offenses against God. It really is amazing Grace!

February 14

"Pleasant words are a honeycomb, sweet to the soul, and health to the bones."
Proverbs 16:24

†††

I have found that it is just as easy to speak pleasant words than angry or combative words. Those pleasant words also have a lot better outcome in my life and in the lives of others. My lips are moving no matter what I say so I might as well direct them rightly. How about you?

Gaze at your favorite color today. Colors are a gift from our Creator.

February 15

"Now when he was in Jerusalem at the Passover, during the feast, many believed in his name after seeing his signs which he did. 24But Jesus did not trust himself to them, because he knew everyone, and because he did not need anyone to testify concerning man; 25for he himself knew what was in man."
John 2:23-25

✝ ✝ ✝

Hello, precious reader. Hmmm, what do you think Jesus knew (verse 25)? Think about this and WRITE down your thoughts. Be thorough, asking God to reveal the meaning of this verse. This can be a great learning experience. Do you think it would a good thing to know what Jesus knew in this regard? How helpful would that be?

Pray today. It will be the most important thing you do.

February 16

"When pride comes, then comes shame, but with humility comes wisdom."
Proverbs 11:2

✝ ✝ ✝

Verse 2 of Proverbs chapter 11 reiterates a common teaching in Proverbs and throughout the Bible. PRIDE is a killer. It's what got Satan kicked out heaven and it's what got Adam and Eve kicked out of Paradise. Sadly, it will keep us from enjoying an intimate relationship with our Creator (James 4:6, 10) and with one another.

How do you safeguard against pride in your life? Is maintaining humility a struggle for you or anyone you know? Prayer and Bible study will most surely HUMBLE those who pursue these things.

February 17

"Wine is a mocker, and beer is a brawler. Whoever is led astray by them is not wise."
Proverbs 20:1

† † †

This is a verse that rings true in my life. Alcohol has destroyed countless lives throughout history, and it almost destroyed MINE. I do not know what delivers others you from the devastation of alcohol, but I was set FREE from captivity when the Lord Jesus saved me. He has power over all things, including alcohol, drugs, and whatever else Satan chooses to wield against mankind, but people will never know this unless someone tells them about Jesus. Perhaps you and I can tell someone today.

I pray you will use this day wisely and enjoy your family and friends.

February 18

A friend called me yesterday to tell me his beloved mother had entered eternity. She had been struggling for several years with cancer and had undergone various treatments, including clinical trials the past six months. Although postponed, the cancer ultimately prevailed. Death, in the final days was an act of mercy.

My friend was understandably unnerved and grieved at her passing. I encouraged him as best I could but in times like this, there's not much that can be said beyond condolences.

Thankfully my friend's mom was a Christian who trusted her Savior until the very end of her life on planet earth. That provided comfort and hope for my friend and her other survivors. Yes, they will mourn her loss, but only temporarily. One day they too will enter eternity and, if born again, will be reunited forever with their loved ones.

As I prayed for my friend, I thought of the billions of people that do not have a Savior. Some have never heard of Jesus, some have rejected Him, and others trust in an alternative. They are from all tribes and people groups worldwide. My heart breaks for those folks as they sail through life like those unfortunate passengers on the Titanic. Merrily, merrily, until it was not. Let us be on the lookout for those "passengers" and offer them the lifeboat of the Cross of Jesus.

If you are able, walk around your neighborhood praying for God to reveal Himself to each person.

February 19

"The foolishness of man subverts his way; his heart rages against the LORD."
Proverbs 19:3

† † †

This verse fleshes itself out daily all over the world. It seems like we humans rarely want to take responsibility for our own failures.

We have a propensity to blame others, even God for our problems. I have seen, heard, and sadly, even said it myself, "how could God let this happen?" In my defense, I made those accusations prior to being saved. I now do not blame God for any bad thing in my life or the life of others. Sometimes they have been caused by my bad behavior. If not me, then another man or woman behaving poorly caused the distress, NOT God. In the end, it is Mankind who is responsible for individual and collective failures.

God has given us the solution; believe exclusively in the Lord Jesus for forgiveness of personal sin, receive the Holy Spirit, trust that truth is found in the Bible, and love one another as yourself. If only the entire population of the world would do these things, we would no longer have crime, poverty, broken relationships, and war. Sadly, men and women all over the world refuse to accept God's directive.

Father, pierce the hardest heart today with the message of the Gospel. Save those closest to hell.

February 20

"...Do not be grieved; for the joy of the LORD is your strength."
Nehemiah 8:10

I have learned not to depend on my own strength. It is just not a sure thing, one day there but gone the next. My strength is subject to failure. However, when I am joyful in the Lord, I have sufficient strength for the task at hand. I am not sure how that works, but it does. Yep, I still tire but it is a sweet exhaustion, satisfying both body and soul.

Spend time with God today. You won't be disappointed. Enjoy admiring the beauty and complexity of a flower today, it's good for the soul.

February 21

"Do not be deceived. God is not mocked, for whatever a person sows, that he will also reap."
Galatians 6:7

✝ ✝ ✝

There are a lot of things people can do that will result in a bad consequence, but mocking God tops the list. Why? Because those consequences are both temporal and ETERNAL. If someone mocks God's instructions on how to live their life, even though saved, they will suffer the consequences of their sinful behavior. Believers have gone to the gallows for extreme sinful behavior. If a person mocks the sacrifice of His Son Jesus by denying it ever happened or saying it did not matter, they will spend eternity separated from God, and the fires of hell burn eternally.

Father, help me to avoid actions, words, and attitudes that mock you. Be quick to reveal those times to me and draw me to the Cross of Jesus for forgiveness.

February 22

"You are my hiding place and my shield. I hope in your word."
Psalms 119:114

✝ ✝ ✝

Not often, but sometimes, I need a hiding place. Not necessarily a physical one but rather one for my soul. When those times come, I know where to go, to the Lord in prayer and meditation. Some would say it is escapism and they are right. I want to escape the madness of this world, the lies, the violence, the hatred, sickness, and those who can think of no one but themselves. I just need time alone with God to strengthen my soul and spirit so I can reenter the battlefield of this world. I pray you also have a hiding place where you can be refreshed.

Pray you will experience a Spirit filled day.

February 23

"David himself said in the Holy Spirit, 'The Lord said to my Lord, "Sit at my right hand, until I make your enemies the footstool of your feet."' (Jesus speaking)
Mark 12:36

✝ ✝ ✝

If ever there was a verse that verified the concept of God speaking through people, this certainly ranks among the highest. Remember, these words came from the very lips of Jesus, the Son of God. There can be no greater endorsement.

Is the Holy Spirit still speaking through people today? Every time the Gospel is uttered, every time God's word is spoken without comment, the Holy Spirit is speaking. At water baptisms, marriages, communion, and other sacred events the Holy Spirit is speaking through people. He sometimes speaks through one believer to another for a specific purpose. What the Holy Spirit will NEVER do is speak anything contrary to the word of God. Be familiar enough with God's word to recognize when the Holy Spirit is speaking.

Why? Because, Satan, our enemy will also speak God's word through people but ALWAYS out of context to advance his agenda and his agenda is to kill, steal, and destroy.

Father, I pray for the peace of Jerusalem today.

February 24

"It shall happen that, before they call, I will answer; and while they are yet speaking, I will hear."
Isaiah 65:24

†††

That is a serious promise from a serious God, our God. I suspect most of us spend far too little time in this important resource our Heavenly Father has provided. Let us be wise and pray often believing our Father is responding in His perfect Will for our lives.

Pray that God will give you a keen awareness of His presence in your life and unwavering confidence in His promises.

February 25

"Your promises have been thoroughly tested, and your servant loves them."
Psalms 119:140

†††

God's Word is perfect. It has stood the test of time. I do not know anything else that I can say is absolutely PERFECT. Do you? How could I not love it? How could I treat it as just another book? How could I not elevate it above all other resources to explain why the world is the way it is, and why mankind is the way it is? It has all the answers to life's questions.

Give your love away to others. When you do God will replenish it with more to give away!

February 26

"You are near, LORD. All your commandments are truth."
Psalms 119:151

† † †

Yes, God REALLY is nearby. If we have trusted Jesus for forgiveness of our sin, He lives in us by virtue of His Holy Spirit. We do not have to climb a mountain, swim a raging river or accomplish some other great feat to fellowship with God, all we have to do is talk with Him. I know, it all sounds so simple, too good to be true, but it is true. The Creator of all things seen and unseen lives in believers, and He is not ashamed to do so. It is no wonder the Bible directs us to pray frequently because the author of the Bible knows how accessible God is to His children. If only we would believe that and act accordingly. Something to think about as this new day unfolds.

February 27

"He is in the way of life who heeds correction, but he who forsakes reproof leads others astray."
Proverbs 10:17

† † †

We can all raise our hands in confirmation of the truth presented in this verse. The times we refuse instruction from parents, teachers, counselors, and most of all, God is countless. We have a propensity, and even a burning desire, to do things our way. Our mantra is too often "my way". Our Heavenly Father knows this and patiently offers advice and guidance to us, but He also ALLOWS us to ignore His advice and SUFFER the consequences. Let us be wise and look into His Word today for that advice and guidance and be wiser still to flesh it out in our lives. We won't be disappointed in doing so!

Spend some time today admiring your favorite color. It just might be the best part of your day.

February 28

"And I will be a Father to you, and you will be my sons and daughters," says the Lord of hosts.

II Corinthians 6:18

† † †

This is one of my favorite promises that God makes to people who trust Him and believe in the Gospel. I know it is hard to imagine being treated like a son or daughter by the Creator of all things seen and unseen, by the God of ALL things, but that is exactly what our status becomes once we are born again. We may, however, need to rethink what it means to be a son or daughter. Because God takes on this role, He expects us to ACT accordingly. Yes, He loves us and will discipline us with the goal of fashioning us to be like His Son, Jesus. Unlike our earthly fathers who were mere men, God is Holy and desires His children to be righteous in our behavior, both in thought and action, just like Jesus manifested His life while on planet earth. That is a sobering charge and one that means we should desire to abandon behavior that offends our Heavenly Father. In doing so we get so much more in return; unconditional forgiveness from our bad behavior, eternal life in heaven, His protection from spiritual enemies, peace of mind and heart, selfless love inspired by God's Holy Spirit that lives in us, and so much more. And because His Holy Spirit lives in us, we now have the ability to live for Him instead of for ourselves. It's little wonder why I love this promise of God. I hope you do, too.

WELCOME TO MARCH

"I am the good shepherd. I know my own, and my own know me"
John 10:14

March 1

"Let us consider how to motivate one another to love and good works, not forsaking our own assembling together, as the custom of some is, but exhorting one another; and so much the more, as you see the Day approaching."
Hebrews 10:24, 25

†††

I am not sure if you are able to attend a worship service because of health issues, but if and when you can, it will be exhilarating. God not only wants us to recognize Him as our Creator with thanksgiving, but He also deserves that acknowledgment and praise. There are so many things that the world offers to us to exalt and worship but they are a counterfeit to the real thing, God Almighty and His Son, Jesus. Before I was a believer, I held so many of those counterfeit things in high regard, including myself. I was a fool then, but God was merciful to me and drew me to Himself by virtue of His Holy Spirit. I pray, dear reader, that you will take every opportunity to worship your Creator and Savior.

Eat your favorite dessert today. It will make your tummy smile.

March 2

> "Set your mind on the things that are above, not on the things that are on the earth."
> Colossians 3:2

✝ ✝ ✝

When we read the stories of people in the Bible, we see the heroes focusing on God's kingdom principles while the villains focused on earthly principles. The greatest example of all was Jesus. His mind was always stayed on the Kingdom of God.

Reading the chronicled events of the Bible should encourage us to have a heavenly minded attitude as we navigate life. Thousands of years of testimony should give us confidence to set OUR minds on things above. The way for us to increase our faith is hiding in plain sight.

Laugh at yourself today. It will be good for your soul.

March 3

> He said to all, "If anyone desires to come after me, let him deny himself, take up his cross daily, and follow me."
> Luke 9:23

✝ ✝ ✝

The very first truth in this verse is that it is necessary for a person to DESIRE to follow Jesus. Without that desire there will be no conviction or motivation to fulfill the other conditions Jesus lists. Is the desire to follow Him something that everyone feels? I think not, otherwise there would be no rejection of Jesus. Jesus says that no one can come to Him unless the Father draws that person to Jesus

(John 6:44). This is one of the great mysteries and dilemmas of scripture that theologians have debated for centuries. Does God really desire for ALL people to be saved from eternal separation from Him? It will certainly seem so if we consider 1 Tim 2:4 and other related verses. Whatever the truth is about God's call to people, the only one we absolutely need to be concerned with is God's personal call to OUR heart. When that happens, we have a decision to make about Jesus. When that call comes, do we answer the call or reject it? Therein lies our personal responsibility that will be tested and revealed on our day of judgement.

Next time we will consider what it means to deny ourselves.

March 4

He said to all, "If anyone desires to come after me, let him deny himself, take up his cross daily, and follow me."
Luke 9:23

† † †

As we continue to explore this verse let us consider what Jesus means in regard to denying ourselves. Why would He even say this? Is He directing us to be contrary to who we are? Yes, if He is referencing our unregenerate nature. When we are born into this world, we have a nature that wants to be INDEPENDENT of God and His authority. We want to be captain of our ship, commander of our souls, first and foremost in all we do. It was the motivation of Eve to be like God when she first ate the forbidden fruit. She believed as truth the lie Satan had told her (Genesis 3). Jesus, by His life, demonstrates that He was DEPENDENT on God, and beyond that, the welfare of others rather than Himself became His highest priority. In fact, it WAS His nature because His father was not a man from whom sin is passed down from one generation to another, but God, hence the immaculate conception.

But how do we assume this new nature? Can we apprehend the nature of Jesus? Jesus says yes, but we must be born again to do so, not physically, but spiritually. When we believe the Gospel, the Holy Spirit comes to live within us providing the resource we need to overcome our base nature. Prior to the Holy Spirit living in us, we neither had motivation (desire) or power to resist our "me first" nature. The key to unlocking the power of the Holy Spirit in our lives is SURRENDER. When we surrender to the leading and guiding of the Holy Spirit, we are denying ourselves thereby fulfilling one of the conditions Jesus lists for those wishing to follow Him. Spending time in God's Word and prayer are essential and these things work in concert with the Holy Spirit of God to change us into the likeness of His Son, Jesus (Romans 8:29).

Next time we will consider what it means to "take up our cross daily."

March 5

> He said to all, "If anyone desires to come after me, let him deny himself, take up his cross daily, and follow me."
> Luke 9:23

☦ ☦ ☦

Today let us consider the third truth Jesus presents in this verse. Jesus says anyone who wants to come after Him will be subject to their own "cross". Although He experienced the pain and humiliation of a physical cross, the one He promises His followers is metaphorical, nonetheless, it can often be wrought with humiliation and emotional pain. But how do we know this and why is it so? Because Jesus told

His disciples just prior to His ruthless execution, "If you were of the world, the world would love its own. Yet because you are not of the world, but I chose you out of the world, therefore the world hates you. Remember the word that I said to you, 'A servant is not greater than his master.' If they persecuted Me, they would also persecute you. If they kept My word, they would keep yours also." (John15:19, 20)

The scary truth is that the world still hates Jesus. If you do not believe me, try talking to a group of unbelievers about Jesus. There is a likelihood you will be mocked and/or ridiculed. Worse than that, in some parts of the world it could actually cost you your life! Still, our love for Jesus compels us to share the love of God with people despite the potential for unpleasant consequences. It is, after all, the very reason Jesus endured His cross; to save a world that is hostile towards God.

Next time we will consider what it means to follow Him.

March 6

> He said to all, "If anyone desires to come after me, let him deny himself, take up his cross daily, and follow me."
> Luke 9:23

Today we will consider the final issue Jesus lists about people desiring to come after Him - 'follow me'. That sounds really simplistic and somewhat vague at the same time. But consider the following verses: "My food," said Jesus, "is to do the will of him who sent me and to finish his work" (John 4:34). So, Jesus said, "When you have lifted up the Son of Man, then you will know that I am he and that I do nothing on my own but speak just what the

Father has taught me. The one who sent me is with me; he has not left me alone, for I always do what pleases him" (John 8:28, 29).

Lots of specificity in these verses. So, we can conclude from these verses Jesus expects us to listen to God and do what God asks us to do, just like Jesus did. Jesus says He was taught by the Father what to say and He always did what pleased the Father. Jesus received His teachings from the Holy Spirit, prayer, and the scriptures - the same resources we have today. To be clear, I have no illusion, or perhaps a better word would be delusion, that I will be able to live a life free from failure. It happens all too frequently, but that is why God gives me, and all of His children, the option of confession and repentance of any and all failures. When we exercise those options sincerely, we are ready to start anew, forgiven and cleansed by God of our failures. Yes, there may be earthly consequences because men and women often choose not to forgive an offense, and those earthly consequences may linger a lifetime, but not in the throne room of God. That is grace!

So now we have considered the four truths Jesus presented in this verse, desire, denying oneself, taking up a cross, and following Him. Much easier to consider than to implement.

March 7

"Every way of a man is right in his own eyes , but the LORD weighs the hearts."
Proverbs 21:2

† † †

It is our human nature to be proud and self-assertive, not meek. Only the Spirit of God can transform our lives through the new birth experience and then make us over again into the image of Christ. He is our example of true meekness. Let us make it our heart's desire to live in His image today and always.

Dear reader, I pray you and your family will have an opportunity to attend a worship service this week. He is worthy of our praise. Sing to the Lord today!

March 8

> "In this is love, not that we have loved God, but that he loved us, and sent his Son as the atoning sacrifice for our sins."
> 1 John 4:10

✝ ✝ ✝

When a young man or woman falls in love for the first time they often feel as though they invented love. I know I did. No one could have ever felt the way I felt about that girl. I surely must have invented true love. But the truth is this, that even though I didn't realize it, I was reflecting an attribute of God, my Creator.

The Bible declares that God is love! So, the next time you express genuine, selfless love for another, know that you are imitating your Heavenly Father. I pray we ALL imitate Him today.

March 9

> "The entrance of your words gives light. It gives understanding to the simple."
> Psalms 119:130

✝ ✝ ✝

Today I would like to ask you several questions. Before that, however, a comment. I prepare a Bible verse accompanied by my understanding of that verse every day. I do this because they are important to me, but that does not mean they are important to you.

So here is what I would like you to consider. Do you read the Bible? If so, how often? If so, what version? If so, what is your favorite verse, favorite chapter, favorite book, and why? Beyond that, do you consider yourself to be born again? Don't get freaked out by these questions. There are no wrong answers. Please just consider what you believe and why you believe those things.

God has given Mankind free will to choose how and why they lead their lives, and I want to be like God in this regard. In fairness to God, however, that does not mean that there will not be eternal consequences for our choices. I want you to consider if Bible verses are important to you, and if you consider them to be infallible in regard to truth.

Be brave and thankful today, it beats the alternative.

March 10

> Jesus said to her, "I am the resurrection and the life. He who believes in me will still live, even if he dies. And whoever lives and believes in me will never die. Do you believe this?"
> John 11:25, 26

A friend mine entered eternity yesterday morning. It saddens me to know I will no longer be able to see him on planet earth. I am saddened yet joyful at the same time. That sounds like a contradiction, I know. Let me explain.

I am saddened that the health issue that took his life ever manifested. I am saddened that his family will now have to adjust to life without him. I am saddened that his wife of many decades has lost the love her life. I am joyful that he is free of the pain and frustration of his debilitating illness. I am joyful that he is now living in the Paradise that Jesus promised his followers. I am joyful he now is face to face with Jesus, his Savior.

I look forward to the day I will see him again.

March 11

"Pilate, wishing to please the crowd, released Barabbas to them, and handed over Jesus, when he had flogged him, to be crucified."
Mark 15:15

✝ ✝ ✝

I am critical of Pontus Pilate every time I read this account until the Holy Spirit reminds me that, at times, I too have behaved similarly. How so, you ask?

To my shame, I have wanted to please the "crowd" by not speaking about my faith. To my shame, I have gratified myself by abandoning the things of God for the things of the world. To my shame, I have ignored opportunities to serve Him for selfish reasons. In an abstract sense, at those times I was "crucifying" Jesus.

There is another person in the story of Jesus' execution - Barabbas. He is the criminal that was set free while Jesus took his place on the Cross. The truth is I am now Barabbas; not a man set free from a Roman prison but rather a man set free from the prison of sin.

Oh, the wonder of grace! Oh, the wonder that a sinner like me could be rescued from the fires of hell. Thank you, Jesus!

March 12

"A word fitly spoken is like apples of gold in settings of silver."
Proverbs 25:11

✝ ✝ ✝

Our words matter. What we say, how we say it, and the spirit in which we say it has an impact on the hearer, either good or bad. Choose your words wisely with the intention of encouraging the hearer. There is way too much of the other in society today. Our tongue can do nothing on its own. It takes direction from our heart.

Do you have a sibling? Call him or her today and tell that person you miss them. Everyone likes to hear that they are missed.

March 13

"You are the light of the world. A city located on a hill cannot be hidden. Neither do you light a lamp, and put it under a measuring basket, but on a stand; and it shines to all who are in the house. In the same way, let your light shine before people, that they may see your good works, and glorify your Father who is in heaven."
Matthew 5:14-16

✝ ✝ ✝

Let us continue being a light to those that are in darkness, but to do that we must REMAIN in the light of Jesus. Let us commit to live in His light through the Word, Prayer, and obedience to Him. I pray our light will overcome the darkness today.

Stand in a completely dark room and then turn on a flashlight. That is a great demonstration of the impact we can have on this unbelieving world.

March 14

> But Jesus said, "Leave her alone. Why do you trouble her? She has done a good work for me. For you always have the poor with you, and whenever you want to, you can do them good; but you will not always have me."
> Mark 14:6, 7

† † †

On this occasion Jesus is rebuking people who had criticized a woman for anointing Him with a costly oil. The critics protested that the oil should have been sold and the proceeds given to the poor. In normal circumstances perhaps their claim would have been valid but there is no normality in Jesus. He was, after all, the Son of God, the King of kings and the Lord of lords. Her gesture was most appropriate.

In His response, Jesus points out that they (and us) will ALWAYS have the poor with them and will ALWAYS have opportunity to reach out to them. I wonder how many of them helped a person in need that very day? Of course, that is the challenge for you and I today. Poor people are everywhere, poor in spirit and poor in resources. Let us look for opportunities to minister to the poor while also following this woman's example of worshipping Jesus.

March 15

"Let the words of my mouth and the meditation of my heart be acceptable in your sight always, LORD, my rock and my redeemer."
Psalms 19:14

✝ ✝ ✝

Today I will speak many words and have many thoughts. Some thoughts will be fleeting in nature while others I will mediate upon.

The Psalmist knew this to be true in his life and prayed that his words and meditations would be honorable and pleasing to God. Even though we will be challenged to do otherwise, let us commit ourselves to the nobility of the Psalmist's prayer. Let us surrender our words and meditations to the Holy Spirit today and always.

Father, I ask you guard my lips today. Use them for good and not evil.

March 16

"With great power, the apostles gave their testimony of the resurrection of the Lord Jesus. Great grace was on them all."
Acts 4:33

✝ ✝ ✝

For the first 35 years of my life, I wandered through this world in spiritual darkness. Like a blind man, I would bump into something or someone and change my direction only to have to do it over and over again. It was like being in the ocean in a tiny boat with no land in sight. But here is the thing, it was only AFTER the entrance of light that I realized my desperate condition.

But then one day I heard that God loved me and wanted to have a father/son relationship with me. I could hardly believe that God could love someone like me after all the ugly things I had done. But on that day My heart was drawn to Him like a moth to a flame, it was an attraction that was irresistible. And then suddenly, in the twinkling of the eye, when I surrendered to Him and believed that Jesus died for my sins, light flooded into my life like water rushing over Niagara Falls, and for the first time ever, I could "see"!

I could see the world and my life for what it really was, interested in self, promoting self, and ignoring the very one who created it. Beyond that, the words in the Bible were like cool water to a man that was dehydrated and dying of thirst. I was so thankful that at last I had found truth and not just opinions about life. Those words really do bring light to my path as I continue to negotiate this world. So, yes, this verse is very real to me, and to this very day I look for the truth of the Bible to provide light to my path.

That is MY TESTIMONY. What is your story, your real story? Share it with someone today.

March 17

"Just to be tender, just to be true,
Just to be glad the whole day through,
Just to be merciful, just to be mild,
Just to be trustful as a child:
Just to be gentle and kind and sweet,
Just to be helpful with willing feet, . . .
Just to let love be our daily key,
That is God's will for you and me."
(Author unknown)

March 18

> "I will meditate on your precepts, and consider your ways. I will delight myself in your statutes.
> I will not forget your word."
> Psalms 119:15, 16

I am not sure what my life will look like today, in fact, I am not even certain that I will live the entire day, no one is. One thing is for sure, however, I will think about many things today and some of those things I will take time to mediate upon. Perhaps it will a dilemma or problem I or another is having, perhaps it will be on something I'm trying to learn, or perhaps it will be on something I see or hear. God has given us the gift of a beautiful mind to imagine and meditate; no other creature has these abilities. So, in the midst of all my thoughts and meditations today, my priority will be to consider and mediate on the One who gave me my mind. He is majestic and the only One worthy of my praise.

How about you? What will you meditate on today? You or Him?

March 19

> "But be doers of the word, and not only hearers, deluding your own selves. For if anyone is a hearer of the word and not a doer, he is like someone looking at his natural face in a mirror; for he sees himself, and goes away, and immediately forgets what kind of person he was."
> James 1:22-24

How many of us would look into a mirror, see ourselves in disarray, and walk away without correcting our appearance? Yet that is exactly what we do in regard to our behavior when we ignore God's Instructions for our lives as revealed in the Bible. There are lots of reasons we CHOOSE to ignore Biblical instruction; a powerful habit, disagreeing with God about what is right and wrong, pressure from friends or family, fear of losing friends or social status, and many other reasons. It seems like we can always justify our choice to ourselves and to others. But here is the thing about our justification, God never accepts our excuses. He is NEVER wrong, ever!

That is the very reason we need a Savior. Without a Savior we will be judged on our choices and behavior, no excuse will be accepted. The exceptionally good news is that Jesus has already experienced the punishment for our rebellion, and when we believe and trust in His death, burial, and resurrection, and trust Him for forgiveness, we experience forgiveness and salvation. Beyond that, God gives us His Holy Spirit that gives us the desire and power to overcome our inadequacies.

It is a great truth that everyone needs to hear. Not everyone will believe it. It is called free will for a reason, God allows us to choose how we live our lives. Sadly, what many choose to forget or ignore is that there are eternal CONSEQUENCES for our choices.

I hope you have an opportunity to tell this story to someone today. Beyond that, I pray you have chosen wisely.

Want to laugh today? Put a piece of your clothing on backwards and look at yourself in a mirror.

March 20

> "And be kind to one another, tenderhearted, forgiving each other, just as God also in Christ forgave you."
> Ephesians 4:32

✝ ✝ ✝

NOTE: THIS IS JUST A MULTI DAY DEVOTION

Unfortunately, forgiveness is not really in the human spiritual or intellectual DNA. We are more inclined to hold a grudge or worse, revenge. Lives have been destroyed, wars have been started, and unspeakable acts of terror have been committed because of unforgiveness. Of course, there would be no need for forgiveness if Adam and Eve had not chosen to succumb to the temptation of pride - in the end they wanted to be like God (Genesis 3:4-6). Had sin not entered the world through them, Mankind would be living in perfect harmony with one another, and unconditional love would be the rule rather than the exception.

So, dear One, is there a solution to our dilemma? Can the human heart TRULY forgive? Words of forgiveness can roll off our lips, but are our hearts synchronized to our words? Others can hear our words of forgiveness, but others can never see what is in our hearts. Those things are only visible to us and God.

What do you think? What has been your experience with forgiveness, both given and received? I'll give you my thoughts in a future message.

March 21 - AN EXTENSION FROM PREVIOUS

"And be kind to one another, tenderhearted, forgiving each other, just as God also in Christ forgave you."
Ephesians 4:32

✝ ✝ ✝

Forgiveness is a NECESSITY and the hallmark of Christianity. It is the specific reason Jesus was manifested in flesh and died. Our God given faith in His death, burial, and resurrection is how we attain forgiveness from our Creator and without forgiveness we would suffer eternal punishment for our sins. Any discussion about forgiveness must start with this truth.

When we agree with God that it is necessary for us to receive His forgiveness, it soon becomes obvious to us that because we are created in His image, it will be necessary for us to forgive others when they wrong us. But how? Sometimes the pain of an offense against us is so intense that we feel we will never recover from our emotional wounds, and even if we can once again gain emotional equilibrium, we will be emotionally stunted for the rest of our lives. I know, I have been there, and you may have been there also.

So, is there some magic formula that will allow us to overcome our reluctance to forgive others? Are there Biblical principles we can apply? Does forgiveness mean we excuse, or worse, endorse bad behavior?

More on this in my next message. I pray you will enjoy this brand-new day and experience the wonder of life!

March 22 - AN EXTENSION FROM PREVIOUS

"And be kind to one another, tenderhearted, forgiving each other, just as God also in Christ forgave you."
Ephesians 4:32

†††

Forgiveness is critically important to God and consequently should be critically important to us. After all, His Son, Jesus, died a brutal death so God could offer, and we could receive forgiveness for our rebellious behavior. That sacrifice was motivated by God's love for humanity, for us, but our forgiveness comes with a condition. Let me explain.

In Matthew chapter 6 we read where Jesus' disciples ask Him to teach them how to pray. What is included in His model prayer should be etched in our hearts and minds because Jesus considered these things to be the most important things to include in our prayers. Think about that. He could have listed anything, dozens or even hundreds of requests, yet He listed very few; so, we can conclude that the things He did list are vitally important, essential for our well-being. Beyond that, Jesus offers explanation for one particular request immediately after His prayer (Verses 14 and 15).

With these thoughts as a backdrop, consider this petition in the model prayer, "And forgive us our debts (sins), as we forgive our debtors (those who sin against us)" - Matthew 6:12. Is Jesus asking us to pray for God to forgive us the SAME way we forgive others? Perhaps, and, if so, that frightens me because far too often I have asked for forgiveness without forgiving others, and that may very well violate the teaching found in verse 12. In an effort to justify my oft times hard heart, I have tried to explain away this verse to myself but to no avail. I still have to deal with verses 14 and 15. "For if you forgive men their trespasses, your heavenly Father will also forgive you. But if you do not forgive men their trespasses, neither will your Father forgive your trespasses" - Matthew 6:14, 15. There is no way I can explain these verses away, they are unambiguous, and crystal clear.

Now do you see and understand why giving forgiveness is so important for us to have a healthy relationship with our Heavenly Father? We only have two choices, to do it or not, and there are benefits or consequences for our choice.

In my next message I'll share with you a "how to" principle I use. Listen to your favorite song today. It will make your heart happy.

March 23 - AN EXTENSION FROM PREVIOUS

"And be kind to one another, tenderhearted, forgiving each other, just as God also in Christ forgave you."
Ephesians 4:32

† † †

By now you have decided what you will do about forgiveness and unforgiveness, both present and future. God will not force you to forgive anyone, He gives us choice in that regard. It is called Free Will. If you have chosen to practice forgiveness, then I will share something I have learned from my Heavenly Father.

My dilemma was that I could speak words of forgiveness but still have unforgiveness, bitterness, or even hatred in my heart. That was especially true for individuals who had wronged me but never asked to be forgiven. Worse, some enjoyed seeing me struggle or suffer emotional or physical pain. Forgiving them seemed like a fool's errand to me, and yet I felt compelled to do so.

Thankfully, in my desire to be obedient to God's direction to forgive, He gave me a solution to my dilemma, prayer. Yes, prayer. What I learned was that if I prayed for that person for just a minute or two three times a day, my heart would eventually and ultimately embrace true forgiveness for that person. For me, it became impossible to hate someone I asked God to forgive and bless in all areas of their life. Sometimes it took many days to come to experience that peace in my heart, but it ALWAYS occurred. Sometimes I felt like a genuine hypocrite asking God to bless someone I hated, but I was always glad I persisted.

So that is my "secret" to forgiving someone who could care less about being forgiven. What I eventually learned was that forgiving others was more for my benefit than the other person. Forgiving others allowed me to regain my emotional stability and experience peace. Perhaps you, too, will discover that when you forgive others from your heart. That's my prayer for you.

March 24:

"For it is God who works in you both to will and to work, for his good pleasure."
Philippians 2:13

† † †

Sometimes it is difficult for me to reconcile the ills and struggles of God's children, of which I am one. I would not want those hardships for my children so why would God allow them for His? It is,

I believe, a legitimate question that has no definitive answer, at least not one that the world would embrace.

Thankfully God provides answers, albeit difficult answers, like the scripture referenced above. Perhaps they are not exactly answers but rather truths. After all, I could challenge an answer, but I cannot challenge truth. I could negotiate an answer, but I cannot negotiate truth. So, I am left with the truth that God is working circumstances and outcomes in the lives of His children for His good pleasure. And that suits me just fine. How about you?

March 25

"The LORD is near to all those who call on him, to all who call on him in truth."
Psalms 145:18

Over time I have concluded that very few God related things happen until I pray. It is like pulling the trigger on a gun. Until then I am subject to the whims of this world and my own craftiness, or lack thereof. But when I petition God, I become subject to His Will, and so do the forces of the universe. When I petition God, hearts change (if only mine), mountains move, seas part, and my God roars. The changes may not be what I asked for, but they will always be what God wants for me. For me, that is victory!

I encourage you to pray frequently. It is our greatest resource.

March 26

"The lips of the righteous feed many, but the foolish die for lack of understanding."
Proverbs 10:21

✝ ✝ ✝

What will our lips "feed" listeners today? Will they hear grace, love, and encouragement or will we "feed" others anger and bitterness?

And what will our response be if we happen upon a fool today? The Bible says: "The fool has said in his heart that there is no God…" (Psalm 14:1). But were we not once all fools? At some point in our lives someone took the time to share Jesus with us. Perhaps we will have that opportunity today.

God's best blessings to you today.

March 27

> "The refining pot is for silver, and the furnace for gold, but the LORD tests the hearts."
> Proverbs 17:3

✝ ✝ ✝

What ways does the Lord use to test my heart, to test your heart? Allowing sickness, health, riches, poverty, faithfulness, unfaithfulness, the lure of the world, the lure of the Holy Spirit, success, or failure? These are just a few of the things that can test our hearts. I am sure you can craft your own list.

But here is the thing; how does our heart respond to each test? Is God ALWAYS our highest priority or does something or someone else occupy that spot? Let us strive to allow the Holy Spirit to give us the desire and power to keep God in the forefront of every situation. Who really knows what God will use to test their heart today? Whatever the test, God is working to refine us for His glory.

March 28

"Therefore I urge you, brothers, by the mercies of God, to present your bodies a living sacrifice, holy, acceptable to God, which is your reasonable service."
Romans 12:1

✝ ✝ ✝

Sacrifices have always been a part of religious activity worldwide. They require giving something of value to the god or gods the person worships. In the eye of the worshipper, the greater the value of the thing sacrificed, the greater the appeasement of the deity and the greater their reward will be. It has been used and abused from the beginning of time.

But here is the thing: Christianity is not a religion; it is a relationship. It is personal, not ethereal. I would argue that it is as tangible today as Jesus was tangible while living on earth. Every believer is now part of the body of Christ. If only we would confidently believe this and act accordingly, who knows the impact we could have on our world.

March 29

"I will meditate on your precepts, and consider your ways. I will delight myself in your statutes. I will not forget your word."
Psalms 119:15, 16

✝ ✝ ✝

At this time in David's life, when he penned these words, it is easy to see and understand why God called David "a man after His own heart." Sadly, later in his life, David fell prey to lust and deceit, somehow wandering far from his previous commitment to God's statutes. We should take careful notice knowing that we, too, are vulnerable to life changing failure if we do not keep Jesus and the Holy Scriptures at the CENTER of our lives. Moving Jesus and God's word to the sidelines will heighten our vulnerability to the enemy and his treachery. If it can happen to David it can happen to us.

Memorize one Bible verse today. Just one.

March 30

"Teach me good judgment and knowledge, for I believe in your commandments."
Psalms 119:66

† † †

Someone once said there is no such thing as teaching, only learning. That is an interesting perspective, and perhaps there is something to that claim. God has provided the Bible to reveal Himself and His will to mankind. He has provided the Holy Spirit to open our hearts and minds to spiritual matters yet the world, for the most part, remains spiritually ignorant. Is that because there is no teacher or because there are few students – people WILLING and EAGER to learn? The question, of course, is rhetorical.

Look again at the verse. King David is anxious to learn what God wants Him to know and if you read through Psalm 119 you will discover that David's source material for learning is God's word. Countless people lived during the time of David, but countless people cared little about God's word, and consequently learned zilch because they were unwilling to learn.

To be sure, I am not discounting the need for teachers. I have had both good and bad and I am sure you have encountered the same. But here is the question: is my assessment of good and bad based on my willingness to learn what was being taught or the teacher's ability to teach it? Perhaps in the final analysis, for success both are necessary.

In conclusion, I pray that my heart and your heart, dear reader, have the same willingness to learn as that of King David. If so, our teacher is ready to teach us!

March 31

"Entrust your works to the LORD, and your plans will be established."
Proverbs 16:3

† † †

Did you ever look at a problem or set a goal that you thought would be impossible to solve or achieve? At some point in our lives, we are all confronted with such dilemmas. It is in the nature of man to reach for the proverbial "brass ring." It is why we put men on the moon and Mount Everest was conquered despite the sad reality that some died trying to overcome those lofty challenges.

Our challenges may be significantly more modest than climbing a mountain or going to outer space, but they are challenges, nonetheless. The really great news is that God has given us the option of handing the challenge off to Him. That does not mean we are to disengage our diligent pursuit of a solution, but it does mean we are to trust His guidance as we move forward to success and victory. Try Him, trust Him and look forward to success, and when it happens, praise Him.

Father, help me to understand that you are ALWAYS with me providing wisdom and guidance.

Happy birthday to my wife today! You can read about her in Proverbs 31.

WELCOME TO APRIL

Jesus said to her, "I am the resurrection and the life. He who believes in me will still live, even if he dies. And whoever lives and believes in me will never die. Do you believe this?"
John 11:25, 26

April 1

"If a wise man goes to court with a foolish man, the fool rages or scoffs, and there is no peace."
Proverbs 29:9

We all know foolish men and women; they are all around us. Perhaps, on occasion, we have been foolish. It happens. But do you know how the Word of God describes a fool? Psalms 14 verse 1 says: "The fool has said in his heart, "There is no God." That is the ultimate failure of a man or woman, in fact, it is the beginning of all foolishness in mankind. Without God we are left to ourselves to determine right and wrong. With God, we are directed and shepherded in right and wrong behavior. Society insists on determining acceptable behavior, but those parameters often ignore the guard rails God has put in place, and so the societal battle continues. Who will prevail? God, of course!

Let us be sure we are on the right side of this battle and trust God above anything or anyone else. It will bring peace to our hearts and joy to our lives. Enjoy your day with THE Savior.

April 2

"LORD, your word is settled in heaven forever."
Psalms 119:89

✝ ✝ ✝

During my many years on planet earth I have never found anything to be forever. Things change, people change, nothing stays the same. Ironically, that is the only thing that stays the same, the fact that life's circumstances will eventually change.

It is not so with God. Jesus Christ is the same yesterday, today, and forever! Beyond that, the Word of God (Bible) is forever. He has promised blessing, both here and eternally for those who follow Him, and warnings for those who deny and live apart from Him.

Let us set our eyes and hearts on that which never changes.

April 3

"Praise the LORD. Praise, you servants of the LORD, praise the name of the LORD. Blessed be the name of the LORD, from this time forth and forevermore. From the rising of the sun to the going down of the same, The LORD's name is to be praised."
Psalms 113:1-3

✝ ✝ ✝

Notice that the call to praise the Lord is directed ONLY to His servants. Unbelievers view being a servant as a big fat negative. What they fail to realize is that everyone is serving someone or something; self, money, career, reputation, you name it. But here is the thing, a master is responsible and has charge over the servant. I am grateful that my master is Jesus. I know He will never abuse or take advantage of me. Instead, He took the punishment for all my bad behavior so that I could spend eternity with Him. What a wonderful master I SERVE.

I know how easily it is to be distracted, it happens, so perhaps today you will consider who or what is your master. Like so many others that live on planet earth, I pray you are serving the only master worth serving, Jesus. He will never disappoint you.

Enjoy listening to your favorite song today. That will bring a smile to your ears.

April 4

"I have gone astray like a lost sheep. Seek your servant, for I do not forget your commandments."
Psalms 119:176

†††

I view Psalm 119 as David's manifesto for life. It is glorious, his thoughts and declarations soaring to spiritual heights unequaled. No wonder God calls him a man after His own HEART. It is fascinating to me that David concludes this epic Psalm with the same declaration I have made many times in my life. David's vulnerability is encouraging to me, and his confession an unforgettable lesson. After all, who would not want to have the heart of God?

Pray for a family member today.

April 5

"I have chosen the way of truth. I have set your ordinances before me."
Psalms 119:30

✝ ✝ ✝

Choices! We make them each day, each and every hour, sometimes minute by minute. Some are routine; what to wear, what to eat, what to say? Others are much more significant; what to believe, how to behave, who to follow? There is simplistic justice in choices; good choices have good results while bad choices bring bad results. Successfully navigating life really is a matter of choosing wisely at every spiritual, moral, and ethical intersection.

David chose to follow God by examining and embracing the truths that God revealed in His holy Word. Every citizen of planet earth will embrace and follow something or someone today. CHOOSE wisely, our present and future, temporal and eternal, are hinged to our choices. My prayer for you today is that you will choose correctly at every intersection.

Think about your favorite childhood friend today. Those will be fond memories.

April 6

> "His disciples did not understand these things at first, but when Jesus was glorified, then they remembered that these things were written about him, and that they had done these things to him." John 12:16

Just like the disciples, our journey to spiritual understanding begins at the Cross of Jesus. When we accept the death, burial, and resurrection of Jesus as God's reconciliation process for our personal sin and surrender to the lordship of Jesus, we are born again. Just like Jesus was given new life we too are given new life that is now guided by the Holy Spirit of our Heavenly Father. A result of His presence in our lives is that we now have the privilege of understanding the scriptures. Let us exercise that privilege today by reading His Holy Word. He has so much to say to us. He really does want us to understand not just Him, but our new life in Him.

April 7

He has said to me, "My grace is sufficient for you, for power is made perfect in weakness." Most gladly therefore I will rather glory in my weaknesses, that the power of Christ may rest on me. Therefore I take pleasure in weaknesses, in injuries, in necessities, in persecutions, in distresses, for Christ's sake. For when I am weak, then am I strong.
II Corinthians 12:9, 10

† † †

I know this verse may sound like a paradox but it is not. The Apostle Paul learned this principle by total surrender to God. Think about this: if we accomplish difficult things in our own strength, we take credit for doing so. If we allow God to accomplish His Will in our lives, then deservedly so, He gets the credit and glory. His love NEVER fails.

April 8

"Therefore I consider all of your precepts to be right. I hate every false way."
Psalms 119:128

† † †

Have you ever desired to find the "silver bullet" that would slay all the vampires and dragons in your life, the Kryptonite that would render evil strongholds helpless? David, the man after God's own heart, considered God's promises and commandments to be such a resource for his life. Could it be that simple? Has it been available to us ever since God first spoke to Adam? What would the world be like today if Adam had obeyed God's one prohibition in the Garden of Eden? Could obedience to God's directions in the Bible be all WE need to conquer evil that threatens us? But how do we first overcome our prideful and often deceitful hearts that we inherited from Adam? Could Jesus' instruction to be "born again" be the solution for our sinful hearts? No, we can not put the "sin" horse back in the barn, unfortunately Adam opened that door and unleashed sin upon this world. Thankfully Jesus provides a way for US to now corral OUR restless and selfish heart. "Not by power, not by might, but by My Spirit says the Lord." If we have surrendered our lives to Jesus, the Holy Spirit of God lives in US. Live victoriously in Him today!

April 9

"He who rejects me, and does not accept my words, has one who judges him. The word that I spoke will judge him on the last day."
John 12:48

According to this verse it would be wise to pay particular attention and be obedient to the words printed in red in our Bibles. Those words will be used as the standard on judgement Day. This verse is both frightening and comforting. Frightening to those who reject the teaching of Jesus and comforting to those who believe and embrace His words. Let's make sure we're on the right side of this equation.

Is there someone you need to forgive but refuse to do so? Forgiveness is for the forgiver, not the forgiven.

April 10

"Therefore I will be ready always to remind you of these things, though you know them, and are established in the present truth. I think it right, as long as I am in this tent, to stir you up by reminding you ..."
II Peter 1:12, 13

☨ ☨ ☨

One of the challenges of being human is that we have itching ears and curious hearts. We long for something new because boredom easily besets us. It is why we compose new music, write new books, climb mountains, or explore new worlds. Inherently, there is nothing wrong with expanding our horizons, adding new to the old, except when it infringes on morality and/or challenges what God has already revealed in the Bible. To be sure, our understanding and knowledge of God does expand as our relationship with Him matures. That is not problematic, but boredom with the scriptures, and consequently our Christian life most certainly is concerning.

The Apostles recognized this and were faithful to remind believers what they already knew and embraced. ("Brothers and sisters, do not be weary in doing what is right." 2 Thessalonians 3:13)

I find myself being reminded by the Holy Spirit of things I believe and embrace every time I read scripture. Those reminders eventually spill on to the pages I write or words I speak. There is nothing new in them, just reminders of what is already known. I encourage everyone everywhere to enjoy the satisfaction of knowing and resting in the truth of the Gospel and all that is included in a relationship with their Creator. As for me, I will, like the Apostles, continue to remind myself and others the most important aspect of life - the death, burial, and resurrection of Jesus. How about you? What message does your life express to others?

Take a walk in a park today and admire what God has made. It will calm your soul.

April 11

"He who dwells in the secret place of the Most High will rest in the shadow of Shaddai."
Psalms 91:1

† † †

There is significant evidence that Moses is the author of Psalm 91. He FOUND the secret place of God and rested there. He did not reveal its location because if he did it would no longer be secret. But here is the thing, if a man or woman GENUILELY longs to find the secret place of God, God will reveal that place to that person. Is it real? Moses believed it to be so and so do countless others. I found it. Have YOU?

Happy birthday to my daughter today!

April 12

Praise the LORD, my soul, and all that is within me, praise his holy name. Praise the LORD, my soul, and do not forget all his benefits; who forgives all your sins; who heals all your diseases;

who redeems your life from destruction; who crowns you with loving kindness and tender mercies; who satisfies your desire with good things; your youth is renewed like the eagle's.
Psalms 103:1-5

†††

This is my heart's song this morning. How about yours? Can you think of a better way to start your day? Can you think of a better way to end your day?

April 13

"LORD, do I not hate those who hate you? Am I not grieved with those who rise up against you? I hate them with perfect hatred. They have become my enemies."
Psalms 139:21, 22 (King David)
(AND)
"But I tell you who hear: love your enemies, do good to those who hate you, bless those who curse you, and pray for those who mistreat you."
Luke 6:27, 28 (Jesus)

†††

If you were asked to reconcile these two verses, would you be able to do so? They could be construed as being in opposition to one another. I encourage you to develop an explanation without using any Bible commentaries. If you cannot do it today, then put it on a bucket list of questions that need answers. There is no rush. You literally have a lifetime to consider God's Word and after this life you will have answers to all your questions. In the meantime, choose which attitude will prevail in your life.

Have you spoken to God today? If not, why not?

April 14

"Praise the LORD, my soul, and all that is within me, praise his holy name."
Psalms 103:1

† † †

This cry by King David seems contrary to our petitions. Our prayers usually focus on God blessing us, not the other way. Is it even possible for us to bless God? After all, how can the lesser bless the greater? When we focus on THINGS, we cannot. God doesn't need any THING.

However, when we focus on attitude, we can most certainly bless God. When asked which is the greatest commandment, Jesus replied, "The first of all the commandments is: 'Hear, O Israel, the Lord our God, the Lord is one. And you shall love the Lord your God with all your heart, with all your soul, with all your mind, and with all your strength. ' And the second, is this: 'You shall love your neighbor as yourself. ' There is no other commandment greater than these."

And there we have it, precisely how we can bless God, but it is not automatic. It is an attitude that only comes by belief that Jesus died for OUR sins and subsequently surrendering to the guidance of the Holy Spirit.

God's best blessings to you today!

April 15

"...in whom we have our redemption through his blood, the forgiveness of our trespasses, according to the riches of his grace..."
Ephesians 1:7

✝✝✝

The "Him" in this verse is, of course, Jesus. He is precious to me and my only hope for peace with my Creator. He is my salvation, and I am His eternally. Oh, that my life would somehow reflect His grace and glory. Oh, that the world would welcome Jesus.

Come Lord Jesus to a broken world. Save us from the evil one.

April 16

"Indeed your statutes are my delight, and my counselors."
Psalms 119:24

✝✝✝

Did you ever seek the advice of a counselor, perhaps in school or a career counselor? They can be helpful, guiding you through the pitfalls of school or a career choice. King David considered God's words as counselors in his life. His life was filled with miraculous successes and some epic failures. In times of failure, he ignored his "counselors" and followed his own passions. If David were writing this message, his advice would be to ALWAYS trust the counsel of God that is revealed in the God's Word. God's counsel will always be the best advice for avoiding the trap doors of life. Just like David, I speak from experience.

Call a family member today and tell them you love them. You may very well hear the same in return.

April 17

"The LORD is my shepherd; I lack nothing. He makes me lie down in green pastures. He leads me beside still waters."
Psalms 23:1, 2

†††

My soul is in constant need of a shepherd. Why? Because it is prone to wander, oftentimes into dangerous territory. Pride, sorrow, greed, selfishness, depression, hopelessness, lust, and every other pitfall of life that seeks after my soul eagerly awaits me and invites me. When I was young, I never thought I needed a shepherd, but now that I am old, I realize how foolish I was in those early days. Thankfully, there came a day when my soul met and trusted in a shepherd that will always guide me into green pastures and give me rest beside peaceful waters. I pray that you also yield your life to that shepherd. His name is Jesus.

April 18

Jesus answered and said to him, "If anyone loves me, he will keep my word; and my Father will love him, and we will come to him and make our dwelling place with him."
John 14:23

†††

Putting aside the Creation event, the rebellion of Adam and Eve, and the death, burial, and resurrection of Jesus, the coming of the

Holy Spirit to born again believers could be the most SIGNIFICANT event in the history of mankind. The fact that the Holy Spirit now LIVES IN the soul of a believer overshadows many other promises made by Jesus. Perhaps that is why He waited until His final hours to make this revelation. The promised Holy Spirit is the SAME one who descended on Jesus at His baptism, the same one who filled the Prophets of Israel, and the same one present at Creation. He is the same one who fell upon Peter and thousands more on the day of Pentecost. He is the same one who guided the writers of the Scriptures, both new and old testaments. He is the same one who is a part of the Trinity of God, being of the same essence of God the Father and Jesus the Son. This same Holy Spirit makes His HOME in a believer, and just like the Disciples were physically with Jesus while He was on earth, the Holy Spirit is continually with us. His presence is why Jesus can say, "Lo, I am with you always, even to the end of the age."

How many times do we fail to embrace His presence in our lives? How many times do we think of God as distant or unattainable when the reality is that He is living within us? How many times do we fail to understand that our body is now the temple of the Holy Spirit of God? How many times do we miss the fact that by virtue of the Holy Spirit, Jesus IS WITH US this very moment? Too many, I suspect. Take time today to embrace the presence of the Holy Spirit in your life. He wants to be more than just noticed; He wants to be paramount in our lives.

April 19

"How sweet are your promises to my taste, more than honey to my mouth."
Psalms 119:103

✝ ✝ ✝

Is this hyperbole being used by King David to illustrate his love for God's words? Perhaps. But what if David was so in love with God that when he spoke God's words, they actually brought a sweetness to his mouth and lips? What if those words actually became tangible to David? I guess we will never know exactly what David meant when he penned these words, it is the reader's choice to decide for themselves. Hyperbole or tangible, I pray to have the same passion for God's words. How about you?

April 20

"Now, Father, glorify me with your own self with the glory which I had with you before the world existed."
John 17:5

✝ ✝ ✝

The meaning of this particular request of Jesus remains a mystery. What was happening in Heaven before the world was? What did the glory that Jesus requested look like? Did the nature of Heaven change when God created the physical universe? The answers to these questions and many, many more may or may not someday be revealed to us.

What we DO know is this; God created the world and all that is in it with Man being the centerpiece of His creation. We KNOW the world was created for Man and all things were perfect prior to Adam and Eve choosing to disobey God, and we KNOW and experience the disconnect that followed that disobedience. What we also KNOW is that God eventually provided a rescue plan for Man by sacrificing His Son Jesus and that each person must PERSONALLY believe that

Jesus died for them to be spiritually reunited with their Creator. What we do KNOW is that God will provide eternal life for those who believe God and that the opposite is true for those who choose to not believe Him.

Was the glory that Jesus spoke of in His prayer restored to Him? I'm certain it was. I encourage you to read the entire seventeenth chapter of the Gospel of John to see what else Jesus asked of His Father. It is most surely worth your consideration.

Gaze at the stars tonight. It will humble even the most proud heart.

April 21

Meanwhile, when a crowd of many thousands had gathered together, so much so that they trampled on each other, he began to tell his disciples first of all, "Beware of the yeast of the Pharisees, which is hypocrisy."
Luke 12:1

†††

There are only a few things that trigger disgust and even anger in me. Hypocrisy, both in MY life and others is most certainly one. It is the "fool's gold" of life. Avoiding those I identify as hypocrites is an easy solution to one half of the problem. It is the other half that is the most troubling - MY own hypocrisy. I find it an easy transition from legitimate to hypocritical, often in a heartbeat, both in thought and deed. There seems to be no solution but there is redemption. King David often asked God to search his heart; I often ask the Holy Spirit to do the same with my heart. When iniquity is revealed to me, I confess and gratefully bathe in the forgiveness that God promises. Without Jesus, I would have no such confidence or resource. Will I fail again? It is an absolute certainty, and that is exactly why I NEED a Savior. Salvation humbles me. How about you?

April 22

> "for the Holy Spirit will teach you in that same hour what you must say."
> Luke 12:12

† † †

Am I teachable? How about you? I cannot speak for you, but I can testify on my behalf. Sadly, there are times when I think I know enough, when there is no need to learn more. "Been there done that" becomes my mantra. I have read that, I have prayed that, I have experienced that, so there is no need for a redo. But then I read the above scripture, I am jolted back to reality. Jesus reminds me that I must remain teachable. Yes, I need to apply the biblical principles I have learned, but I also need to allow the Holy Spirit to show me how to CORRECTLY apply those principles and to give me additional understanding. Being zealous does not necessarily make me wise. I pray I will remain teachable this day and always.

April 23

> "I tell you, my friends, do not be afraid of those who kill the body, and after that have no more that they can do. But I will warn you whom you should fear. Fear him, who after he has killed, has power to cast into hell. Yes, I tell you, fear him."
> Luke 12:4, 5

† † †

Fear is a powerful emotion that can prompt us to do unimaginable things, both good and bad. It can be an enemy or friend. If we must fear, let us be careful that the object of our fear is none other than God.

However, as believers, we have a better option than fear, we have the power to love. Knowing that we have friendship with God because of our faith in Jesus gives us freedom from fear and the joy of love. Let us focus on love for God and others today. It is a much better neighborhood than fear.

April 24

"Be therefore imitators of God, as beloved children."
Ephesians 5:1
(AND)
Jesus said to him, "Have I been with you all this time, and still you do not know me, Philip? He who has seen me has seen the Father. How can you say, 'Show us the Father?'"
John 14:9

✝✝✝

The Holy Spirit of God inspired the Apostle Paul to pen the first verse. It has inspired countless Christians throughout history to live their lives accordingly. The second verse makes clear what that life would look like. No ambiguity in these two verses, just opportunity. How about you, dear reader, who will you imitate today?

God's best blessings to you this new day. It is a day that the Lord has made!

April 25

"I have called to you. Save me. I will obey your statutes."
Psalms 119:146

Let's make a Deal! It is a fun game but one that God does not play. Just like the Psalmist in this verse, I too on occasion have tried to play that game with God and perhaps you also have tried. But here is the truth, the ONE and ONLY deal God has made with mankind is the sacrifice of Jesus for our sins and if we accept that deal, we are adopted into the family of God. The good news is that it is a GREAT deal!

Jesus says, "I am the way, the truth, and the life. No one comes to the Father except through Me." TAKE the deal, it is the only way to win the "game" of life. Beyond that, share it with others so that they too can be winners.

Read one page of the dictionary today. You will learn a lot for free.

April 26

"If I speak with the tongues of humans and of angels, but do not have love, I am a noisy gong, or a clanging cymbal. If I have the gift of prophecy, and know all mysteries and all knowledge; and if I have all faith, so as to remove mountains, but do not have love, I am nothing. If I dole out all my goods to feed the poor, and if I surrender my body so that I may boast, but do not have love, it profits me nothing."
I Corinthians 13:1-3

So, what is the Apostle Paul, and by extension, the Holy Spirit saying to me in these passages? My understanding is that it is possible, very possible, for me to accomplish good works with WRONG motives. Self-serving, self-righteousness, and pride manifesting rather than a pure and legitimate desire to place the needs of others above my own come to mind. Yep, been there done that, and I do not mean that in a cavalier manner. It is a confession from a repentant heart.

Forgive me, Holy Father, and help me accomplish good and worthwhile works motivated by Godly love. Let others see YOU and not me in my outreach to them. Allow my heart to be like yours.

Stand facing the wind today and think about where that wind came from and where it is going.

April 27

"Love is patient and is kind; love does not envy. Love does not brag, is not proud, does not behave itself inappropriately, does not seek its own way, is not irritable, does not keep a record of wrongs; does not rejoice in unrighteousness, but rejoices with the truth; bears all things, believes all things, hopes all things, endures all things."
I Corinthians 13:4-7

Someone once suggested substituting "God" for the word "love" in these verses. Although that does give me a better understanding of my Heavenly Father, I do not think that is why Paul penned these words. The Holy Spirit, through the writings of the Apostle Paul, wants me to understand what true love, Godly love, looks like. He also wants me to embrace that love and share it with others unconditionally. The very next verse declares, "Love never fails..." and in my final analysis, I believe that to be true.

Holy Father, help me to love others selflessly. I want to, but I cannot do that without You.

April 28

"Oh that my ways were steadfast to obey your statutes. Then I wouldn't be disappointed, when I consider all of your commandments."
Psalms 119:5, 6

✝ ✝ ✝

Someone recently asked me why I often write about my spiritual failures. I directed them to the above verse. Just like King David, I am sometimes ashamed when I consider God's Holy Scriptures. I embrace that reaction as a good thing for two reasons. First, the Apostle James (James 1:23, 24) says that reading the Bible and not recognizing a need for correction is like looking in a mirror and not correcting any disarray in my appearance. Second, my Savior comes into crystal clear focus when I realize my failures. That prompts both praise and humility in me.

I do not know how others respond to God's Word, perhaps it is entirely different than my response, but their reaction is between them and the Father, it is personal and beyond my purview. My testimony is this; experiencing personal awareness and Godly sorrow over my failures usher in repentance and gratitude for my Savior, and that has strengthened and purified my faith.

April 29

"But I will warn you whom you should fear. Fear him, who after he has killed, has power to cast into hell. Yes, I tell you, fear him."
Luke 12:5

✝ ✝ ✝

Hell is real! Jesus talked about it on a many occasions giving validity to the fact that it is not just a frightening concept, it is an ACTUAL place. Revelation chapter 20 reveals a vivid portrayal of the horrors of such a place. So why do so many people live their lives as if it does not exist? Perhaps they have never heard about Hell and if that is true the church must accept failure in that regard. We, the church, are called to teach others everything Jesus taught while on earth. True, some of His teaching is downright scary and may be uncomfortable, but nonetheless it needs to be said. Sadly, unbelief is most likely the overwhelming reason people reject the reality of Hell. We need to pray that God will unravel their unbelief.

For decades I brought Jesus to jails and prisons and shared God's love and forgiveness to those who would listen. There were times I would teach about the reality of Hell and that those without Jesus are destined to spend eternity there. Occasionally other Chaplin's would criticize that approach because they felt it inappropriate to "scare people" into believing in Jesus. I always found that odd because Jesus never acted like teaching about Hell was unnecessary. In fact, to this very day I am convinced that making people aware of Hell is an act of mercy. It should not be our first approach with the unsaved, but neither should it be avoided. We have warning labels and road signs that help people be aware of dangers in this world so why would we not want to warn them about the eternal consequences of rejecting the love and forgiveness of the Cross of Christ? I can think of no valid reason. Can you?

Happy birthday to my son today!

April 30

"Now the fruit of righteousness is sown in peace by those who make peace."
James 3:18

†††

Making war is easy, both literally and figuratively. It is in the human spiritual DNA, it is in my spiritual DNA and its name is PRIDE. Every time it manifests in my life it wars against God - sometimes overtly but often covertly. Ironically, the fact that a reader would be offended by this assertion only proves its validity. The effect of this war is the fruit of unrighteousness.

But there is a superior spiritual DNA residing in me, that which was given to me when I was born again. My flesh opts for the old DNA but my spirit longs for the new. Someone once observed that, "the dog that is fed is the strongest." Feeding my Godly DNA with prayer, scripture, and the fellowship of like-minded believers allows me to be a peacemaker and manifest the fruit of righteousness. I want that in my life. How about you?

Holy Father, direct my thoughts and steps in the way of a peace maker. Guide me to a place that pleases YOU.

WELCOME TO MAY

"If anyone serves me, let him follow me; and where I am, there will my servant also be. If anyone serves me, the Father will honor him."
John 12:26

May 1

"For with God nothing will be impossible."
Luke 1:37

†††

This is such a short verse for such a BIG truth. It seems to me that an entire book should have been written on this ENORMOUS truth. But then I remember that such a book has been written. Beyond that, it has been written by God who inspired men by His Holy Spirit to write about the "impossible" works of God. Even that seems impossible and is often characterized as such by skeptics and unbelievers, nonetheless, it exists.

It is hard for me to wrap my mind around the impossible being possible. Suddenly the possibilities are endless. I am privileged to be a servant of this great and awesome God. More than that, however, is that I am blessed to call Him Father. That is an impossibility that He made possible. So, yes, it is true. NOTHING is impossible for God.

May 2

"Praise the LORD, my soul, and all that is within me, praise his holy name. Praise the LORD, my soul, and do not forget all his benefits"
Psalms 103:1, 2

✝ ✝ ✝

How about you? As a child of God, what benefits can you name? Enjoy those benefits today and always. They were purchased for you by Jesus at a price that is incalculable in human understanding. If you need a reminder of those benefits, I encourage you to read the Gospel of John and then the book of Ephesians. Lots and lots of promises and benefits listed there.

Help a stranger today. You will become a benefit to someone else!

May 3

"For my thoughts are not your thoughts, neither are your ways my ways, " says the LORD. For as the heavens are higher than the earth, so are my ways higher than your ways, and my thoughts than your thoughts."
Isaiah 55:8, 9

✝ ✝ ✝

The key that unlocks understanding to prayer is couched in these Isaiah verses. It is a secret hidden in plain sight for those of us who are born again. Ironically, what the key reveals is that because God is infinite and omniscient, there are times when it is IMPOSSIBLE for us to understand God's choices for us, however, trusting that God's thoughts and ways are better than ours, AND embracing His response to our prayers allows us to be at peace with our circumstances. Consider this, if He answered all our prayers according to our will, God would not be God, we would, and that would be disastrous.

The dilemma with embracing this is that it sometimes yields results like pain, suffering, and even sorrow and it is in these times when we can experience a disconnect with our Father. We are tempted to believe He has not answered our prayer and seek alternative solutions to our issues. Indeed, our spiritual enemy will be quick to level that accusation. We are unable to reconcile these results with God's will for our lives. After all, why would God allow these things, there must be other factors at play, we reason. Although possible, it is likely that it is unlikely. It is in this reasoning that we have abandoned our faith in the truth revealed in the Isaiah scripture. The truth is that oftentimes there is NO earthly explanation for God's response to our prayers, but we are bound by faith to believe they are for God's glory and our ultimate benefit. That faith honors God and triggers the peace that passes all understanding.

Jesus demonstrated His trust in this principle when He asked His Father to find another way during His journey to the Cross. Ultimately He prayed, "NOT My will, but Yours, be done." It would certainly be advantageous for us to also have this trust that God's will is better than ours. It is also our admission and proclamation of servitude.

To be clear, I am not suggesting prayer is an exercise in futility. The believer is directed by Jesus, the Prophets, and the writers of both the New Testament and Old Testament, all of whom were inspired by the Holy Spirit to pray frequently and even unceasingly. Indeed, Jesus spent an inordinate amount of time in prayer. Prayer is essential to a Christ-like life, it is a privilege, not an obligation. What I am suggesting is God will always answer our prayers according to His

Will, and like Jesus, we should readily embrace His choice as the best choice. Here is something to contemplate; each of Jesus' disciples, except John, died a martyr's death. It is not a stretch of the imagination to think they and others prayed for their personal safety and deliverance.

May 4

> "You ask, and do not receive, because you ask with wrong motives, so that you may spend it for your pleasures."
> James 4:3

†††

When I first truly believed in the Gospel of God, I was zealous to share that faith with others, but sadly I would become irritated or even angry when people mocked my newfound faith. I somehow forgot that I had lived thirty-five years before believing. Nonetheless, I wanted everyone to experience a relationship with their Creator, the same relationship that I now enjoyed. Over time God turned my anger to sorrow and like King David, I too found myself weeping for lost souls. That continues to this very day and my prayers are often directed in this regard.

Perhaps you feel similarly. If so, know that you have become like Jesus who wept over Jerusalem (Matt 23:37) for this same reason and like Jesus, let us commit to be faithful to the end.

May 5

> And he said to her, "Daughter, your faith has made you well. Go in peace, and be cured of your disease."
> Mark 5:34

† † †

Sometimes people make the mistake of having faith in THEIR faith rather than the OBJECT of their faith. The truth is we demonstrate faith every day when we sit in a chair, start our car, answer our phone, or even flip a light switch. We have faith those things are going to work. Did our faith make those things work as we intended or was it because they were correctly engineered to do so? We believed they would work because they had been reliable in the past, so reliable in fact that every time we flip a light switch, we never stop to consider whether or not it will turn on a light. But here is the thing; our belief that the light would come on did not cause it to do so. Our belief just caused us to take advantage of the resource. Without believing those things would actually work, we would never use them for their intended use and miss their benefit to our lives.

God want us to have that same kind of confidence (faith) in Him. But notice something important about the foregoing scenario. We had experience with those things and that experience bolstered our trust that they would actually work. When we read the Bible, we can see how God has always been faithful to His promises. Time after time He makes good on His promises and that strengthens our faith in Him, and when we WALK with God according to His word, we understand His promises can be believed. In the verse above, the woman believed the object of her faith (Jesus) would be the solution to her problem. God wants us to have that same kind of faith.

Father, please help me to always remember the object of my faith – YOU!

May 6

> Now there were some present at the same time who told him about the Galileans, whose blood Pilate had mixed with their sacrifices. And he answered and said to them, "Do you think that these Galileans were worse sinners than all the other Galileans, because they suffered these things? Or those eighteen, on whom the tower in Siloam fell, and killed them; do you think that they were worse offenders than all the others who dwell in Jerusalem? I tell you, no, but, unless you repent, you will all perish in the same way."
> Luke 13:1-2, 4, 5

There are not a lot of scriptural details that surround these two events Jesus references. To be sure, they were both a tragedy and apparently well known to His audience.

Perhaps the lack of scriptural details is purposeful due to the emphasis of the teaching - REPENTANCE. Jesus could very well use the same analogy to current events if He were physically with us today. What was Jesus calling the people to repent of in this story? Bad behavior, unbelief, or trusting a foreign god all come to mind. Perhaps it was all these things or none of these things, let the reader decide. In the simplest explanation, repent means to change direction, moving one way and then moving in the OPPOSITE direction, the optimum word being MOVING. Theologically it means to move towards God rather than away from God. The teaching is still relevant today for both believers and unbelievers alike.

Here is what makes the story personal; is God calling us to repentance? If so, how will we react to God's call? Jesus told His original hearers that unless they repent, they would likewise perish. God has given us Free Will - let's be sure we choose wisely.

Sing a chorus of your favorite song today. You will remember why it is your favorite.

May 7

"A disciple is not above the teacher, but everyone when he is fully trained will be like his teacher."
Luke 6:40

I recently tripped over this verse and ever since then the Holy Spirit continues to remind me of these words of Jesus. So, what did Jesus mean by being perfectly trained? To be sure, those under His tutelage were perfectly trained, but what about us who claim to be disciples of Jesus yet are living thousands of years after His return to heaven? How can we be perfectly trained? As a reminder, the definition of a disciple is one who embraces and assists in spreading the teaching of another.

Focusing on the four Gospels is a great place to start and persist. The Holy Spirit has preserved and made available to believers the essence of Jesus' life and teaching. Being more than casually familiar with the Gospels is akin to sitting at the feet of Jesus or traveling with Him. His words are comforting, challenging, and sometimes frightening.

The question I have asked myself in light of this verse is: do I REALLY want to be like my teacher or just enjoy the eternal benefits of salvation? If I want to be like Him, then I am obliged to an unconditional pursuit and loyalty of and to His teaching. That likeness also makes me subject to the persecution Jesus promised His first disciples. It is all part of being like the teacher.

Remember His promise; "everyone perfectly trained will be like his teacher." The Gospels and the rest of the Bible could be the key to fulfillment of this promise. Give grace to all because all need grace.

May 8

"The entrance of your words gives light. It gives understanding to the simple."
Psalms 119:130

† † †

Have you ever been in an uncomfortable or even desperate situation and suddenly the right person enters the room, the one who can solve your problem and rescue you? Or have you ever been in a dark room or building and been confused or frightened but suddenly a light comes on and everything becomes visible? That is the imagery in this verse. The ENTRANCE of God's Word, the Bible, is that deliverer and light.

Sure, we can choose to fumble along in darkness or continuously struggle to find a solution to a desperate situation, but why? Why not let God via His Word, and consequently His Holy Spirit, provide light to the darkness and dilemmas of our lives?

That is a question each person must answer for him/herself. Our Creator has given us "Free will." Depending on how it is wielded, that is a sword that can both save and kill. Someone once remarked, "there are none so blind as those who will (choose) not see." Sadly, that is the choice of many people.

Here is my testimony: there was a time when I lived in the darkness but now, I live in the light, and I can say with all sincerity that the light is a much better neighborhood than the darkness. I encourage everyone to pursue God's Word with greater vigor than they pursue a career. That pursuit will yield a much better outcome than a successful career.

May 9

Yesterday I heard Frank Sinatra sing "I did it my Way." It is a conundrum that I both love and hate this song. To be fair, Paul Anka wrote the lyrics, but Sinatra sings it with such passion that he takes ownership. The lyrics are the epitome of the Anthro-centric approach to life and that is what appeals to my flesh, but my spirit wants it to be "God's way." In the seventh chapter of Romans the Apostle Paul writes about this same struggle in his life. Truthfully, even the most ardent believer falls through the "my way" trap door occasionally, some more often than others. It is certainly one compelling reason why we need a Savior.

Is there some sure-fire way to change "my way" to ALWAYS "His way?" I cannot speak for others but for me, no. Like Paul, my only option is to trust Jesus for forgiveness and the Holy Spirit to direct me in "God's Way" through His Word and His power in my life. Still, I know "my way" will, at times, prevail. That is my shame but also the glory of the Cross of Jesus, forgiveness, and reconciliation with my Creator. If God can do this for me, He can do it for anyone, and He will if only we believe that God so loved the world that He gave His only begotten Son, that whoever believes in Him should not perish but have everlasting life.

Father, help me make my way YOUR way.

May 10

Recently I was exploring popular Bible APs and the many contributors available for personal spiritual growth and edification. Some names I recognized but most were new to me. The thought came to me that these are men and women who have something to say about Christianity, perhaps about their own faith. I am confident the Holy Spirit of God encouraged them to share what He had laid on their hearts, and now they are being obedient to that call.

Why am I writing about this? It is because I am one of those people that cannot keep the things of God to myself, the things that jump from scripture to my mind and ultimately my heart, eventually jump onto a page I am writing or out of my mouth. It is who I am, it is my place in His Kingdom. Each of us has a specific place in God's Kingdom, it is part of His plan for us. It does not matter whether your spot is in the front or the back. Those are judgments rendered by man, not God. He only sees His own working according to His Will, keeping the body of Christ functioning effectively.

I have found my place, and I am writing this to encourage you to find your "sweet spot" in His Kingdom. Perhaps you have already found it. GREAT! Enjoy your spot and be the very best you can be. Life on planet earth is so much shorter than we anticipate. Perhaps you have yet to find yours. Perhaps you are afraid to find it. It is true that others may not understand and find fault in what you find beautiful, it can be risky in that regard. It is also true that some people view Christianity as an Alice in Wonderland experience with all the weirdness in that rabbit hole. It has in the past and will in the future be that which separates people, even friends. Be assured, however, that the temporal and eternal benefits of finding your place in His Kingdom far outweigh any temporary loss or anxiety you may experience.

One final thought. Have you found YOUR sweet spot in His Kingdom?

The Beginning, the Fall, the Solution, the End, the Gospel

THE NEXT 6 DAYS

Read and *meditate* on each scripture then pray

May 11

The Beginning –
"In the beginning God created the heavens and the earth."
Genesis 1:1
(AND)
"And God commanded the man, saying, "Of every tree of the garden you may freely eat; but of the tree of the knowledge of good and evil, you shall not eat of it; for in the day that you eat of it you will surely die."
Genesis 2:16, 17

May 12

The Fall–*Think about it!*
Genesis 3:6

† † †

"When the woman saw that the tree was good for food, and that it was a delight to the eyes, and that the tree was to be desired to make one wise, she took of its fruit, and ate, and she also gave some to her husband who was with her, and he ate."
Genesis 3:6

May 13

The Solution–*Think about it!*
John 19:30

†††

When Jesus therefore had received the vinegar, he said, "It is finished." He bowed his head, and gave up his spirit. John 19:30

May 14

The Solution–*Think about it!*
Matthew 28:5, 6

†††

The angel answered the women, "Do not be afraid, for I know that you seek Jesus, who has been crucified. He is not here, for he has risen, just like he said. Come, see the place where he was lying." Matthew 28:5, 6

May 15

The End–*Think about it!*
Revelation 21:1

†††

"I saw a new heaven and a new earth: for the first heaven and the first earth have passed away, and the sea is no more." Revelation 21:1

May 16

The Gospel—*Think about it!*
John 3:16

† † †

"For this is how God loved the world: he gave his only Son, so that everyone who believes in him will not perish but have life without end."
John 3:16

May 17

"The fear of the LORD is to hate evil. I hate pride, arrogance, the evil way, and the perverse mouth."
Proverbs 8:13

† † †

It is hard to get more explicit than this, the word hate is used twice. This verse makes it clear that just personally avoiding evil is not sufficient in God's economy. Notice also that pride, arrogance, and a perverse mouth are part and parcel to evil. God is holy and expects us to hate evil, but to be clear, He doesn't expect us to hate people, but He does expect us to hate evil behavior. Often, it is a challenge to separate the two. Jesus was a master at separating evil behavior from the evil doer. After all, Man in the beginning was created in the image of God. That truth helps us to understand WHY GOD loves us.

So, why do some people become evil doers and continue in that behavior until death? That is a subject for another discussion. What this verse is calling us to is a recognition of evil and hatred towards it. Evil is what necessitated the sacrifice of God's Son, Jesus. That single act should be sufficient for us to understand and embrace this verse. Sometimes we do not have to look very hard to find evil, sadly the mirror is all that is necessary. Let us be sure we are honest with both God and ourselves in that regard. Remember, forgiveness is only a confession away.

May 18

"The soul of the sluggard desires, and has nothing, but the desire of the diligent shall be fully satisfied."
Proverbs 13:4

†††

I consider this unequivocally true when it comes to prayer and Bible study. How about you? When I become a sluggard in regard to spiritual issues, my soul becomes impoverished.

Father, help me to be energetic in my pursuit of You.

May 19

"I opened my mouth wide and panted, for I longed for your commandments."
Psalms 119:131

†††

When I read these words of King David, I am reminded of God's love for him. God tells the Prophet Samuel that David is a man after His own heart. What an endorsement! It is no wonder why God graciously honored and used David's devotion to make David such a big part of Israel's history.

Yes, David did have failures in his life, sometimes big failures, but when he was made aware of those failures he repented and sought his first love. Psalm 51 and Psalm 32 are great examples of David's repentant heart when confronted with his sin surrounding Bathsheba and Uriah.

I pray for that same repentant heart in my life. No excuses, just confession and personal accountability. How about you?

May 20

> One of the criminals who hung there insulted him, saying, "Are you not the Christ? Save yourself and us." But the other answered, and rebuking him said, "Do you not even fear God, seeing you are under the same condemnation?"
> Luke 23:39, 40

And so, it continues today, a world full of condemned people. They may not be nailed to a cross, but their death is a certainty. It also continues that some see Jesus on His Cross and believe He has the power to save them while others mock Him with disbelief even as they slip into eternity. As Solomon astutely observed; "There is nothing new under the sun."

Let us do all we can do to present Jesus as the Savior to the dying men and women of this world. Let us use our talents and treasure to bring the Gospel to everyone everywhere. Some of Jesus' final words include the following: "Go therefore and make disciples of all the nations, baptizing them in the name of the Father and of the Son and of the Holy Spirit, teaching them to observe all things that I have commanded you; and lo, I am with you always, even to the end of the age."

A lofty goal? You bet it is but one that WE can be part of if we choose to do so. Opportunities are everywhere!

May 21

"Wisdom is before the face of one who has understanding, but the eyes of a fool wander everywhere."
Proverbs 17:24

†††

Our God, the one who created it all has wrapped wisdom in a book, His book, the Bible. Between the covers we discover the glory of our Creator, His Will for us, and how to live at peace with Him and each other. His Word truly is a lamp unto our feet and a light unto the path of life.

Without it we are like the fool who searches the earth for wisdom but finds only counterfeits that provide the illusion of a successful life. Jesus asks His followers, "What does it profit a man to gain the whole world but lose his very soul?" Success has many faces but ultimately only one matters. Thankfully, God reveals that one way in His book. I encourage you to make it your highest priority (John 6:63; 17:3).

May 22

"Send men, that they may spy out the land of Canaan, which I give to the children of Israel. Of every tribe of their fathers, you shall send a man, every one a prince among them."
Numbers 13:2

†††

I really like spy stories. I confess that sometimes I have imagined myself part of the Mission Impossible team or even as James Bond. It is funny, I know, but we all have our fantasies.

But here is a reality, I really have at times, lived a clandestine life. Let me explain. All too often those around me never knew my true identity - a born again follower of Jesus. Whether it was a business associate, an old friend or new acquaintance, they never knew because I never told them, or worse, my actions would have indicated otherwise.

For those times I am truly ashamed and have sought forgiveness. The scary part is that I fear there will be similar times in the future. I will once again be the chameleon that blends perfectly with my surroundings. These past and potentially future failures lead me to challenge the Apostle Paul's claim to be "the chief of sinners." I certainly must be near the top of that list. Sadly, I really am a repeat offender.

Maybe you have also been a secret agent of the Lord. Let us purpose together that we will reveal our true identity by both our actions and confession. I will pray for you while you pray for me.

May 23

"Whoever listens to you listens to me, and whoever rejects you rejects me. Whoever rejects me rejects him who sent me."
Luke 10:16

† † †

These words of Jesus ring true today and they continue to levy eternal consequences on those who reject the Gospel. I sometimes struggle to believe that God has given us His authority as we present the Gospel to others, but my struggle does not negate the truth.

In my lifetime I will speak millions of words but none so important as the Gospel. The same goes for hearing. Some would say it is impossible to pick one thing in life that stands above all others. For me it is the story of a Father who rescues His rebellious and wayward children from the fires of hell. How about you?

May 24

"Let another man praise you, and not your own mouth; a stranger, and not your own lips."
Proverbs 27:2

† † †

Pride is a killer and God hates it. Beyond creating an obstacle between God and us, pride will also skew our human relationships. Very few people enjoy the company of a prideful man or woman. Pride is common and chronic to Man, but why?

It first manifested when Eve believed the Serpent in that she could be like God if she ate the forbidden fruit. Sadly, Adam was quick to follow and ever since that fateful moment pride has become part of our soul's DNA. Without the regeneration of the Holy Spirit pride will continue to enjoy a prominent place in the human heart. "Me first and foremost" will be the mantra of men and women worldwide.

Thankfully, our Creator has provided a solution for the malady of pride. First, the Cross of Jesus, and then our own cross. Jesus says, "If anyone desires to come after Me, let him deny himself, and take up his cross daily, and follow Me." Jesus demonstrated humility by always trusting His Father's Will rather than His own. We can genuinely choose to do likewise if the Holy Spirit has sway in our lives. He will give us both the desire and the power to overcome pride. Trust Him!

May 25

"But if I by the finger of God cast out demons, then the kingdom of God has come to you."
Luke 11:20

† † †

Yes, there really are demons just like there really are angels. Jesus talks about both and if He acknowledged their presence, we would be wise to do likewise. We cannot see them, but both are all around us, in fact, some actions by people are so evil that demonic influence is the only explanation.

Should we fear them? Not if we are born again but we should not ignore them either. The Bible reveals that, You are of God, little children, and have overcome them; because greater is he who is in you than he who is in the world" (1 John 4:4). The "He" who is in us is the Holy Spirit of God who has authority over all things in heaven and on earth. Yep, the same Holy Spirit that lived in Jesus lives in us! Hard to fathom, I know.

Nonetheless, demonic activity can manifest at any moment in our lives. Be on guard and ask the Holy Spirit to guide and protect you. Remember, a demon will push you away from the Cross of Jesus while the Holy Spirit will draw you to that same Cross. Also remember and be confident that we have permission and authority to plead the blood and the name of Jesus when we rebuke evil spirits.

Tell a stranger that God loves them.

May 26

It came to pass, as he said these things, a certain woman out of the crowd lifted up her voice, and said to him, "Blessed is the womb that bore you, and the breasts which nursed you." But he said, "On the contrary, blessed are those who hear the word of God, and keep it."
Luke 11:27, 28

† † †

According to Jesus keeping (doing) God's Word is what triggers a heavenly blessing. So, the question I must continually ask myself is; "Do I want to be blessed by God today?" The question is rhetorical; of course, I always want to be blessed by God; which one of us would not? The commitment to KEEP His Word today is another matter. Pride, greed, lust, fear, and other enemies are lurking at my door, ready to pounce. The "door" is who I am trusting? Do I trust God or will I, like Adam and Eve, believe the enemy's lies about the goodness and trustworthiness of God? I must confess that too many times I have opened the door and allowed the enemy into my house, my mind. Thankfully, I have a Savior who forgives my sometimes lack of faith in His promises. Without Jesus I would be doomed. With Him, I am saved from the enemy of my soul and my own fickleness in faith.

May 27

"But Jesus did not trust himself to them, because he knew everyone, and because he did not need anyone to testify concerning man; for he himself knew what was in man."
John 2:24, 25

† † †

Although Jesus was a man, He was also God, and His Devine nature knew that people are not trustworthy. Even the best among us fails, some more than others, but no one scores 100% on that test. We all have a trail of broken promises in our past. Our untrustworthiness is just one sad part of Man's sinful nature and one of many compelling reasons why we need a Savior.

Think about it. We declare and even boast that Jesus is our Lord but often choose our will rather than His, and we end up occupying the throne of our heart that rightfully belongs to Him. It all seems so harmless, even natural until we consider the Cross. It is then that we are vividly confronted with the devastation caused by sin, OUR sin!

So, what can we do with our past and inevitable future failures? Nothing, life is not a dress rehearsal. We cannot undo what has been done. That is why God does not offer us a way to turn back the clock, He offers us forgiveness. I pray that I will be quick to recognize failure, confess it, repent, and not live a life of regret and remorse, but instead the abundant life Jesus promised.

May 28

"For the grace of God has appeared, bringing salvation to all people, instructing us to say "No" to ungodliness and worldly desires, and to live soberly, righteously, and godly in this present age."
Titus 2:11, 12

† † †

The grace of God has appeared in so many ways to mankind. Jesus most certainly is grace in person, the Bible is grace in print, the

Holy Spirit is grace invisible, the Creation, family, the Church, and friends are all part of the grace of God afforded to sinful men and women. The very fact that He holds ALL things together is a silent demonstration of God's grace. None of these things would be available if it were not for the grace of God. Someone once defined grace as unmerited favor, and so it is. Grace does not consider our behavior, good or bad.

According to this verse, there is something else about grace that we need to understand and embrace, grace is PURPOSEFUL. It has a teaching aspect that guides or even directs us to a life that reflects the character and nature of God. Jesus most surely did that and so does the teaching in the Bible. The other manifestations of grace also witness to order, community, and creativity, and when we gather all the demonstrations of grace together, we most certainly are encouraged to live a godly life. Our very soul is bent toward righteousness.

Father, teach me by your grace to be the man you want me to be.

May 29

> "Now may the Lord of peace himself give you peace at all times in all ways. The Lord be with you all."
> 2 Thessalonians 3:16

☨ ☨ ☨

Are these just pleasant words the Apostle Paul offers his readers or is there substance to them? Is peace only an illusion or can it become the reality of our lives? Heck, nature itself strives for equilibrium as evidenced in the laws of thermodynamics, so is it not reasonable to want the same in our lives?

The principle that unlocks true peace is not the absence of conflict. Jesus speaks of this in John 16:33. Instead, TRUE peace is found exclusively in having peace with our Creator, and that can only be achieved once that which separates us, the sin issue, has been resolved. Until then, conflict remains, and our spirit will never be at rest. Thankfully, that issue has been settled at the Cross of Jesus and expressed in the Gospel. When we truly believe the Gospel, spiritual equilibrium occurs; our sin, past, present, and future is both absorbed and eliminated by Jesus while His righteousness flows to us thusly creating spiritual equilibrium. Our conflict with God ends. Period!

Nonetheless, unrest and even turmoil can prevail in our lives when we fail to understand AND embrace the spiritual equilibrium afforded by faith in the Gospel. Unlike the laws of gravity and thermodynamics that are independent of our recognition, it is necessary that we embrace spiritual equilibrium to achieve it.

May 30

"The proud and haughty man, "scoffer" is his name; he works in the arrogance of pride."
Proverbs 21:24

✝ ✝ ✝

We all know this man or woman. Perhaps at some point in our lives we were this person, but regardless of who we once were we need to focus on who we are now. If we have been saved by Grace, and that is the ONLY way we can be saved, then we should leave pride behind like we would leave a bag of garbage in a trash can. One problem with pride is that it is often covert, we do not recognize it in OUR lives. It is so easy to identify in another person, it is obvious, overt in nature, but like a secret agent it masquerades in our lives as self-confidence or positive assertiveness. Like a secret agent, however, it is not working on our behalf but on the behalf of another. Satan is manifested to the world in prideful behavior.

Is there a way to determine if pride is problematic in our life? One way is to ask your family and friends for an honest opinion; however, those can be turbulent waters. The best way is to ask the HOLY SPIRIT to reveal this to you. The way He will do this is through the Word of God, the Bible, especially the Gospels. As you read about Jesus and His interaction with the religious leaders of His day, you will see what true, God honoring humility looks like versus the dastardly pride of man. Yes, you will need to spend time in the Bible, but your life will be better because of that time.

Father, I ask you to reveal to me whether pride is a secret agent in my life.

May 31

> "He put all things under his feet, and gave him to be head over all things for the church, which is his body, the fullness of him who fills all in all."
> Ephesians 1:22, 23

† † †

The poet John Donne once wrote, "No man is an island, entire of itself." From the very beginning Man was not meant to be alone as demonstrated by the creation of Eve to accompany Adam in his journey. We are created in the image of a God who lives in community, the Father, Son, and Holy Spirit. Born again believers become members of the worldwide community of the church. Even without a single person around we are never alone. Jesus says, "I will never leave you or forsake you."

WELCOME TO MAY

Our Heavenly Father understands our need for community and made certain a community of believers is available to His sons and daughters. I encourage the reader to take advantage of those resources for fellowship. Join a church, join a Bible study, visit a friend or family member, say hello and have a conversation with a neighbor or become a volunteer. It will be good for the soul and an encouragement to others. You will not be disappointed.

WELCOME TO JUNE

"I have come as a light into the world, that whoever believes in me may not remain in the darkness."
John 13:46

June 1

"Do you think that I have come to give peace in the earth? I tell you, no, but rather division."
Luke 12:51

There is no doubt this is one of Jesus' most controversial proclamations. It sounds militant and radical because that is the nature of His ministry. Jesus calls His followers to both rebellion and peace; rebellion against the works of Satan including hypocrisy and bad doctrine, but He also calls His followers to seek peace with God through repentance and belief in who He is, the Son of God. He condemns the core sin of Satan, a sin that to this day plagues mankind, the sin of PRIDE. He asks His followers to live a humble life of service to both Him and those around them, to trust Him exclusively for their salvation, and to understand they are, on their own, helplessly separated from their Creator. Is there any wonder why that message brings strife to even the strongest familial relationship?

Nonetheless, that is His message and the teaching of the Cross. Can anyone have pride in themselves after viewing the brutality of the crucifixion knowing it was done for their sake? Pride? Yes, not in ourselves but rather in our Savior!

June 2

"The spirit of a man will sustain him in sickness, But who can bear a broken spirit?"
Proverbs 18:14

† † †

The most important thing about any training is not how good or bad you do, but that you NEVER give up. As long as you continue trying, you have not failed. Yes, proficiency is the goal but proficiency without participation is impossible.

Can we relate this principle to life in general? I believe we can. When we find ourselves without hope, our spirit is broken, and when our spirit is broken we GIVE UP. Our Creator understands this and continuously extends the hope of the Gospel to all mankind. No matter what our circumstances are, no matter how dire they may appear, the HOPE of the Gospel eclipses them all.

Do you know someone who has lost all hope? Share the hope of the Gospel with them TODAY! God loves to heal a broken spirit.

June 3

"Do not be overcome by evil, but overcome evil with good."
Romans 12:21

† † †

Overcome evil? Is that even possible? After all, ever since the beginning, evil has lurked in the shadows and manifested in both obvious and veiled ways. On a global scale the answer is no. Wars, both big and small, have been waged in an effort to eliminate evil, but to no avail. Evil continues to be resilient, often vigorously so.

In his letter to the church in Rome, the Apostle Paul is speaking to individuals, not the collective. For those who argue that evil starts with the individual and then like a contagious virus quickly spreads to the collective, I agree. But here is the thing. We are called to combat evil with good in our own souls first. Jesus tells His followers, "For out of the heart come evil intentions, murder, adultery, fornication, theft, false witness, slander." So how do we overcome the things that are imbedded in our heart? Jesus tells a man named Nicodemus that he needs a new heart, that he needs to be "born again" if he expects to see the kingdom of God, a kingdom void of evil. What was true for Nicodemus is also true for everyone else on planet earth.

With our new heart we actually can wage the war of good versus evil, and by the power of the Holy Spirit win those battles. God gives us both the desire and ability to sow and reap peace and goodness rather than evil. The Apostle was not asking the impossible, but instead pointing us to a choice we can make with confidence.

Perhaps you need a new heart. Sincerely ask God to give you one, He will.

June 4

"Whoever guards his mouth and his tongue keeps his soul from troubles."
Proverbs 21:23

✝ ✝ ✝

This is true for people everywhere and of all ages. How many of us have regrets over what has come out of our mouth? I suspect we have all found ourselves regretting something we said, wishing we could somehow take back cruel, unkind, or careless words. But it does not work like that because once they leave our lips they are gone forever—no take backs possible. People usually recover from physical injuries, but emotional injury caused by careless words can last a lifetime. Perhaps you remember a hurtful word that was carelessly said to you when you were a child. Sadly, that is not uncommon.

The Apostle James says, "And the tongue is a fire, a world of iniquity..." That is a scary assessment of the potential pain we could cause others and ourselves with a careless tongue. Let us make a covenant with our lips to speak the truth in love, and to look for opportunity to speak encouraging words that build up and not tear down.

June 5*

"I the Lord have spoken."
Jeremiah 1:19a

†††

Three times in one chapter God says to Jeremiah, "I have spoken!" Three times he offers comfort to a worried and resistant young man and closes his words with, "I have spoken."

When God created the universe, He "spoke" it into being (Gen 1:3); when he came to Earth as the God-Man Messiah, John referred to Him as "the Word" (John 1:1); and when the author of Hebrews began his letter, he wrote that in these new days, God has "spoken" to us through His Son (Heb 1:2). When God speaks, universes literally spring from nothing, cosmic powers are overthrown, and human beings can pass from death to life.

When I was a music teacher, I would tell my students there was a difference between "hearing" and "listening". Hearing is a physiological function of the ear – sound waves pass through the ear canal and cause the ear to vibrate, and we "hear" a sound. Listening, however, is a function of the mind – it requires attention, intention, and thought. And when it comes to God, listening also involves the heart.

God's words have the power to transform us – if we will only listen to them (which means we put them into practice (Matt 7:24)). We know from the gospels there are many who "heard" Jesus' message, but not everyone "listened."

Father, give me a heart and mind to listen to your word, to find peace, comfort, encouragement, challenge, forgiveness, and acceptance in what you say. Train me to listen, for your words have power. Help me be like Peter, who proclaimed, "Your words have life!" (John 6:68).

June 6

> "Teach me good judgment and knowledge, for I believe in your commandments. Before I was afflicted, I went astray ;but now I observe your word. You are good, and do good. Teach me your statutes."
> Psalms 119:66-68

† † †

To be sure, there are times when bad things happen to us. King David understood that the bad in his life could, in fact, be good because it brought him back to focusing on his relationship with God rather than focusing on the world. He learned that God could use the bad to help him understand what is truly good. We should all pray for that same understanding.

Notice in these verses that David, in his AFFLICTION, recognized that his prayer to know good judgment and knowledge is being answered in the affliction he is experiencing while straying from his relationship with God. Did God cause that affliction? That's an age-old question. Perhaps, or perhaps it was a result of David's bad choices. Either or both can be true; we'll never know for sure. The one thing we can know for sure is that God used that affliction to help David return to a RIGHT relationship with Him. It is what David prayed for and what he received.

Are we asking God to teach us what David longed for in his life? If so, be prepared to be taught by a teacher that David declares is not only good but does good. There are occasions to fear God, but this would not be one.

Share the Gospel with someone today. At the very least, look in the mirror and share it with yourself.

June 7

"Trust in the LORD with all your heart, and do not lean on your own understanding."
Proverbs 3:5

Notice that this teaching instructs the reader to trust God and His instructions with "ALL" their heart. This is especially important because elsewhere the Prophet Jeremiah says that the "heart is deceitful above all things, desperately wicked" (Jeremiah 17:9). This reality presents a clear and present danger.

The danger is that without surrendering to God ALL our understanding of how to live our lives, we will live according to how we feel, and the odds are those feelings and desires will focus on OUR will and not the will of God. We will act out our selfish priorities, not His best practices. Countless individuals will mock this instruction as being "imagined danger." I ask them to consider the condition of the world to understand the danger of following an unregenerated heart. Can anyone say we live in a utopian world, or at least a safe world?

Some will argue that it is impossible to legislate morality. I agree, but society has legislated laws to protect itself against those who are following their own heart in regard to criminal behavior. Here is something to consider: Imagine what the world would look like if people everywhere followed Jesus' instruction to love God with our WHOLE heart and love our neighbor as ourselves. Occasionally we are confronted by people who want to know why God has not provided a solution for the ills of the world. He has, but people choose to ignore it. Being "born again" is the solution. It is why we pray for God's will to be done on earth as it is in heaven.

Until that day manifests, we can rely on God's Word to teach us how we should conduct our lives. We may die never seeing the people of earth living in harmony, but we can be assured that in heaven it will be so.

June 8

"But love your enemies, and do good, and lend, expecting nothing back; and your reward will be great, and you will be children of the Most High; for he is kind toward the unthankful and evil. Therefore be merciful, even as your Father is also merciful."
Luke 6:35, 36

†††

These words of Jesus haunt me. They are the most troubling for me in all the Bible. Why? Because on my own, I have no inclination, leave alone any desire, to love my enemies or be kind to evil people, but that is exactly what Jesus asks me to do.

What was He thinking when He spoke these words? What could possibly motivate Him to say such things, I question? But then I am reminded by the Holy Spirit of the truth expressed in Isaiah 55:8, 9:"For my thoughts are not your thoughts, neither are your ways my ways, " says the LORD.

For as the heavens are higher than the earth, so are my ways higher than your ways, and my thoughts than your thoughts."

So, there it is, the explanation, one I can easily hide behind. I cannot be expected to have His thoughts. Or can I? 1 Cor 2:16 says: "For, Who has known the mind of the Lord? Who will instruct him? But we have the mind of Christ." Uh Oh, my conceived cover is now blown. I can no longer plead ignorance, and I realize I must choose between MY will and His. It is then that the Holy Spirit reminds me of Proverbs 3:5, 6:"Trust in the LORD with all your heart, and do not lean on your own understanding. In all your ways remember him, and he will make your paths straight."

Like the Apostle Paul, I now cry out: "What a wretched man I am. Who will deliver me out of the body of this death? Thanks be to God through Jesus Christ, our Lord. So then with the mind, I myself serve God's law, but with the flesh, the sin's law." (Romans 7:24-25).

Does all this sound confusing. For those without the Holy Spirit dwelling in them, the answer is "of course!" For those with the Holy Spirit, the answer is "no, " but it is nonetheless challenging. For me,

Jesus' words in Luke are a vivid reminder of why I need a Savior, I again realize without a Savior I am doomed.

Jesus sacrificed himself to be the Savior for all people. Encourage those without a Savior to ask Jesus to forgive their sins. He is the only one that can save from the coming wrath of God.

June 9

"Inasmuch as it is appointed for people to die once, and after this, judgment,"
Hebrews 9:27

†††

We all have an appointment with death, and it is one we cannot postpone or reschedule. There is no escape from this appointment, it is an absolute certainty. Like it or not, death hangs over our head like low hanging fruit in an imagined garden. Some people think physical death is the conclusion of a person, they simply cease to exist in any form. Others believe they will be reincarnated as another person or life form, while others believe the spirit of a person roams the earth and heavens. There are other beliefs, but you get the idea. All, however, are speculative beliefs lacking proof.

Thankfully, the One who created life has provided the truth about death, and the truth is that physical death is not the end of our story. God, our Creator, has graciously provided definitive information so we will not have to speculate. It is all in His words to mankind, the Bible, a book given to us so we can avoid misunderstanding both life and death. It is only meant for our time on planet earth, there will be no need for a Bible in heaven.

Some will argue that the Bible is no more authoritative than any other religious manifesto. Conceivably, that argument may have merit except for ONE glaring validation. The resurrection! The resurrection of Jesus, God's Son, is an historical fact, documented in both Christian and secular historical accounts. Only the hardest of hearts would ignore the evidence. One can choose to ignore it but that does not negate that it actually happened. Denying that it never happened is akin to saying that gravity is not true while stepping off the roof of house. Unbelief does not change a fact. Jesus died on a Roman cross, crucified, yet God resurrected Him from the dead as witnessed by many.

A person can choose to believe the proof of the one resurrected from the dead or speculate otherwise. God has given mankind "free will" to choose to believe Him or call Him a LIAR. Choose wisely because both choices have eternal consequences. Believing the proof and the teachings of Jesus provide eternal life while those rejecting the invitation to eternal life (living eternally in His presence in heaven), will be separated from God eternally and spend a conscious eternity in Hell from which there is no escape or reprieve.

June 10

"As clouds and wind without rain, so is he who boasts of gifts deceptively."
Proverbs 25:14

†††

We have all been there, a promise made to us never fulfilled. Perhaps we vividly remember an employer, a friend, or even a loved one who reneged on a promise. Sadly, we need only to look into the mirror to find a guilty party. How many times have we failed to keep a promise or commitment? It happens to the best of us, and if it never happened to or by you, you are one in a million. I caution you, however, that there is a likelihood it will someday become a reality in your life.

It is in the backdrop of this truth that God stands alone. Jesus says, "For truly I tell you, until heaven and earth pass away, not one letter, not one stroke of a letter, will pass from the law until all is accomplished." His promises that reflect both good and bad will ALL be accomplished in His timing. And therein lies our oft times misunderstanding. We expect His promises to be accomplished during our lifetime on planet earth. But we forget that with God, "a thousand years is like a day."

To be sure, EVERY promise of God will be kept whether in our limited time in this world or in our eternal life in heaven. It is a certainty.

Thank someone today for the things they do.

June 11

"It happened on one of those days, as he was teaching the people in the temple and preaching the Good News, that the chief priests and scribes came to him with the elders."
Luke 20:1

† † †

Often times we think of the gospel as the death, burial, and resurrection of Jesus. It is certainly the essence of the gospel, but in this passage, we learn that Jesus "taught the people in the temple and preached the GOSPEL." At this time, Jesus was very much alive, so although the gospel without the resurrection is incomplete, what gospel was Jesus preaching?

Most people know that the word gospel means good news. The good news started when the angels declared to the shepherds, "Glory to God in the highest, and on earth peace, goodwill toward men!" The very fact that God chose to live among us is good news. The very fact that He lived a sinless life, extended grace to sinners, corrected bad doctrine, exposed religious hypocrisy, revealed the true nature and will of God for humanity, and fulfilled every prophecy of His first coming is very much part of the gospel. Jesus, His entire life and glorious conclusion, IS THE GOSPEL! Don't miss this.

Every word in the gospels (Matthew, Mark, Luke, John) is part of the gospel of God. Read those beautiful words expecting to find truth, forgiveness, salvation, love, instruction, the past, present, and future, joy, peace, and, most of all, God. After all, Jesus tells Philip, "Have I been with you all this time, Philip, and you still do not know me? Whoever has seen me has seen the Father."

Good news? To me it is GREAT news. How about you?

June 12

"Do good to your servant, according to your word, LORD."
Psalms 119:65

✝ ✝ ✝

There are a couple of things that the Psalmist declares in this verse. First, the Lord has dealt well with him, a SERVANT. Perhaps, just perhaps that is why the Lord was kind to him, because the Psalmist considered himself to be the Lord's SERVANT. To truly embrace that understanding requires humility. Sometimes, even in the church, it is difficult to find humble folk. Rarely do I hear someone aspiring to be a SERVANT of God. Pride is a powerful enemy of God, and it lies dormant in every human. It waits patiently to manifest itself in words, attitude, thought, or deed. Secondly, the Psalmist declares that the blessings he has received are all promised in God's Holy Word, the Bible. He realizes this because he is familiar with God's Word; he knows the promises. Is this a teaching verse? I think so, how about you?

Father, help me to overcome pride in my life. Help me to truly consider myself to be your SERVANT and bless me according to your Word.

June 13

"Praise the LORD, my soul, and all that is within me, praise his holy name. Praise the LORD, my soul, and do not forget all his benefits"
Psalms 103:1, 2

† † †

How about you? As a child of God, what benefits can you name? Enjoy those benefits today and always. They were purchased for you by Jesus at a price that is incalculable in human understanding. It will be a good spiritual exercise to create a list of the benefits of being a child of God and then to thank Him for those benefits.

June 14

"For the Son of Man also did not come to be served, but to serve, and to give his life as a ransom for many."
Mark 10:45

† † †

This proclamation was made by Jesus in response to a request from several of His disciples for a place of prominence in His coming Kingdom. When I contemplate this verse, I think about what it will be like in heaven. Will all those in heaven be anxious to serve one another, more concerned about the other than themselves? With a new body, heart, and soul unencumbered by sin, will my greatest joy be derived from serving others? Will my heart finally be the same as the heart of Jesus? In this life I have learned that there is much more satisfaction and joy in giving than in receiving. Perhaps this realization is just a preview of coming attractions.

I doubt that His disciples embraced His proclamation, heck, I am not even sure I do, and I am living on the other side of the Cross. Nonetheless, whether I embrace it or not, it is true.

Father, help me to be a servant to all but especially to you.

June 15

"Therefore, you should pray this way:' Our Father in heaven, revered be your name."
Matthew 6:9

✝ ✝ ✝

There have been many excellent earthly fathers in the history of the world. However, the Greatest Of All Times (GOAT) father is the Heavenly Father. All others pale in comparison. To be sure, honor your EARTHLY father, it is the fifth of the Ten Commandments, but remember what Jesus said was the greatest commandment; "You shall love God with all your heart, with all your soul, with all your mind, with all your strength."

If you are able, fly a kite today. It is so fun to do so.

June 16

He looked up, and saw the rich people who were putting their gifts into the treasury. He saw a certain poor widow casting in

two lepta. He said, "Truly I tell you, this poor widow put in more than all of them, for all these put in gifts from their abundance, but she, out of her poverty, put in all that she had to live on."
Luke 21:1-4

✝✝✝

Have you ever wondered if God really does know who you are and what you are doing? After all, billions of people live or have lived on planet earth, so how could we possibly be noticed?

I do not know if the widow in this story wondered these things but clearly Jesus knew her, her life situation, her actions, and her heart. The parallel truth is that He knows these same things about you and me.

So, which one am I in this story and which one are you? Yes, the story focuses on money, but it is really about the hearts of those Jesus referenced. Have we given God our whole heart or are we holding something back? This story is a great reminder that He knows us personally and intimately.

Try to smile for fifteen continuous minutes today. It will make a difference in how you feel.

June 17

And he answered them, saying, "Who are my mother and my brothers?" And looking around at those who sat around him, he said, "Look, my mother and my brothers. For whoever does the will of God, the same is my brother, and my sister, and mother."
Mark 3:33-35

This is an astonishing declaration by Jesus. Here is the background: Jesus is teaching inside a house, and a very large crowd has gathered. It is so large that His mother and brothers are unable to come inside and have access to Him. Someone from outside calls to Jesus alerting Him that His family is outside wanting to come to Him and His response can be found in the verses above. Jesus identifies His FAMILY as those who DO THE WILL of God.

So, we have from the very lips of Jesus a critical truth. When a person genuinely believes that Jesus is the Son of God, they become a family member of Jesus with ALL the rights, responsibilities, and privileges that family affords, but notice the verse again. His family DOES the will of God, it is what verifies and identifies a person as being a family member. What is the Will of God? First and FOREMOST, BELIEVE on the Lord Jesus Christ and you will be saved. There is no greater Will of God than this. Beyond this, love God with all your heart and your neighbor as yourself.

June 18

> "And he will wipe away every tear from their eyes, and death will be no more, nor will there be mourning, nor crying, nor pain, anymore, for the first things have passed away."
> Revelation 21:4

† † †

This is a promise that EVERY human being yearns for in their lives. No more death, no more sorrow, no more pain; who would want otherwise? This is EXACTLY what awaits those who believe that God has sent His Son, Jesus, to redeem the world. Some would question why the world needs redemption while ignoring the ugly realities of life on planet earth, and those ugly realities are a result of the sin of men and women.

Are there some people who will not experience the promises of this verse? Sadly, YES. Just like you and I would not invite people who hate us into our house, so God will not allow those who hate Him into His. But who are those who hate God? All those who do not BELIEVE Him, who choose to believe what is contrary to His teaching. Especially offensive to Him are those who reject and even mock the death, burial, and resurrection of His Son, Jesus. It is, however, the will of God that ALL people will experience the promises in this verse. If that is true, why will some people be excluded, some will ask? It is because God has given each of us a freedom to CHOOSE how we LIVE our lives and what we will BELIEVE, and it is because of that free will why God will Judge every person. With that in mind, let us be very CAREFUL what we believe and how we live. It really does matter.

Color a picture in a coloring book today. It will take you back to your childhood.

June 19

> and said to them, "Why do you sleep? Rise and pray that you may not enter into temptation."
> Luke 22:46

There are times when I may as well be asleep when I consider my prayer life. Perhaps I am too busy, too tired, or just plain disinterested in prayer. Perhaps I do not believe prayer will make a difference. Whatever the reason or excuse, my time spent in prayer is too often minimal or anemic at best.

However, when I consider this entire verse, it becomes crystal clear to me that I heighten the risk of temptation by ignoring the privilege of prayer. That is what Jesus told His disciples and I believe it to be true. I realize that when I neglect to pray and read the Bible, I tend to be attracted to the "shiny" things in life rather than the substance of a healthy relationship with my Creator. I tend to focus on myself and my wants rather than the needs of those around me. I once asked God to MAKE me pray regularly, but I know deep down that will never happen any more than I can MAKE someone love me. Like love, prayer is a choice. Perhaps when it comes to God the two are intricately related - love and prayer.

Father, forgive my casual attitude about prayer. By the power of the Holy Spirit, help me to understand the value that regular and passionate prayer brings to my relationship with you.

June 20

"Thus says the LORD who made the earth, and who formed it to establish it; the LORD is his name: 'Call to me, and I will answer you, and will show you great and hidden things, which you do not know."
Jeremiah 33:2, 3

† † †

This invitation from God seems too good to be true. It invites His children to a personal and intimate relationship with Him. It is intimate because He knows our deepest thoughts, emotions, fears, joys, and even our secrets. How does He know such things? It would be well to remember that He is our Creator and knows EVERYTHING about us. To be sure, the intimacy is lop sided, we will never know Him as fully as He knows us, especially on this side of eternity.

Nonetheless, He has written a book about who He is and how He relates to humanity. The Bible was penned by 40 different authors who were inspired by the Holy Spirit of God to chronicle creation events through re-creation events and everything in-between. Beyond that, He has given every born again believer His Holy Spirit to guide, direct, and explain His holy book. He has provided all the details we NEED and all that we can UNDERSTAND with a finite mind. Yes, there are some details that we will not be able to understand fully, and for those instances He asks us to BELIEVE what He has written. Trusting Him is a powerful way to develop intimacy.

There will come a day when we will know so much more than we are ABLE to understand while on planet earth. In that day we will see clearly the things that we now see dimly. In that day our minds will not be confused by temptation and sin. In that day we will no longer need faith because our faith will have realization. In that day all the mysteries of life will disappear and never spoken of again. That day is coming, dear reader, and that day can happen either individually or collectively. Are you ready?

June 21*

"I the Lord have spoken."
Jeremiah1:19a

†††

Three times in one chapter God says to Jeremiah, "I have spoken!" Three times he offers comfort to a worried and resistant young man and closes his words with, "I have spoken."

When God created the universe, He "spoke" it into being (Gen 1:3); when he came to Earth as the God-Man Messiah, John referred to Him as "the Word" (John 1:1); and when the author of Hebrews began his letter, he wrote that in these new days, God has "spoken" to us through His Son (Heb 1:2). When God speaks, universes literally spring from nothing, cosmic powers are overthrown, and human beings can pass from death to life.

When I was a music teacher, I would tell my students there was a difference between "hearing" and "listening". Hearing is a physiological function of the ear – sound waves pass through the ear canal and cause the ear to vibrate, and we "hear" a sound. Listening, however, is a function of the mind – it requires attention, intention, and thought. And when it comes to God, listening also involves the heart.

God's word has the power to transform us – if we will only listen to them (which means we put them into practice (Matt 7:24)). We know from the gospels there are many who "heard" Jesus' message, but not everyone "listened."

Father, give me a heart and mind to listen to your word, to find peace, comfort, encouragement, challenge, forgiveness, and acceptance in what you say. Team me to listen, for your words have power. Help me be like Peter, who proclaimed, "Your words have life!" (John 6:68)

June 22

"And I, when I am lifted up from the earth, will draw everyone to myself."
John 12:32

† † †

Sometimes it feels to me like the Church is a rudderless ship at sea being tossed about by the wind and waves. A myriad of denominations, worship styles, doctrines both "progressive" and conservative, music aimed at one age group or another, dozens of Bible translations, on-line ministries, and TV and radio ministries exist. Seminars on everything from how to grow a church to how to manage church finances are common. Are these things bad? Not if they are viewed in the right perspective and proper context. Sometimes, however, inappropriate disputes within a congregation over these issues arise and spawn ridicule from an already skeptical world. Individual congregations become Satan's playground. Denominations and local congregations are often reduced to ORGANIZATIONS rather than the ORGANISM it was designed to be – the BODY of CHRIST on planet earth.

Read the verse again. Jesus has already told us how to reach the world. When HE is lifted up in proclamation and service, when HE remains the focus of a congregation and individuals rather than music, Bible version, service projects, or social issues, HE will draw ALL peoples to Himself. That is His promise. To be sure, there are many, many Biblically sound congregations proclaiming the Biblical Gospel while also meeting the physical needs of people in need. Conversely, there are many proclaiming a social gospel or worse, a gospel void of Jesus. Choose wisely where you worship because both God and the world are watching.

June 23*

Thus says the LORD, "Do not let the wise man glory in his wisdom, neither let the mighty man glory in his might, do not let the rich man glory in his riches; but let him who boasts boast in this, that he has understanding, and knows me, that I am the LORD who exercises loving kindness, justice, and

righteousness, in the earth: for in these things I delight," says the LORD.
Jeremiah 9:23, 24

✝ ✝ ✝

A key aspect of my job is to train leaders; and, given that I'm in the education field most have advanced degrees, with many holding doctorates. It's probably no wonder then that a common struggle many admit to is the belief that wherever they are, they're the "smartest person in the room." And as one who teaches many of the "smartest people in the room, " I fall prey to the same struggle (after all, if I'm teaching the smart people, doesn't that make me "smarter"?). But the fact is I'm not the smartest in the room – not by a long shot. In fact, given some of the things I come up with I'm not sure I'm the smartest person in the room when I'm the only person in the room!

I say that partly tongue-in-cheek, and partly I'm saying a deep truth. Even when I'm physically alone, I'm not alone – God is always with me; and I'm certainly not smarter than Him. Remember the Garden of Eden and the temptation our ancestors finally gave in to? It was to "know" what they were not to know, because in the "knowing" they would "be like God." Knowledge is a gift, and it can also be an idol we worship, pursue, and serve.

According to God, the only knowing we should boast in is that we know God. And the more I learn about Him, the more I realize how little I know – how small I am and how large He is. Lately, God has been correcting and redirecting me.

Father, change my mind – help me to be one who boasts only in you and never in myself. And, as Jeremiah prayed, be gentle in your correction. I am reminded that "[my life is not my own]"and [I am] not able to plan [my] own course. So, correct me, Lord, but please be gentle. Do not correct me in your anger, for I would die" (Jeremiah 10).

June 24

"Honor your father and your mother, that your days may be long upon the land which the Lord your God is giving you." Exodus 20:12

✝ ✝ ✝

Why did God include this in the Ten Commandments? Perhaps it was to train us to be submissive to authority. Think about it: if we are unable to obey the Father we CAN see, how can we be expected to obey the Father we CANNOT see? I suppose God could have other reasons for directing obedience to our parents but I can think of none that make more sense than my earlier premise. Whatever the reason, it is to our advantage to obey.

If your parents are still living, contact them today and check on their welfare.

June 25*

"For thus says the LORD, 'Do not enter into the house of mourning, neither go to lament, neither bemoan them; for I have taken away my peace from this people, says the LORD, even loving kindness and tender mercies." Jeremiah 16:5

✝ ✝ ✝

Throughout history God has held back evil – both the spiritual powers and the sinful desires of man. And there have been times He didn't hold back and instead allowed people to be given over to their desires. Here God is saying it will happen again. Only in the Lord will people find refuge and survive the coming judgement (see Jeremiah 16:19,17:7-8), and only in Him will they thrive even through it.

God has done it in the past and He will do it again! The only salvation available to us is Jesus – He alone is our rock and fortress. But people can't turn to Him if they have never heard of Him.

If we think things are bad now, I can't imagine what they will be when God pulls back His hand. That thought should frighten me for those who don't know Jesus or trust in Him. It should motivate me to share His good news of salvation – while there is still time.

Father, give me courage to speak words of truth to those around me, to share the good news of your salvation to others while there is still time. Soften their hearts to hear your message so they will turn and trust in you. We don't know the hour of judgement – but I know we will all face it when we die. Only in Jesus is hope found, so give me courage and words to share Him.

June 26*

"Simon Peter answered him, 'Lord, to whom would we go? You have the words of everlasting life.'"
John 6:68

† † †

This is certainly one of the more famous verses in scripture. I remember as a child it appeared in weekly church services as part of the sung liturgy. The teaching here is so simple – He is the one way to the father (see also John 14:6). So many people will not accept this simple truth, though, and the more I consider it the more it breaks my heart.

There are many things in this life about which we can legitimately disagree, and it will not impact eternity. But on this point, there is no disagreement – like Peter, we must come to the realization that Scripture is focused on no one else but Jesus. We can choose to accept and believe this, or we can reject it, but if Jesus is who He claims to be, it will not matter at the end of life if we think differently.

This truth should bring comfort to those who believe and sorrow when we think of those who don't believe – as well as motivation to share Him. If it does not, I wonder how deep the truth as really penetrated.

Pray for an old friend today.

June 27*

"For I know the plans that I have for you, ' says the LORD, 'plans for your welfare, and not for calamity, to give you hope and a future."
Jeremiah 29:11

This is one of those classic Bible verses many of us learn as children - it's shared at birthdays, graduations, and other milestone events. I think it has appeared on several wall plaques and maybe it's even been embroidered onto a few pillowcases or blankets! These observations are not to diminish God's promise in any way - He does have a plan for us. But as I reread these verses recently, I was struck by what surrounded them: God is in the middle of proclaiming judgment on the people in response to their sin, telling how he is sending Nebuchadnezzar to destroy them and take them captive to a foreign land for 70 (yes, 70!) years!

So even in the midst of judgement, God is demonstrating his gracious and mercy. As He sends His people off into of slavery (something He had originally rescued them from, which led to the founding of the nation itself), He still offered hope and a promise for salvation! God stays true to His original promise to Abraham, Isaac, Jacob, and even David: He continued to care for, love protect, and pursue His people even when he was punishing them.

And, He hasn't stopped - God continues to pursue us! He sent Jesus to die for us so we could be redeemed, restored, and forgiven. And He has also promised to come back again in glory. Just like the Jews' banishment to Babylon was temporary (70 years), so our time on earth is only a temporary assignment.

How will I spend this time He's given me? Will I be like David and show people the Lord? Or will I be like those who became so connected with the culture they refused to even return to Jerusalem when given the chance after the exile? (see Ezra and Nehemiah).

June 28*

> "Call to me, and I will answer you, and will show you great and hidden things, which you do not know."
> Jeremiah 33:3

God invites us into relationship - He wants us to know Him. And He has revealed Himself to us through His word. Jesus tells us that His words are life (John 6:63) and the author of Hebrews proclaims that God's word is "sharper than any two-edged sword."

But even though I know this, so often I look for wisdom in other places than to simply ask a God for it. I often forget that God lives in me; His Holy Spirit dwells in me, giving me a new heart and a new mind. Too often, though, when I face decisions, I look only to man to guide me. Don't get me wrong - God has revealed much through other men, and it is good to seek it out. But why do I so often start and end there? Why do I go to God as a last resort? God invited Jeremiah to ask Him questions, and James writes that we do not have because we do not ask (and this writing is in the context of his writing on wisdom). Could it be my vision of God is too small? Or maybe perhaps it's that my vision of me is too big? I want to figure stuff out on my own; it's the same independent streak we faced in the garden of Eden.

Father, teach me to seek you first, to ask you before I ask of others. For in you I find all I need – be all that I want as well. Reveal to me your secrets, so I can know you like you want me to.

June 29*

> "For thus says the LORD: "David shall never want a man to sit on the throne of the house of Israel; neither shall the priests the Levites want a man before me to offer burnt offerings …"
> Jeremiah 33:17, 18

† † †

In the preceding chapters of Jeremiah, God told the people to prepare for judgment and destruction as they were to be sent to Babylon for 70 years of exile. He told Jeremiah all of the sins the people committed, and He promised to destroy them for it. And yet He still offered hope and a promise of peaceful future, and that future involved a King and a Priest. Jesus is both king and high priest! God is fulfilled this prophecy in Jesus! All scripture points to Jesus, and I believe this verse is a prime example. Paul wrote that all God's promises come true in Jesus (2 Cor 1:20)! He is our salvation, our savior, our king, and our priest. Through his death the final sacrifice was made, and the full debt has been paid; in his resurrection, both death and sin are overcome!

Why do we so often look elsewhere for fulfillment? God has provided a way for us to be right with Him, to have our sins forgiven. He has provided the king and high priest He promised millennia ago!

Lord, help us rest 100% in you and your work.

June 30*

> The LORD said to him, "Go through the midst of the city, through the midst of Jerusalem, and set a mark on the foreheads of the men that sigh and that cry over all the abominations that are done in its midst."
> Ezekiel 9:4

In this vision, God sent death and destruction on everyone in the city, but He spared those with the mark. How and why did they receive the mark? It was given to them because they grieved over the city's sin. Do I grieve sin like God does? Or do I explain it away as someone's "bad choice, " not recognizing what they are choosing? When I see sin around me - and there is much - do I respond in love, in judgment, or in ambivalence.

Too often it's the latter. "It doesn't impact me," I say. Yet God looks at people and grieves because He knows the price they are paying. He knows and understands what they are missing. So, He grieves.

Father, give me a heart like yours that sees sin for what it is, and grieves over it. Help me see the world through your eyes.

WELCOME TO JULY

"A new commandment I give to you, that you love one another. Just as I have loved you, you also must love one another."
John 13:34

July 1*

"Son of man, you dwell in the midst of the rebellious house, who have eyes to see, and do not see, who have ears to hear, and do not hear; for they are a rebellious house."
Ezekiel 12:2

† † †

God here tells us that rebellion leads to us being (or at least becoming) both blind and deaf to the truth. Jesus often said of the religious rulers that they had eyes but could not see and ears but could not hear. They, too, were a rebellious group. The gospel is obvious to anyone who will look and listen to what God has done and said, but to rebellious people the truth is hidden.

But let's get to the heart of the matter: what about you and me? Am I like Ezekiel who hears and responds in humility and obedience to God? Or am I the blind and deaf person who doesn't perceive God because I've tuned Him out? One of my regular prayers is "Father, open my eyes so I can see what you see, my ears to hear what you hear (and hear year), my mouth to speak what you would have me speak, my mind so I would understand your message, and my heart so I would choose to respond like you respond."

July 2*

"The soul who sins, he shall die: ... the righteousness of the righteous shall be on him, and the wickedness of the wicked shall be on him."
Ezekiel 18:20a, c

✝ ✝ ✝

God told the people of Israel - who were in exile at the time - that judgment and salvation was personal and individual. He also told them it was based on what they did and how they behaved. I know many people who would say they are "good" people, and yet all of them will say they are not perfect – few would use the word "righteous" to describe themselves. How can we ever be "righteous" enough for the reward God promised here? Doesn't Paul write in Romans that "all fall short of God's glorious standard"? (see Romans 3:23)

Only in Jesus. The message of the gospel is simple, but that doesn't mean it's easy.

I was reminded of this recently while talking with a colleague who doesn't understand the basic promise of the gospel or of the doctrine of substitutionary atonement. God told us in Ezekiel that the wicked will die for their wickedness and the righteous are rewarded for their righteousness. Yet we know none of us can be (or are) righteous. This is why we need Jesus.

The apostle Paul wrote that when Jesus died, He did more than simply pay for our sins; He became sin itself! Why? So, we could become the righteousness of God! (2 Cor 5:21)

The gospel is that God is willing – He wants - to do a great switcheroo! He takes my wickedness and gives it to Jesus, who then suffers for it because it becomes His. And He takes Jesus' righteousness and gives it to me so I can be rewarded, and it becomes mine. Is this fair? No. It is merciful, loving, and gracious? Yes!

Even more amazing is that this does not start at Easter, or Christmas; it doesn't start when Adam and Eve sinned or even when the world was created. It started before the world was formed before sin entered the world. God planned it long ago - before we even were! Or what a glorious God we serve!

July 3*

"You were perfect in your ways from the day that you were created, until unrighteousness was found in you."
Ezekiel 28:15

☩ ☩ ☩

Without context, it would be easy to think these words were spoken to Israel, God's chosen people. But they weren't. God spoke to them through the prophet Ezekiel to the pagan king of Tyre, and many scholars believe they are also a reference to the angel Lucifer before he fell and became Satan.

My focus here is on the earthly object (king of Tyre), not spiritual (Lucifer). Throughout the prophets, God sent words of destruction and judgment on other nations for their disobedience to God's law. I've often struggled with this because I wanted to say, "The Law was given to the Jews, his chosen people – how could He also hold other nations to account for it?"

Here's the deal, though… The Jews were His chosen people, and the law was given to them. But they were not given the law to keep to themselves, they were given it to share with others! All mankind was expected to keep it and are held accountable for it – and it was the Jews' responsibility to share and spread it!

Fast forward several hundred years... Jesus came to save us, and not just us but all mankind. And all mankind will be held accountable for their response. You see, just like the Israelites we were not given Jesus to keep Him for ourselves, but to share Him with everyone.

Which raises the question: to whom have I shared the message of Jesus lately? Who needs to hear it? Who will be held accountable and doesn't yet know him? And what will I do about it?

July 4*

"I am the good shepherd..."
John 10:11

†††

Jesus claims to be the "Good Shepherd," but good in contrast to what (or whom)? Several hundred years before Jesus spoke these words, God gave a message to Ezekiel for the people, comparing the rulers to bad shepherds. The rulers failed to protect the sheep.

I can't help but believe that when the crowds heard Jesus' words at least some of them were reminded of Ezekiel 34. Jesus promised to be their good shepherd, the one who would go and care for the sheep, to look for them, and even separate sheep from goats. These are all images used in Ezekiel, yet in Ezekiel it was the ruler's lack of doing them that led to judgement, and here Jesus promises to do what others did not. I imagine the first century Jews knew Ezekiel's words by heart, and I can understand the comfort (and, for some, the challenge) they found in Jesus' claim to be the fulfillment of that prophecy! But Jesus did fulfill it – and continues to fulfill it – because He is our Good Shepherd.

When God can fulfill promises like this, why do I struggle so often to believe He'll continue to fulfill others? My faith is often too small. Father, give me faith and a new spirit; give me hope in you.

Watch some fourth of July fireworks tonight.

July 5*

"And I will also give you a new heart, and I will put a new spirit within you. And I will take away the stony heart out of your flesh, and I will give you a heart of flesh. I will put my Spirit within you, and cause you to walk in my statutes, and you shall keep my ordinances, and do them...you shall be my people, and I will be your God. I will save you from all your uncleanness . . ."
Ezekiel 36:26, 28b-29a

† † †

These promises were delivered to Israel, and they were fulfilled in and through Jesus for all mankind. Think about that for a moment. . . These promises are for us!

Paul tells us that in Christ we are new creations (2 Corinthians 5: 12), and in Hebrews 8: 10) we learn that we are given new hearts because all things are given us in Christ.

Before his death, Jesus told us he had to leave so the Holy Spirit could come, and then we also learn in 2 Corinthians that our body is the temple of the Holy Spirit! And let's not forget John, who writes that God cleanses us from all unrighteousness (1 John 1:9)! The promises are fulfilled in Jesus!

The good news – the gospel – is that Jesus does this for us, and that it was not just for one nation (Israel) but for all people and nations! It's not about being in the right family or nation, it's about following Jesus. The promise for a new heart, for a new spirit, to be someone God calls His own, to be cleansed of filthy behavior... That's for me. And you.

And if that doesn't get us excited, I'm not sure what will.

July 6

"Seek the LORD and his strength. Seek his face forever more."
Psalms 105:4

Seek! I love that word. It conjures up visions of sailing ships on high seas seeking new worlds and pioneers in covered wagons seeking a new life in unsettled lands. Men and women seeking the adventure of the unknown.

But how can we seek the face of one who cannot be seen? That is the greatest adventure of all. Jesus tells a woman that we are to seek God in spirit and in truth. He tells His disciples that His words are spirit and life, that He is the truth, and if they have seen Him, they have seen God. Armed with this information we do have the ability to accomplish the directive of the Psalms verse.

God has recorded all things necessary to know Him and His will for our lives in the Bible. Like those adventurers that set their hearts to seek a new world or unsettled land, we can set our heart to exclusively seek God and His will as revealed in His word. The key that unlocks Biblical truth is abandonment of our prideful opinions and yielding our understanding to align with what God has revealed in His word. No more, no less. And just like those sailors and pioneers experienced hardship, so will we as we commit to trust God and not our own self-centered heart. Our selfish heart will not surrender without a fight, and unless the Holy Spirit empowers us, our hearts will cling to what we want God to be like rather than who He actually is.

He is knowable and is hiding in plain sight. Trust him exclusively and you will see Him in all His glory.

July 7

"Your word is a lamp to my feet, and a light for my path."
Psalms 119:105

☦ ☦ ☦

As a soldier in Vietnam, I was keenly aware of the pitfalls of land mines. They were deadly. That awareness was like a lamp and a light as I navigated the terrain. When I became a believer, God revealed, through His word, that this world is full of spiritual "landmines" that can have equally devastating consequences. Pride, unbelief, love of money, greed, lust, lying, unforgiveness, hatred, revenge, and so many other spiritual land mines lurk all around me, and frequently tempt me.

I recognize these dangers by virtue of the Holy Spirit who gives me understanding of what God has revealed in His word. Without the lamp and light of His word and the Holy Spirit, I would just assume these are acceptable reactions to life's ever-changing scenarios. After all, movies, books, and songs have all glamorized these land mines so why would I think otherwise? I now realize that the darkness of this world is ever present. The bad news is that recognizing these landmines and AVOIDING them are two different matters. The really good news, however, is that when I do step on one, restoration is possible. Jesus has already suffered the penalty for my failures, and when I unconditionally trust that truth, confess and repent of my failure, I am restored to whole.

I pray that you, too, would have the light of God's word to be a lamp for your path today, and if per chance you trip a land mine, you now know how to be restored.

July 8

"Come now, and let us reason together," says the LORD:
"Though your sins are like scarlet, they shall be as white as snow.
Though they are red like crimson, they shall be as wool."
Isaiah 1:18

† † †

Reason together? Wow! The Creator of the universe, my Creator, invites me to reason together with Him. Unbelievable! There are times I cannot even get my wife or kids to reason together with me, although that may be more my fault than theirs.

Nonetheless, what would reasoning with my Creator look like? There was a time when it would be me offering excuses for my bad behavior rather than reasoning to find the truth of why I behave the way I do. Beyond that, I had no interest in reasoning with Him to find a solution for my sinfulness. But then one glorious day He changed all that. He invited me to become His son by believing exclusively in Jesus for my salvation. It was an offer I could not refuse. My heart was compelled to believe.

After that day, I realized that I really could reason with God by virtue of His word and His Holy Spirit that now lived in me. In His word He explains it all; how the world was created, how I was created, why the world is the way it is, why I am the way I am, His activities throughout history to reveal Himself to us, His ONLY permanent solution for the sin problem, and what the future of this world looks like. So now everyday God reasons with me through the Bible. Sadly, there are times when I reject His reasoning, but He always encourages and allows me to reconsider my choices. That is what He is like.

Perhaps you have a need to reason with your Creator today. Take another look at the verse. His invitation is still valid today.

July 9

"For if you forgive people their wrongdoing, your heavenly Father will also forgive you. But if you do not forgive people, neither will your Father forgive your wrongdoing.
Matthew 6:14, 15

† † †

Jesus says a lot of things that challenge me, but this statement ranks near the top of the list. I love and rely on the fact that, in Christ, God forgives all my offenses against Him, but sometimes struggle to do likewise. There are some offenses that are so deep and painful that my heart actually aches. To my shame, I want to lash out at those people and cause them more pain than what I experienced. Thankfully God has placed a throttle in me that keeps me from doing so. Ironically, there are times when I ask God to forgive my unforgiveness. Nonetheless, if my wounded heart remains untreated, it will become infected with bitterness, anger, and hatred.

Just like an infected flesh wound must be treated to prevent deadly consequences, so must my wounded heart be treated to restore it to health. But how? Fortunately, the Apostle Paul, inspired by the Holy Spirit, writes;" And be kind to one another, tenderhearted, FORGIVING one another, even as God in Christ forgave YOU."

This is a poignant but GENTLE reminder that God has forgiven me even when my behavior deeply wounded His heart. It is that reminder that allows me to apply the "medicine" of forgiveness to my wounded heart, and when I forgive others, the medicine works.

Perhaps you need to apply the medicine of forgiveness to your heart. This medicine will not cost you any money, just your pride.

July 10

"The LORD redeems the soul of his servants. None of those who take refuge in him shall be condemned."
Psalms 34:22

✝ ✝ ✝

So why does the Lord (our Creator) need to redeem a soul? The truth is that the Lord rescues or recovers the souls of those men and women who trust Him. But from what is a soul being rescued, people ask? Therein lies the problem. A person who is not aware of their need to be rescued will not seek a rescuer. They are unaware of their current dilemma. It is like a fish swimming in the sea. Because the fish is always surrounded by water, the fish never understands that there is more to the world than water. The fish does not realize there is an alternate reality until removed from the water. Unfortunately, removal means death.

The opposite is true for humans. When we are made aware of the reality of a spiritual dimension to our lives, we realize physical death does not bring finality to our existence. We continue to exist in another dimension. It is in that awareness when we determine where we will spend eternity, heaven or hell. At some point in every person's life our Creator makes us aware that we are more a than a physical being; we have an eternal soul. In that moment He also reveals that we are separated from Him because of our selfish behavior, a choice we make daily. But then He gives us the good news of how His Son Jesus has paid the penalty for our sins, and if we believe that glorious truth, we will enjoy eternal life and friendship with Him. He gives us the opportunity to surrender our life to Him, and if we surrender, He RESCUES our soul!

Do you know someone whose soul needs rescuing? Tell them about the rescuer and redeemer today.

July 11

"Ask, and it will be given to you. Seek, and you will find. Knock, and it will be opened for you. For everyone who asks receives. He who seeks finds. To him who knocks it will be opened."
Mathew 7:7, 8

I can only imagine how many times this verse has been misused or how many people have been disillusioned because their prayers were not answered according to their expectations. Does Jesus mean we can have ANYTHING we want by asking God to provide those things; can we really ask anything of God? Of course, but our asking does not obligate God to accommodate our request any more than asking our earthly parents for something obligated them to grant our request. Most certainly, Godly prayer, anchored in faith, is mysteriously powerful and effective. Wars have been won, societies and individuals transformed, new worlds, medicines, and countless inventions discovered, all because of prayer. Beyond that, some of the smallest details in our lives are the result of answered prayer. Prayer is our conduit to our Creator.

These verses teach us to be persistent in our prayers; ask, seek, knock, and to resist discouragement when a prayer seems to go unanswered. Reiterating a prayer is not reminding God of a request but rather a reminder to us that He is aware, and His will is being accomplished in His timing. Earlier in Mathew's gospel, Jesus tells His followers to pray that God's will would be done on earth like it is in Heaven. Asking God to exercise His will, in regard to a concern we have, assures that God will act accordingly. He will never violate principles or laws He has put in place. Nonetheless, He asks us to share our will with Him. Remarkable, indeed! Also, He factors in His foreknowledge when answering our prayer, and that foreknowledge oft times conflicts with our expectations. His knowledge of both the present and future is infinite while ours is finite. Armed with this truth, we have confidence that however He answers our prayer, it will be according to His will and good pleasure. That assurance allows us to have peace in our hearts, knowing that the answer to our prayer is appropriate.

Read some classic poetry today. It is good for your heart and soul.

July 12

"Most certainly, the evil man will not be unpunished, but the descendants of the righteous will be delivered."
Proverbs 11:21

†††

Generally, joining forces allows us to overcome overwhelming forces that could potentially move against us. It is a well-known military, police, national, and even societal tactic. The ancients had tribes; we have political parties. People do it because it works, it keeps the opposition at bay. Not many of us want to be the Lone Ranger; we prefer the cavalry instead. We want the security of additional people to reinforce our position because it can be downright scary to stand alone.

There is one exception to this scenario. GOD is an army of ONE. Jesus demonstrated it in His resurrection. The powers of this world nor the powers of Hell could not stand against Him. The man (or woman) who aligns with God, though he be but one, will never be alone. That person's invincibility is not because they are on God's side but rather because God is on their side. Jesus proclaimed, "ALL authority has been given to Me in heaven and on earth." Theologians call this authority Omnipotence, and it is defined as having UNLIMITED power and the ability to do ANYTHING. Jesus also said, "and lo, I am WITH you always, even to the end of the age."

So, if you feel as if you are standing alone as you stand for the promises and principles revealed in the Bible, think again. The Omnipotent One is always with the believer, and regardless of the outcome on earth, your victory is assured in Heaven. Remember, you will not spend eternity on earth but rather in Heaven. His promise is sure: "Do not be afraid, for I am with you. Do not be dismayed, for I am your God. I will strengthen you. Yes, I will help you. Yes, I will uphold you with the right hand of my righteousness."

July 13

"For our wrestling is not against flesh and blood, but against the rulers, against the powers, against the world's rulers of this darkness, and against the spiritual forces of wickedness in the heavenly places."
Ephesians 6:12

† † †

Who are these mysterious entities that the Apostle Paul references in this verse? They were certainly real to him, and they should be real to us. In His time on planet earth, Jesus both encountered and overcame demons, and, just after His water baptism, Jesus had a PERSONAL encounter with Satan. You can read about that encounter in the opening verses of Luke chapter four.

Beyond reading about Satan, we can SEE his influence in the world today. Jesus tells His disciples that Satan comes to steal, kill, and destroy. I will leave it to the reader to determine all that Satan has stolen, killed, and destroyed in both the world and their OWN lives. He has mocked God while dangling death over mankind since his deception of Eve in the Garden of Eden. Believe it or not, Satan is REAL.

The Bible tells of a time when Satan, and ALL who follow him will be cast into the lake of fire for eternity. Until that glorious day we will continue to live in a world where physical death and destruction are a certainty. The good news is that Jesus defeated Satan and death - His tomb is empty, and He is now seated next to God in Heaven where He is the believer's Savior and advocate. One day, perhaps soon, He will return.

Believe in Him, trust Him, worship Him, and resist Satan's beckoning, and you too will spend eternity in Heaven. Jesus says that nothing can snatch a believer out of the loving hands of God the Father.

July 14

"In the same day Noah, and Shem, Ham, and Japheth, the sons of Noah, and Noah's wife, and the three wives of his sons with them, entered into the vessel ...and God shut him in."
Genesis 7:13, 16

✝ ✝ ✝

Another GREAT flood is coming to this world, but it has nothing to do with water. It will be God flooding the world with His JUDGEMENT and the purging of evil and unbelief from mankind. There will be no escape for those who have not trusted Jesus as their Savior, NONE! And just like God shut the door to Noah's Ark to protect Noah from the flood while keeping others out who had rejected Noah's call to repent, those who are not found in the ark of Christ will likewise PERISH. Those who have trusted Jesus for the forgiveness of their sins will rest safely in the ark of Jesus while the fate of those outside that ark will be eternal separation from God, doomed to eternal torment in a lake of fire. It will be a frightening conclusion to this present world and a day of reckoning like no other.

That terrible day is difficult to talk about, few people do because it makes them uncomfortable. But if people do not understand the CONSEQUENCES of rejecting God's provision for their redemption from hell, they would not have the desire to surrender their lives to God. Jesus talked about it without apology. Even so, countless people will CHOOSE to reject the FREE gift that their Creator offers in regard to their salvation. Although free to us, it cost our Creator the grief of sacrificing His Son so mankind could be reconciled to Him.

We all know someone who is not in the "ark" of Jesus. Today would be a good day to tell that person about the coming flood, and to invite them to join us in that ark. Tomorrow may be too late!

July 15

"For You, Lord, are good, and ready to forgive; abundant in loving kindness to all those who call on You"
Psalms 86:5

A HOLY GOD REACHES DOWN

✝ ✝ ✝

Guilt is a killer! It often preoccupies the mind, eclipsing even the ability to reason. It is a burden heaped upon us by ourselves, others, and Satan. Conversely, do not consider the conscience as a bad thing, it is a gift from our Creator. Without a conscience to remind us of a behavioral misfire, we would have no deterrent preventing us from future misfires. To be clear, a failure in an honorable effort is entirely different from a MORAL failure. Surely, we have all attempted something worthwhile and failed, and some would argue that is part of the maturation or learning process. Failure often allows us to recalibrate our attempt and ultimately succeed. A MORAL failure is an offense against our Creator who detests unrighteous behavior. Although against people, they are ultimately against the One in whose likeness we have been created.

The really good news is that our Creator is not like us, He is ready, even willing to forgive. His forgiveness, however, is not without condition. We must CONFESS that our offense IS wrong, and beyond that, we must take OWNERSHIP in the offense. We must also desire in our heart to avoid repeating the offense. Will God tire of forgiving our offenses, even repeated ones? Not according to Jesus. Peter once asked Him if he should forgive someone up to seven times. Jesus replied: "Not seven times, but seventy times seven." I will not go into Biblical numerology here, but Jesus essentially told Peter that there is NO limit on how many times he should forgive someone. And remember this, Jesus told His disciples that if they had seen Jesus, they had seen God.

Are you carrying around unnecessary guilt? If God has forgiven you then jettison that guilt and live in the light and peace of the Cross of Jesus. If you are burdened with the guilt of UNCONFESSED sin, ask God to forgive you. Look at the verse again: "He is ready to forgive."

July 16

"If it seems evil to you to serve the LORD, choose this day whom you will serve ..."
Joshua 24:15

†††

Every day we make choices, what to eat, what to wear, etc. Many of our choices do not really matter in the grand scheme of life, except one. That choice has temporal and eternal consequences. In life, we are going to be guided by and serve someone, either ourselves or our Creator. God gives us the free Will to choose Him or another. Choose wisely and encourage others to do the same because it will be the most important decision we can ever make.

Know God or no God? Choose wisely because your choice has eternal consequences.

July 17

And God commanded the man, saying, "Of every tree of the garden you may freely eat; but of the tree of the knowledge of good and evil, you shall not eat of it; for in the day that you eat of it you will surely die."
Genesis 2:16, 17

†††

Mankind is once again limited to ONE command to have life eternal. Just like Adam had only ONE prohibition keeping him from death, mankind has ONE choice to reverse the consequence of Adam's failure. That ONE choice is BELIEVING in Jesus, nothing else will do, nothing else can do because all mankind is infected with sin from birth and has no ability to save himself/herself. While on earth, Jesus lived a sinless life, both in His heart and body. He was truly sinless in thought and deed! Nonetheless, He experienced physical death and temporary separation from God to satisfy the consequence of Adam's rebellion. He experienced that punishment on our behalf, but death could not prevail on Him because death is hinged to sin and Jesus' sinlessness thereby nullified death. Consequently, He was resurrected from the dead (separation from God) and given a brand-new body. One sweet day, all born again believers will be given a body like Jesus' body, free from sin, and one that will live forever. The exceptionally good news is that our spirit has already been born again if we have placed our faith in the Gospel.

Let us never falter in our personal and unconditional faith that Jesus has reconciled us to our Creator. As Peter, filled with the Holy Spirit, once proclaimed: "Nor is there salvation in ANY other, for there is NO other name under heaven given among men by which we MUST be saved." Yes, we are called to "work out our salvation" but remember that we are working out something that we have ALREADY received, and by virtue of God's Holy Spirit living in us, we have the ability to do so. We serve a great and awesome God!

July 18

"For in him all the fullness of Deity dwells in bodily form, and in him you are made full, who is the head of all principality and power."
Colossians 2:9, 10

† † †

Did you ever pour water into a glass that was already full to the top? Of course not. The Bible, God's revelation of absolute truth, reveals that His Holy Spirit comes to reside in us at the moment of our conversion from SPIRITUAL death to spiritual life. The problem is that the Holy Spirit now competes with our flesh for attention. Prior to salvation we were filled to the brim with the world and led by the works of the flesh. God says those works include adultery, fornication, uncleanness, lewdness, idolatry, sorcery, hatred, contentions, jealousies, outbursts of wrath, selfish ambitions, dissensions, heresies, envy, murders, drunkenness, revelries, and the like. Those things all seemed so natural; not that we necessarily participated in all those things, but often times we had a desire to so.

But God had bigger aspirations for mankind. He wanted us to experience the fruit of the Holy Spirit in our life. That fruit is love, joy, peace, patience, kindness, goodness, faithfulness, gentleness, and self-control. Who would not want those qualities and experiences in their life?

Look again at the verse and take careful notice of the completeness of God in Jesus. Many times in the Bible we are told that WE are IN Jesus by virtue of the Holy Spirit living in us. WE are complete in Him. So here is the challenge from God to us; "And do not be conformed to this world, but be transformed by the renewing of your mind, so that you may prove what is the good, well-pleasing, and perfect will of God." Let us determine to have more of Him and less of the world.

Read something by your favorite author today.

July 19

> To Adam he said, "Because you have listened to your wife's voice, and have eaten of the tree, of which I commanded you, saying, 'You shall not eat of it,' cursed is the ground for your sake. In toil you will eat of it all the days of your life."
> Genesis 3:17

† † †

What if Adam had hearkened ONLY to God's voice and not been swayed by Eve? Think about it. By hearkening to Eve, God's original warning to Adam triggered. There was no alternative. Unlike man, God ALWAYS does what He says He will do.

This verse is a critical reminder to be mindful of who we listen to in regard to life matters. No one can eclipse the validity of God's holy words as absolute TRUTH. Death and sin found entrance into the world by Adam CHOOSING to believe someone other than God. Now think about this: "For God so loved the world that He gave His only begotten Son, that whoever believes in Him should not perish but have everlasting life." It's a DONE deal for believers, nothing or no one can change this TRUTH!

Find something to LAUGH about today. Laughter is good medicine!

July 20*

> ... says the LORD, 'and work, for I am with you... says the LORD of hosts. and my Spirit lived among you...'Do not be afraid.'
> Haggai 2:4c-5

† † †

The people of Israel were called out by God through the prophet Haggai because they were choosing self over God. Rather than build the temple, they were focused on building their own homes and fortunes, spending money carelessly as fast as they earned it ("Your wages disappear as though you were putting them in pickets filled with holes!" (1:6)). God tells them to get to work, promising He is with them, and so they shouldn't fear.

It seems so simple, really. God says to do some things and we look back and think, "Why didn't they obey? How could they be so foolish as to focus on their own comfort rather than God's call? Didn't they learn from their exile to Babylon (and Egypt) this disobedience leads to destruction while obedience to life and blessing?"

And then I pause myself on the page. I always want to be the hero – I want to be (and think I will be) Haggai who calls them out.

But let's be honest… Aren't I – aren't most of us – like the people who get lost focusing on our own needs? Who try to build our own kingdoms instead of His – reasoning we'll do that tomorrow once we are secure? Don't we (I) often spend money as fast – or faster – than we (I) make it? As if we're putting our earnings into "pockets with holes"?

And God's words are the same for us today…Remember He is with us and let that bring confidence and remove fear. And go and do.

How can you (I) build His temple today – His kingdom rather than your (my) own?

July 21*

…for the day of the LORD is great and very awesome, and who can endure it?"Yet even now," says the LORD, "turn to me with

all your heart, and turn to the LORD, your God; for he is gracious and merciful, slow to anger, and abundant in loving kindness, and relents from sending calamity."
Joel 2:11-12a, 13b-c

☩ ☩ ☩

God knows what is coming – not just in this life but also the next. And He is coming in judgement. But he wants to save people from that judgement! Think about that – He does NOT want to send people away! Why? Because He loves us – we are His children.

I see so many Christians – even myself at times - who are eager to punish and bring judgement, being slow to love and quick to judge. When my heat is most like His, though, I should be slow to anger and full of love; I should be eager for Him to redeem and rescue, and for others to not perish. I should be calling to people to Him in love.

But am I? Are you?

July 22*

> "The LORD looks down from heaven on the descendants of Adam, to see if there are any who are wise, who seek after God. They have all turned away. They have together become corrupt. There is no one who does good, no, not one."
> Psalm 14:2, 3

☩ ☩ ☩

So often we seek wisdom in the wrong places, but there is really only one place to find it: in God. Scripture tells us that wisdom is found in a person, not a book or an experience. And His name is

Jesus. Paul writes in 1 Corinthians, "And because of him you are in Christ Jesus, who became for us wisdom from God, and righteousness and sanctification and redemption." (1:30b)

Where are you looking for wisdom? Where am I? Is it in books, articles, podcasts, mentors, teachers, or others around us? Or is it in Him? Yes, God speaks in and through all those mediums – but the key word there is "God". He is the one speaking. And He will never contradict what He's already told us in His word. How can we know if what we read or hear is from God? We have to measure it against what He has already told us. And how can we measure it against His word if we don't know it? And how will we know it if we don't read and study it?

Wisdom – true wisdom - is found in a person; and His name is Jesus, the "word made flesh."

July 23*

LORD, who shall dwell in your sanctuary? Who shall live on your holy mountain? He who walks blamelessly and does what is right, and speaks truth in his heart.
Ps 15:1, 2

It's so easy to read a verse like this and conclude that we can earn our way into relationship with God – that we can be "good enough." But can we really be blameless? In the very preceding chapter, the Psalmist declared that "There is no one who does good, no, not one"(14:3)

Yet here in chapter 15 we are told that there are "blameless" people. How can this be? Is it because of their own goodness? Have they somehow arrived?

No! It is only in Jesus! If you've ever wondered what Jesus did for you when he died, look at Psalm 15. We are blameless – not just forgiven but wiped clean and pure. He gives us new hearts, new desires, and new natures.

The question is, how often do I follow that new nature? How often do I follow the old one?

July 24*

"I have called on you, for you will answer me, God. Turn your ear to me. Hear my speech."
Psalm 17:6

†††

David makes this statement in a Psalm where he calls on God to rescue him – to declare him innocent. David calls on the Lord why? Because he knows God will answer.

Why is it that prayer for me – and many I speak with – seems to be a last resort rather than a first step? Could it be a lack of faith or a lack of belief that God will hear and answer? Jesus tells us that if we pray anything in His name that we will receive it – but so often I don't even bother praying.

Father, as the man who had a sick son said to you, "I believe; help my unbelief." Give me faith and confidence that you not only hear my prayer and will answer it, but that you care. Remind me that you want to hear from me and answer me. Build a discipline of prayer in my life.

July 25

"If then you were raised together with Christ, seek the things that are above, where Christ is, seated on the right hand of God.

For you died, and your life is hidden with Christ in God. When Christ, your life, is revealed, then you will also be revealed with him in glory."
Colossians 3:1, 3, 4

† † †

Maybe today, just maybe He will return today! Are YOU ready? If not, why not?

July 26

"Wait for the LORD. Be strong, and let your heart take courage. Yes, wait for the LORD."
Psalms 27:14

† † †

There is a certainty to life that people everywhere experience - a series of highs and lows. Call it what you want, good and bad days, seasons of life, sickness and health, peaks and valleys, or any other tag. King Solomon aptly reminds us that there is a "time" for everything.

King David also understood this and penned the above verse. He knew that in times when he was experiencing pain, sorrow, loss, rejection, failure, or any low point in his life, it would be best to saddle himself to waiting for the Lord to manifest His purpose. And according to the Bible, God always revealed His purpose to David. Sometimes by giving David supernatural power or wisdom while in other times to discipline David, but whatever the purpose, David embraced it.

In our lives we will have ebbs and flows, it is a certainty. We live in a fallen world. Let us purpose in our heart to "wait on the Lord and be of good courage" and embrace His will and presence. That commitment will lead us back to the mountain top!

Remember, if you want to see the view, you have to climb to the TOP of the mountain!

July 27

"Let your eyes look straight ahead. Fix your gaze directly before you. Do not turn to the right hand nor to the left. Remove your foot from evil."
Proverbs 4:25, 27

Believers in Jesus are called to keep their eyes on Him, but how do we do that? There are so many distractions, the "shiny" things of this world, that compete for our attention that it is often difficult to focus on Jesus. To be sure, our eyes, ears, and heart, often yearn for things other than Jesus. Consider this analogy; life is like walking on rocky terrain. When we walk upright (in righteousness), we have the ability to see over the rocks (temptations) and focus on the end of the trail, our destination. We can carefully walk over the rocks (shiny things) because we can see beyond them. Now consider this; the serpent cannot see over the obstacle because it does not walk upright and is constantly turning to the right or the left. It never really sees the destination but instead is always searching.

So here is the question or perhaps the challenge: who do YOU want to imitate? The man or woman who walks upright or the serpent? It really is a matter of choice.

July 28

> Tell them, 'As I live,' says the Lord GOD, 'I have no pleasure in the death of the wicked; but that the wicked turn from his way and live: turn, turn from your evil ways; for why will you die, house of Israel?'
> Ezekiel 33:11

† † †

Most people think God is pleased with the death of a wicked person. Although the death of a wicked person may be necessary, it brings no pleasure to God. After all, He is the Creator of human life, it was His idea and His doing. Beyond that, He created us in His image, but, sadly, that image is now distorted and at times barely recognizable. Death intruded in life because of human SIN and was never part of God's plan for mankind. Think about this, no normal, well-adjusted person would find pleasure in the death of a son or daughter that he or she participated in creating.

What our Creator finds pleasurable is a wicked person turning from their wickedness and asking to be forgiven. God loves a repentant heart. Fortunately, He provided a way for anyone, INCLUDING the wicked, to be reconciled to Him. Yes, God's grace is controversial, offensive, and even outrageous, but it's also TRUE. Jesus died for everyone, including the wicked. Let us pray that EVERYONE chooses life by trusting in Jesus' substitutionary death. That trust will bring pleasure to God.

Wear two different colored socks today. Although awkward, it will give you a giggle! Remember, you are never too old to laugh at yourself, in fact, it is therapeutic.

July 29

"Your statutes have been my songs, in the house where I live."
Psalms 119:54

✝ ✝ ✝

We are all on a pilgrimage to eternity and everyone will ultimately arrive at that destination. No one will be left behind. But where will we live in eternity? King David was confident that he would spend eternity in the presence of his Creator. His confidence was fastened to the promises that the Creator revealed in His Holy Scriptures. According to the above verse, those promises became songs David would sing as he approached eternity. Perhaps in those times he felt he was already living there.

God has been kind and gracious to preserve those promises for all mankind. In fact, those of us living today have a completed book that reveals the past, present, and future for us - the Bible. In that God inspired book we learn how we too can spend eternity with our Creator in His celestial kingdom. Beyond that, we can learn His will for our lives as we make our own pilgrimage. Spend time in that precious book, you will not be disappointed. You will discover truth that will set you free from uncertainty.

July 30

"I have been crucified with Christ, and it is no longer I that live, but Christ living in me. That life which I now live in the flesh, I live by faith in the Son of God, who loved me, and gave himself up for me."
Galatians 2:20

✝ ✝ ✝

This statement by the Apostle Paul captures the essence of his understanding of being born again. It is both personal and definitive. There are many places in his writings that he elaborates on this understanding, but I find this verse to be the pinnacle of his belief. For those who have never experienced this phenomenon, Paul's statement is foolishness, delusional, or just plain crazy. How can a person be born again, the critics mock? Does Paul really think he has been crucified along with Jesus; they question? The man needs serious therapy, they reason.

Before I was born again, I was one of those people. I mocked it and totally disregarded the concept of being born again. But then one glorious day it happened to me. It is a mystery, to be sure, it is what Christians call a "God thing", and that makes it way above my pay grade to explain the how. What I can tell people is the why. Jesus says that a person MUST be born again if they want to see the kingdom of God. Millions of words have been written on this subject, but here is the thing; if you are being drawn by God to be born again, just DO IT. Believe that Jesus is the Son of God and He died a substitutionary death for YOU because you are a sinner in need of a Savior. Beyond that, believe that God raised Jesus from the dead and that He is now seated at the right hand of God in heaven. If you do this in sincerity, you too will understand what it means to be born again.

If possible visit a pet store today. You will be glad you did.

July 31

"Why do you set your eyes on that which is not? For it certainly sprouts wings like an eagle and flies in the sky."
Proverbs 23:5

† † †

Chasing after worldly riches is a fool's errand. Instead, set your eyes on the riches of the Kingdom of God. Remember, Jesus said, "No one can serve two masters...."

Give some of your money to a stranger today, someone in need. It will be good for them and you.

WELCOME TO AUGUST

Jesus said to him, "I am the way, the truth, and the life. No one comes to the Father except through me."
John 14:6

August 1

"You are my hiding place and my shield. I hope in your word."
Psalms 119:114

†††

There are many "hiding places" that people use to escape the pitfalls of life. Some, like professional therapy can be helpful while others, like illegal drugs and alcohol, are destructive. The truth is everyone uses some physical or psychological mechanism to relieve the overwhelming pressures of life, and just like everything else in life, there is a right and a wrong way to negotiate life.

It only makes sense to turn to the One who created life when we are unable to cope. After all, our Creator KNOWS what the one He created needs. In fact, He promises to provide a "peace that passes all understanding" when we focus on Him. Here is the promise: "Be anxious for nothing, but in everything by prayer and supplication, with thanksgiving, let your requests be made known to God; and the PEACE of God, which surpasses all understanding, will guard your hearts and minds through Christ Jesus."

I choose His peace. How about you?

August 2

"My son, do not forget my teaching; but let your heart keep my commandments."
Proverbs 3:1

Both my heart and spirit genuinely desire to keep God's commandments, but not to add to the redemptive work of Jesus on the Cross. Nothing can add to that glorious work. My behavior (works), good OR bad, does not determine my salvation. ONLY faith in the death, burial, and resurrection of Jesus can accomplish peace with my Creator. I can only plead my helplessness to my merciful God and trust in the promises of Jesus.

So WHY do I desire to keep God's commandments? Primarily because the Holy Spirit lives in me, but also because doing so leads to a better life, a MUCH better life. Greed, lust, jealousy, anger, unforgiveness, and all the other sinful temptations in life never lead to peace or happiness. Quite the opposite. Loving God as best I can, and loving others similarly really does make my life infinitely better. It is God's way!

Take an opportunity to experience a sunrise. It is an amazing sight!

August 3

"If a wise man goes to court with a foolish man, the fool rages or scoffs, and there is no peace."
Proverbs 29:9

We all know who they are, heck, at one time WE were one. Fools are everywhere, on the highways and byways of life and are unavoidable. God has a singular definition of a fool, a very simple one: "The fool has said in his heart, 'There is NO God...'" (Psalm 14:1). In believing so the fool is free to craft his or her own life based on their own selfish desires, and we all know the pitfalls of selfish desires. Fools imagine themselves FREE from any responsibility they have to their Creator, but what they fail to understand is that ultimately, they will be judged by their Creator, and the consequences of that judgement are both FINAL and ETERNAL.

Fools come in all shapes, sizes, sexes, and nationalities. Although difficult, because a fool can be difficult, always remember that Jesus died for EVERYONE. Not every fool will believe that, but let us continue to pray that God will open the hearts and minds of the fools in our lives. Truthfully, we are obliged to do so. Billions of fools have been rescued, I know because I am one!

August 4

> He said to them, "Do not be amazed. You seek Jesus, the Nazarene, who has been crucified. He has risen. He is not here. Look, the place where they put him."
> Mark 16:6

EASTER and the EMPTY tomb: the controversy continues to this very day. "Hallelujah!" cries the believer. "Nonsense" scoffs the unbeliever. The opposing beliefs reflect that of the two men crucified with Jesus. One mocked while the other believed. One was promised Paradise that very day while the other died without that promise.

A writer never is certain of who might read his/her work; perhaps you received this from a friend. So, I ask the reader; which one are YOU? Do you believe or do you mock? Do you have a promise from your Creator of where you will spend eternity, or do you have only YOUR hope? Do you believe the words of Jesus or, by unbelief, do you call Him a liar? The consequences of your answers could not be more significant; literally eternal life or death!

Jesus was crucified so that anyone could spend eternity in heaven, but residence in heaven is not automatic, it is a choice. Our Creator has given us FREE WILL to believe or reject Him through unbelief, but free will is a two-edged sword. One side saves while the other kills. Choose carefully, dear Reader, your choice determines your eternal home.

August 5

"For I know that in me, that is, in my flesh, dwells no good thing. For the desire is present in me, but the doing of the good is not."
Romans 7:18

✝ ✝ ✝

NOTE: THIS IS A MULTI DAY DEVOTION

The Apostle Paul echoes what every believer has thought or said at one time or another; a heartfelt desire to live righteously but feeling helpless to consistently do so. It is THE fundamental flaw or root problem of mankind, and it is called Sin. Sin (yes, with a capital S) is not an act, it is a condition that causes a person to act in a sinful manner (sin). It is a malady that we inherited from our ancestor Adam, and, with the exception of Jesus, every person ever born has inherited it. It is why it was necessary for Mary, the mother of Jesus, to be impregnated by the Holy Spirit of God rather than a man. If by a man, Adam's Sin would have been passed to Jesus thus negating His sinlessness and consequently His resurrection from the dead. Death would have had a valid claim on Jesus. Inherited Sin resides in our flesh, it is the reason we all die physically, and the reason believers need a brand new body in heaven, a body that is not infected with Sin. It is the reason God excluded the first couple from the Garden of Eden less they ate of the Tree of Life and be forever doomed to live in a body of Sin. But what are we to do until we transition from earth to heaven? Is there any relief from the rebellious nature living within us? We will consider this next time.

August 6 – AN EXTENSION FROM PREVIOUS

"For I know that in me, that is, in my flesh, dwells no good thing. For the desire is present in me, but the doing of the good is not."
Romans 7:18

Jesus tells us we need a complete do over, a radical solution to the problem of Sin. He tells us that we MUST be born again, our spirit must be reconciled and made alive to live in harmony with its Creator. But how? Confessing to (agreeing with) God that we are a sinner in need of forgiveness is the first step, but our base nature (Sin) will vehemently resist that need. We will judge ourselves by comparing ourselves with others whom we judge less righteous than us. That nature will insist that our good deeds far outweigh our bad and that God will surely take that into account on Judgement Day. That is just not true. The standard of His judgement is PERFECT

(Divine) righteousness and, with the exception of Jesus, is simply not attainable by any human.

Thankfully God has provided a solution to this dilemma. A person must believe that JESUS, God's Son, died to pay the penalty for their personal Sin and sins, and believe that God raised Him from the dead. When a person whole heartily, genuinely, and humbly confesses and believes, God forgives ALL their offenses, including the root cause, Sin, and gives them a new spirit that yearns for righteousness and fellowship with God, and that fellowship is made possible by His Holy Spirit living in them. But sadly, and at times surprisingly, just like the Apostle Paul, believers continue to struggle with sinful thoughts and behavior, and on their worst days consider if they really have been born again, speculating if they need to be born again, AGAIN. But is that even possible? We will examine this next time.

August 7 – AN EXTENSION FROM PREVIOUS

"For I know that in me, that is, in my flesh, dwells no good thing. For the desire is present in me, but the doing of the good is not."
Romans 7:18

† † †

The most important TRUTH to remember is that it is NOT possible to be born again, AGAIN. Once is and always will be sufficient. If you grew up in a rational family, disobedience did not mean that you were disinherited or removed from the family. It is true that is how some disingenuous mothers and fathers react when their child violates family norms, but that is NOT how God reacts to a child of His who has become disobedient (sins). To do so would disrespect and nullify the sacrifice of His Son Jesus. To do so would mean breaking so many of His promises, and unlike Man, it is impossible for God to break a promise. Nothing can separate a genuinely born again believer (His child) from the His love. Jesus died to make that a certainty. This is only one of three challenges the believer experiences in his or her effort to shun sinful behavior. The second, and equally important, will be revealed next time.

August 8 - AN EXTENSION FROM PREVIOUS

"For I know that in me, that is, in my flesh, dwells no good thing. For the desire is present in me, but the doing of the good is not."
Romans 7:18

There is another critical principle to embrace when seeking to understand Sin and the believer, and that principle is that fully understanding God is just not possible. God reveals this truth when He uses the Prophet Isaiah to tell the people of Israel (and now us) the following: "For My thoughts are not your thoughts, nor are your ways My ways," says the Lord. "For as the heavens are higher than the earth, so are My ways higher than your ways, and My thoughts than your thoughts." Although Jesus, God incarnate, brought much needed clarity about God's ways and will for mankind, often His ways continue to leave even believers questioning why He allows what He allows. In times like this, believers are called to believe, not understand. Faith will always eclipse understanding in a believer's walk with God. In fact, if a believer were able to fully understand God, God would not be God. Believers can only understand what He allows them to understand.

There is yet one more challenge we need to understand about Sin, sin, and the believer, and we will examine that challenge next time.

August 9 - AN EXTENSION FROM PREVIOUS

"For I know that in me, that is, in my flesh, dwells no good thing. For the desire is present in me, but the doing of the good is not."
Romans 7:18

The final thing believers need to consider in regard to sins is the spiritual enemy, Satan (adversary). He is the believer's enemy because he is God's enemy. He knows he lacks the power to attack God directly, but he can attack those created in the image of God, humans. Although a created angel, he wants to be God. That is how he tempted Eve in the Garden of Eden, by telling her to disregard the command of God not to eat the fruit of the Tree of the Knowledge of Good and Evil. If she would eat of that tree, she would become like God, he promised. Sadly, both Eve and Adam ate the forbidden fruit and sin entered the hearts, minds, and bodies of the first couple. No longer did they want to be dependent on their Creator, but instead wanted independence from Him, and so they got what they wanted, and we now live in a world skewed by Sin manifesting in a myriad of "me first" behaviors.

The sad reality is that Satan continues tempting men and women, including believers, by appealing to their base nature, and that nature responds easily to his appeals. He lies to believers like he once lied to Eve, tempting them to disregard the Word of God in favor of their own understanding and desires. He appeals to the flesh while the

Holy Spirit living in born again believers appeals to their born again spirit. The battle is relentless but winnable when believers surrender to the Holy Spirit. Satan's ability to successfully tempt a believer is his ability to skillfully lie. He continues to this very day to encourage believers to disregard God's word and promises found in the Bible.

Armed with these three important truths; it is impossible to be born again, AGAIN, God's thoughts and ways are HIGHER than ours, and the influence of SATAN, a believer can now consider sinful behavior and the born again believer. Next time we will consider another important Biblical truth.

August 10 - AN EXTENSION FROM PREVIOUS

"For I know that in me, that is, in my flesh, dwells no good thing. For the desire is present in me, but the doing of the good is not."
Romans 7:18

†††

What happens to a born again person when he/she manifests sinful behavior (sins)? Are they separated once again from the Creator? Are they again destined for hell as they once were prior to trusting in Jesus' death, burial, and resurrection? Does their status as a son or daughter of God change, reverting back to a person in void of a Savior, hopeless of meaningful fellowship with God, our Creator? Does God abandon them?

The truth about Sin and the born again believer is this: "There is therefore now NO condemnation for those who are in Christ Jesus" (Romans 8:1). People who are not in Christ Jesus are condemned to eternity in Hell. To be sure, this is a truth that is hotly debated by the unbelieving community, but the truth remains the truth. That condemnation is inherently applied to ALL humans because of the Sin humanity inherited from Adam. The Apostle John inspired by the Holy Spirit of God offers this truth: "Indeed, God did not send the Son into the world to condemn the world, but in order that the world might be saved through him. Those who believe in him are not condemned; but those who do not believe are condemned ALREADY, because they have not believed in the name of the only Son of God" (John 3:17, 18). There are many scriptures that reinforce these truths in the Bible, and I encourage the reader to search them out.

August 11 - AN EXTENSION FROM PREVIOUS

"For I know that in me, that is, in my flesh, dwells no good thing. For the desire is present in me, but the doing of the good is not."
Romans 7:18

☨ ☨ ☨

The difference between the sinful behavior (sins) of those "in Christ" and those outside of Christ is that Sin (root cause) in the unbeliever has NOT been forgiven. Consequently, the unbeliever has not been born again and Jesus says that a man or woman must be born again to see the Kingdom of God. It is true that Jesus paid the penalty for every individual sinful act (sins), past, present, and future, but also for Sin (root cause) that is present in EVERY human being. However, accepting that forgiveness (believing) is necessary to receive forgiveness. The Bible describes it thusly: "So if anyone is in Christ, there is a new creation: everything old has passed away; see, everything has become new!" and "For our sake He (God) made Him (Jesus) to be sin who knew no sin, so that in him we might become the righteousness of God" (2 Cor 5:17, 21). Just like all humans inherit the Sin of Adam, BELIEVERS now inherit the righteousness of Jesus Christ. Our Creator now sees those who BELIEVE in the death, burial, and resurrection of His Son, Jesus, as being "in Christ" and subsequently a new a righteous creation. It may seem outrageous, unbelievable, unfair, or non-sensical, but it is nonetheless true. The lingering question remains; are there consequences for(s) sin (unrighteous behavior) for those "in Christ?" The conclusion next time.

August 12 – AN EXTENSION FROM PREVIOUS

"For I know that in me, that is, in my flesh, dwells no good thing. For the desire is present in me, but the doing of the good is not."
Romans 7:18

† † †

Yes! There are consequences for the believer when he or she sins. Someone once said: "The consequence of sin is the sin itself." Someone else observed: "Good choices result in good consequences while bad choices result in bad consequences." Both of these statements are true and just like sin often creates a stumbling block between people, it also creates a stumbling block between the believer and God. Consider the first couple. The immediate response of Adam and Eve when they FIRST sinned was to hide from God. They were both afraid and ashamed. The intimate relationship they previously enjoyed with their Creator was now skewed. In the same way, sinful acts disrupt the intimacy of fellowship with God for the believer. Fortunately, and mercifully, God has made provision for immediate restoration for intimate fellowship, and that restoration is hinged to forgiveness. The provision is found in the Bible (1 John 1:9) "If we confess our sins, he is faithful and righteous to forgive us the sins, and to cleanse us from all unrighteousness." It may sound like a simple fix to a complex dilemma, but confession requires humility, and often humility is a difficult challenge even for a believer. Perhaps that is why God is inclined toward the humble while He rejects the proud.

For a final explanation of Sin, sins, and the believer, I encourage the reader to read chapters six, seven, and eight of the letter the Apostle Paul writes to the church in Rome. In the Bible, it is listed as "Romans" and is in the New Testament. It is in these words, inspired by the Holy Spirit, that the reader will discover God's perspective on this issue and consequently truth. God has preserved the Bible for millenniums for just this reason. He wants us to understand the significance of the Cross of Jesus, and what glories and benefits it provides for His most prized creation, Mankind. Be prepared, however, this should not be a casual read. Ask in faith and He will open your heart, eyes, and mind to the greatest event in the history of the world.

August 13

"My soul is weary with sorrow: strengthen me according to your word."
Psalms 119:28

† † †

Have you ever been so spiritually broken, so devoid of hope, so broken hearted, so famished for the light of life, that you felt like king David when he authored this verse? It can happen, even to believers.

Psalm 119 is the longest chapter in the Bible, and it records David's meditations on the Word of God. In it, David praises God, thanks God, pleads with God, presses God, bargains with God, confesses sin, rejoices in deliverance, humbles himself, exalts himself, expresses a fear of God, and unashamedly reveals how authentic his love for God and His words are to David. They are David's hinge to God. Even a casual reading reveals why God once called David "a man after my own heart."

A study of the chapter will prove priceless. Look again at the verse. Even in his lowest point David knew that he needed to rely on God's Word to restore his emotional and spiritual footing. For David there was NO alternative, and that truth begs us to question who or what WE trust in OUR hour of hopelessness. If we were to ask King David, his answer would most certainly be to trust God's Holy Word.

Look for someone to encourage today. People who need encouragement are all around us.

August 14

"Righteousness exalts a nation, but sin is a disgrace to any people."
Proverbs 14:34

How many societies have fallen because they abandoned righteousness in favor of selfish pursuits? How many nations have followed the beckoning of a charismatic leader as they marched to war for nefarious reasons? The history books are filled with nations past while nations present fill today's headlines. King Solomon was right: "There is nothing new under the sun." Does it have to be this way? Sadly, the kingdoms of this world will continue to fall because too often their "kings" neglect the King of Kings, but is there any alternative to the kingdoms of this world?

Thankfully there is ONE kingdom that will never fail because of a corrupt King and that kingdom is the Kingdom of God. It is real even though some say it does not exist because they cannot see it. But there are many things that exist even though we cannot see them. Love, hate, pride, electricity, the air we breathe are just a few. We know, however, they exist because we see or experience their manifestations, and it is the same for the Kingdom of God. If the Holy Spirit lives in you, then you are experiencing God's Kingdom every time you embrace His leadership. To be clear, currently the Kingdom of God is IN us, but a time is coming when WE will be in the Kingdom of God. Until that day, stay humble, pray, read and embrace the King's words, love God and others with all your heart, and you will always enjoy the Kingdom of God while here on planet earth.

Experience a sunset someday soon. They are soothing to your soul.

August 15

"Praise the LORD, my soul, and do not forget all his benefits"
Psalms 103:2

† † †

In Psalm 103 King David reminds his SOUL of all the benefits the Lord has provided: forgiveness of sin, healing for all diseases, redemption from Hell, steadfast love and mercy, personal satisfaction and peace for a lifetime, and even a renewal of youth. You can find these in the verses of the Psalm.

To be sure, David is not only speaking of the present, but also the future. That is why he reminds his SOUL (which is eternal) and not his body. David views life from the correct perspective - eternal.

Too often I limit my perspective to the present or what I believe to be my attainable future; tomorrow, next week or month. In doing so I focus on ME instead of Him. When I consider eternity, I am forced to consider Him, and the mysteries eternity holds in store for me. In doing so, present troubles, diseases, and unrest are obscured by future glories. So, just like David, today I am going to remind MY soul of the benefits the Lord has provided for ME. How about you? What perspective will you have today?

Sing out loud your favorite song today, either publicly or privately. There is a reason it is your favorite!

August 16

"The secret things belong to the LORD our God; but the things that are revealed belong to us and to our children forever, that we may do all the words of this law."
Deuteronomy 29:29

This verse alerts us to the truth that there are things God keeps to Himself while allowing mankind to understand others. But why? Perhaps because the things He keeps to Himself are just not understandable to the human mind. Think about it: our understanding is bound by time and space, and we can only speculate on eternity. We measure based on time and those measurements are limited to our past and present. It is not so for God because He knows the future. He provides another reason: "For my thoughts are not your thoughts, neither are your ways my ways, " says the LORD. "For as the heavens are higher than the earth, so are my ways higher than your ways, and my thoughts than your thoughts." So, are we to navigate life blindly, void of His instruction? Emphatically, NO!

God sent His Son Jesus to give us discernable understanding about His will for mankind. Yes, some of the teachings of Jesus are about future events while others are difficult to hear and even more difficult to embrace. We can only take by faith the future events of which He spoke while making a choice to accept or reject His hard sayings. Beyond this, God has given us the Creation that witnesses to His creativity and detail, and He has given us the Bible that teaches us His will in regard to how we should live our lives. Finally, He has given believers His Holy Spirit to unlock the Bible, comfort and encourage, and keep believers until they enter eternity. Here is the conclusion: focus on what God has made understandable and have faith that He will accomplish that which He keeps secret. The truth is that He has given mankind everything necessary to know Him and His will.

August 17

"As far as the east is from the west, so far has he removed our transgressions from us."
Psalms 103:12

† † †

How far is the east from the west? Truthfully, the two never intersect. No matter how far a man goes east, he will never reach a point where he begins to go west. It is impossible to do so and that is why the Psalmist is inspired to use these words. And so it is with our sins when God forgives them; we are ETERNALLY separated from them. Remember, although our offenses are against other people, they are ultimately against God because ALL humanity is created in His image. He, and only He can fully absolve us of guilt, and without His forgiveness we remain in debt to our Creator and one day be required to make good on that debt.

The Cross of Jesus is all about forgiveness. In His death and burial, Jesus paid the penalty for OUR sins through HIS death and separation from God. He did so to pay a sin debt that was impossible for mankind to repay to their Creator. To avail ourselves of that forgiveness, however, a person must acknowledge their need to be forgiven; it is not automatic. For the reader who has not yet done so, I encourage you to do so now. God tells us how in His Holy Word, the Bible: "if you confess with your lips that Jesus is Lord and believe in your heart that God raised him from the dead, you will be saved." If a reader is genuinely sincere in their confession and belief, he or she will share in the resurrection of Jesus and be born again. A brand new life awaits those who are without Jesus! Claim yours today.

August 18

"All the ways of a man are clean in his own eyes; but the LORD weighs the motives."
Proverbs 16:2

† † †

Have you ever believed with all your heart that something is true only to discover you were mistaken? Do you remember how surprised you were? That is how it will be for many at the end. The end I am referring to is that time when an individual stands before their Creator and is judged on the works of their lives. The surprise will not be about how good a person has been but instead how bad they actually were. God will not grade (judge) on a curve but rather by comparing the demands of the Mosaic Law to the actual behavior, both THOUGHTS and deeds, of the individual. EVERYONE will fail the examination! None will be judged acceptable by a Holy God because the unequivocal standard will be HIS holiness. Again, NONE will measure up!

That sounds like bad news because it really is bad news. Eternity in Heaven or Hell is what is at stake for the individual. But, like many things in life, good news is hiding in plain sight. Our Creator has provided a Savior to keep us from the fires of Hell, and His name is Jesus. If a person has trusted Jesus for forgiveness of their cradle to grave sins, they will be ushered into Heaven. All others will enter into an eternity without the grace of God and suffer the consequences of trusting in their righteousness instead of the forgiveness and resulting righteousness afforded by faith in Jesus. Rejecting the sacrifice of Jesus is like giving an obscene finger gesture to God. Perhaps you know someone that is living outside of the grace of God or maybe, just maybe, you are. It is never too late or too early to repent of the bad behavior and trust Jesus for your eternal salvation.

August 19

"You are our letter, written in our hearts, known and read by everyone."
II Corinthians 3:2

† † †

What the Apostle Paul is telling believers in Corinth is that THEY have become living letters (epistles) for the world to "read" and gain understanding of what it means to be a Christian. Other teachers were seeking to gain acceptance with the newly formed church in Corinth by providing written letters of commendations and references. Some of those seeking recognition may have been contrary to the pure Gospel advanced by Paul. Paul tells the local church that HIS commendation is their lives that witness to his teaching about Jesus and His love for them. They have, in fact, become "letters" from Christ for all to "read" and consider.

But what if now I am a letter (epistle) written by Jesus to the world, or at least to my world? What if YOU are a "letter" that Jesus has written to those in your world, family, friends, neighbors, strangers, or even enemies? Have WE become beautiful love letters from Jesus to those around us? At some point in most lives, a person receives a love letter from someone they adore. Those letters are saved and read over and over again, and each time they are read, the heart of the reader sings for joy and soars to new emotional heights. So, the question is this; what kind of a letter are we? As we go about our daily lives let us remember that people are "reading" the "letter" of our lives. We are making a difference one way or another.

Wear two different colored socks today. You will laugh at yourself all day long!

August 20

> "But it is good for me to come close to God. I have made the LORD my refuge, that I may tell of all your works in the gates of the daughter of Zion."
> Psalms 73:28

† † †

Life is full of choices, way too many to list here. Some choices are good for me while others are not. In fact, some choices can be disastrous. Notice in this verse the Psalmist has declared that it is to his advantage to draw near to God. He goes on to declare that he has put his TRUST in the Lord. People put their trust in many things; other people, governments, loved ones, money, intellect, career, influence, and popularity are just a few things that people anchor (trust) their lives to. Everything on this list, or any other worldly list, has the potential to fail, sometimes failure that leads to devastating consequences. Sadly, failure is imminent, it is only a matter of time. Also sad is the reality that those who put their trust in US will be disappointed, we will eventually fail. At times, even the best of us stumble.

It is not so with God. He never fails, He never stumbles, EVER! We may think that He has failed us but what we interpret as failure is a misunderstanding on our part. Jesus says that in THIS life we will have tribulation but also encourages us to be of good cheer because He has overcome the world. When we consider the perspective of eternity, we realize that in God's perfect timing, ALL His promises will be fulfilled. We will enjoy sufficiency in ALL aspects of life eternal. There will be no misfires or misunderstandings, no tears. Perhaps that is why the Psalmist ends his statement by saying that he will declare all God's work to anyone who will listen. How about us? Are we declaring the works of God, especially the Gospel to anyone who will listen? Like the Psalmist, it will be GOOD for us, too!

August 21

"A new commandment I give to you, that you love one another. Just as I have loved you, you also must love one another."
John 13:34
(AND)
"Neither do I condemn you. Go, and sin no more."
John 8:11

WELCOME TO AUGUST

✝ ✝ ✝

Both these verses record the words of Jesus. The first is given to His disciples near the end of His earthly ministry while the second is given to a woman who was caught in adultery. Is it possible to harmonize the two? Someone once said that a Christian is to love the sinner and hate the sin. That sounds harmonious to me, how about you? Throughout the Gospels we see this principle being fleshed out in Jesus as He encounters both saints and sinners. To be sure, Jesus HATES sin, it is the REASON He is making His journey to the Cross. Also a surety, Jesus wants everyone to live a righteous life that will first honor His Father, but also bring peace to their lives. Chronic sinful behavior never provides peace. It may satisfy the flesh momentarily, but just like hunger for food is cyclical, so is the flesh as it hungers for carnal satisfaction through a variety of behavior, good or bad.

King David, a man that God once called "a man after His own heart" writes in Psalm 23 that the Lord LEADS him in the paths of RIGHTEOUSNESS. Make no mistake about this, God does not LEAD people into sin, nor does He condone it. The world and the church today are filled with people who want to legitimize sinful behavior, even justify it in the name of love. God will have nothing to do with that attitude and neither should we. Love the sinner, YES! Encourage them to continue sinning, GOD FORBID! Let us agree with Jesus to love one another and to sin no more. When (not if) we do stumble, let us be quick to confess and repent. God promises to restore us if we humble ourselves.

Wear your favorite shirt or blouse today. It will brighten your day.

August 22

"Be subject therefore to God. But resist the devil, and he will flee from you. Draw near to God, and he will draw near to you…"
James 4:7, 8

†††

Wherever you are right now, focus your eyes on an object. If in a room, pick something unfamiliar and small on the other side from where you are sitting or standing. Do the same for wherever you are. Now think about that object, its size, color, perceivable details, perhaps letters that are printed or written on it. That is now your understanding of that object, but is that a good understanding? Would you now be able to accurately describe it to another person? Now slowly move closer to the object. Are you gaining greater understanding and clarity? Now hold it in your hand and examine it for cracks, crevices, printing, blemishes, hues of color, and any other details that were not visible when you first spotted it. Would you now be able to ACCURATLY describe it to another person?

In this verse the Holy Spirit, through the writings of the Apostle James, tells us to "draw near to God." How, specifically, do we draw near to someone we cannot see? How is it possible to know the details of someone we have or never will see in person while living on planet earth? The truth is I know an awful lot of details about historical figures, both heroes and villains. But how? Because I have read their autobiographies or biographies. I have listened to their music, seen their paintings, enjoyed their inventions, or otherwise know more than just their name. All this is because I have "drawn near' to them through various resources. The same is true for our

God. He has given us His autobiography while prompting others to write biographies of Him. He has given us His Holy Spirit that "speaks" to our hearts and listens to our prayers. Look again at the verse. Humble yourself, reject the enemy of God, and draw near to Him through every available resource He has provided. The best part of this verse is the last part: "He WILL draw near to you!"

Father, give me a desire to draw near to you this day and always.

August 23

> "Your hands have made me and formed me. Give me understanding, that I may learn your commandments."
> Psalms 119:73

✝ ✝ ✝

We are all created with specific DNA that makes our bodies unique. Sadly, sin has corrupted the DNA of mankind and now obscures the perfection of Adam and Eve. Their bodies were perfect, ours are imperfect; so imperfect that eventually our body will stop functioning properly and die. Someone once said: "No one gets out of here alive!" That may have been uttered in jest, but it is nonetheless true.

Our SOUL is different from our body and is the essential part of the "me" that this verse references. Beyond that, our soul is eternal. From our beginning, our soul is housed in our physical body thereby allowing us to interact with the physical world into which are born. Our mind and emotions are part of our soul and, for the most part, influence how our bodies act. We may consider our bodies autonomous, but without the direction of the mind they are really just an organism. A miraculous organism to be sure, but generally useless without the mind to prompt activity. So, what does any of this have to do with the verse we are considering today? Lots! In this verse the Holy Spirit reveals that we (body, soul, and spirit) have been created and FASHIONED, we are not an accident of nature or a random result of evolution. We have been given a SPECIFIC body, mind, and personality with both strengths and weaknesses. We have all been created for a PURPOSE! Armed with this understanding, ask your Creator what is YOUR purpose? If you humble yourself, both body and soul, He will reveal that purpose to you, and as you embrace that God ordained purpose, He will give you the power to harness both your strengths and weaknesses to bring glory and honor to Him. In doing so, you will find fulfillment in your life while on planet earth. With this perspective, reconsider the verse.

August 24

"So then, have I become your enemy by telling you the truth?" Galatians 4:16

† † †

It happens. Hearing or telling the truth sometimes separates even the best of friends, especially if that truth reveals something undesirable or calls for corrected behavior. Pride rears its ugly head and views the truth as offensive. Anger ensues and before long the relationship is in jeopardy. I know because I have been on both sides of this equation, and I suspect every reader has also experienced similar dilemmas.

When the Apostle Paul sought to correct bad teaching within the churches of Galatia, some people were angered. The truth that Paul presented did not fit their narrative and became an offense to some. They had their own "truth" and rejected THE truth and sought to ostracize Paul from any credibility. The same thing happened to

Jesus when He presented truth to the Jewish people, and we all know how that ended. Is there a lesson for us in this verse? Of course! When we share the Gospel (THE Truth) many people will be offended and some will be angered. Some will separate from us while others may persecute us. However, a precious few will accept the truth of the Gospel and be saved from eternal separation from the one and only God. The saved souls of those precious few will make any hardship we experience worth enduring.

Tell someone today the God loves them. It can a friend or foe, just DO it.

August 25

"Buy the truth, and do not sell it. Get wisdom, discipline, and understanding."
Proverbs 23:23

† † †

Buy truth and wisdom? Is that even possible? What currency is used in such a transaction? The good news is that if you are reading this you already have the currency, and I am not referring to money. There is one common currency among the living – TIME. We all have twenty-four hours a day and then on to the next. We "spend" our time working, eating, sleeping, recreating, and all the other things in life that compete for our twenty-four hours. Sometimes we spend our time wisely while other times we squander it.

But where do we go to buy Truth, yes, Truth with a capital "T"? There are a lot of people, groups, and institutions offering truth, but oftentimes it is only what they perceive to be truth. To be Truth, something must be true always and everywhere – no exceptions. Gravity is Truth; on planet earth it is true always and everywhere. By the way, we do not need to purchase gravity, it is free, but I caution the reader to use it wisely. The Truth about God and Mankind is found in the Bible (WORD of God) and to obtain it we must spend OUR currency of time. The more currency we spend the more Truth we obtain. Jesus once proclaimed that "I am the way, the TRUTH, and the life." That makes sense when we read the Apostle John's declaration that "the WORD became flesh and dwelt among us." Perhaps it would be prudent to examine how we are spending OUR currency of time. Let the words of Jesus echo in our hearts: "Sanctify them by Your truth. Your WORD is truth." Remember, once your currency (time) is gone it is gone forever. There are no do-overs.

August 26

> But the LORD said to Samuel, "Do not look on his face, or on the height of his stature; because I have rejected him. For man does not see as God sees, for man looks at the outward appearance, but God looks at the heart."
> I Samuel 16:7

This is a powerful principle to which we should pay particular attention. It should be considered a flashing red light when we are tempted to hastily judge another person based on appearance. When God was selecting a new King for the nation of Israel, He told the Prophet Samuel to go to the house of Jesse and there he would find the new King among the sons of Jesse. The problem was that Jesse had eight sons. Samuel first thought that Jesse's first born son was the one because of his stature, but the Lord rejected not only him but the next six brothers. Finally, David, the youngest, was summoned from the field where he was tending sheep and the Lord revealed to Samuel that David was the chosen one. It was after rejecting the first son that the Lord spoke the words we are considering today.

But what about us? Have WE ever rendered judgement on appearance? Surely, they do not know the Lord based on their sloppy clothing or rag-tag appearance, we reason. A mature Christian once taught me this same principle when I was first saved. I was reluctant to sing during service because I really do not have a good singing voice when compared with some that were sitting around me. He somehow noticed my reluctance and told me that God does not listen to my voice but rather my HEART. After that I no longer hesitated to sing in a service. So, here is the lesson: without getting to know someone, we cannot know their heart regardless of their appearance. The words that the Lord spoke to the Prophet are recorded for a reason – so WE would not make the same mistake.

August 27

"But far be it from me to boast, except in the cross of our Lord Jesus Christ, through which the world has been crucified to me, and I to the world."
Galatians 6:14

Pride is a killer! It is what got Satan kicked out of Heaven and Adam and Eve kicked out of the Garden of Eden. Pride will skew our relationships with friends and family, and it is a stumbling block between us and the Lord. The Apostle Peter reminds us that "God resists the proud but gives grace to the humble."

Few people want to be around a prideful man or woman and yet they are everywhere. They are in our families, our workplaces, our schools, on TV and radio, in every walk of life, and even in our Churches. Their objectionable behavior is obvious to all except them. The Apostle Paul had much to be proud of but, according to this verse, rejected boasting except in the Cross of his Savior, Jesus. When we REALIZE that everything we have is a gift from our Creator; life itself, our salvation, our body, mind, personality, abilities, and provisions, we are humbled. When we realize that God could, at any moment, stop our heart and call us to give an account of our lives, we can only respond with humility. Let us CHOOSE humility over pride as we live out the plan that the Lord has for each of us.

Pray for people in another country today. Ask God to draw many to Him.

August 28

"Therefore if anyone is in Christ, he is a new creation. The old things have passed away. Look, new things have come."
2 Corinthians 5:17

† † †

NOTE: THIS IS A MULTI DAY DEVOTION

Do you remember that day? The day you heard the call of the Holy Spirit and recognized the need for Jesus to be your Savior; you surrendered your life and asked God to forgive you of your sins. In that instant your life was changed; you were resurrected from the (spiritually) dead and became a new creation (spiritually alive). The reality is you were born again; you were forgiven, pardoned, redeemed, and resurrected from death to new life. You were not given just a second chance but rather a brand NEW life!

"But what happens now?" you probably questioned. How do you negotiate your new life? Did God expect anything from you? Did you expect anything from Him? Until now your attitude and behavior had been based on your understanding of life and that was now an outdated understanding of God. Even though you may not have been aware of it, you had been changed in a way that was unlike anything you had ever experienced or will ever experience again, and maybe you were wondering what this new life was supposed to look like. Everything you knew or once believed was about to be challenged. Your spirit had been awakened and God's Holy Spirit had now taken up residence in your heart. The journey you had just begun was a very personal one and you were not certain that everyone would embrace it.

August 29 - AN EXTENSION FROM PREVIOUS

"Therefore if anyone is in Christ, he is a new creation. The old things have passed away. Look, new things have come."
2 Corinthians 5:17

As a child of God, you now lived in two kingdoms. By virtue of your physical birth, you were a citizen of the KINGDOM OF THIS WORLD (system) but because you were "born again" you were now a citizen of the KINGDOM OF GOD. But here's the thing, even though you had dual citizenship, where should your allegiance and priorities be rightly directed? Could you meld the two together? Were they compatible with one another, did they harmonize? Was citizenship in the two kingdoms permanent or would one prevail; which one was permanent, and which one was only temporary?

Someone once said, "You cannot put a round peg in a square hole." Most likely you soon discovered that the two kingdoms were mutually exclusive. Although both kingdoms are governed by love, it is the OBJECT of that love that separates the kingdoms. In the kingdom of this world the object of love is SELF, which often creates contention, jealousy, and even hatred for others. However, God and others are the objects of love in the Kingdom of God. The only hatred in the kingdom of God is the hatred of sin. Beyond that, the principles of the kingdom of the world are energized and directed by pride, fear, death, and money. In opposition to that, the Holy Spirit enables the principles of the Kingdom of God in you, and those principles include love for God, love for others, forgiveness for self and to others, and everlasting life.

August 30 - AN EXTENSION FROM PREVIOUS

> "Therefore if anyone is in Christ, he is a new creation. The old things have passed away. Look, new things have come."
> 2 Corinthians 5:17

† † †

So, the question remains; to which kingdom should your allegiance belong? Fortunately, the Bible gives clear advice on this issue. Through the writings of the Apostle Paul, the Holy Spirit directs believers to allow their mind to be renewed, and that renewal comes through faith stimulated and nourished by the Holy Spirit, renewal also comes by studying God's Word, prayer, forgiving others, worship, fellowship with other believers, and continual personal surrender to Christ (A word of caution is necessary here…believers can both grieve and quench the Holy Spirit). Beyond that, the Holy Spirit reveals that believers are now ambassadors for

Christ, and the role of an ambassador is clear; represent their home country honorably and extol the virtues of their homeland while practicing the attitude and behavior of that homeland. Staying true to their commission often stands as a stark contrast to their country of residence. That is also the goal of an ambassador for Christ, to offer better life options than the world offers, including ETERNAL life. The ambassador knows that they have the full force and support of their home kingdom, and as an ambassador for Christ, the believer is NEVER alone even though they may stand alone in their witness. The kingdom is ALWAYS with the believer. Let me ask you again; do you remember that GLORIOUS day when you were born again? It is a day worth remembering.

August 31

> "Therefore I urge you, brothers, by the mercies of God, to present your bodies a living sacrifice, holy, acceptable to God, which is your reasonable service."
> Romans12:1

† † †

Someone once noted that the problem with a living sacrifice is that it keeps jumping off the altar. Funny? Yes, but also true, at least in my experience. Although the Apostle Paul writes that it is our "reasonable" service, it often does not feel reasonable. Surrendering MY will, praying for others, turning the other cheek, trusting that God is in control of a world that seems to be out of control certainly stretches my ability to stay on the altar. Nonetheless, that is the call of imitating our Savior, and that imitation both honors and glorifies Him!

Father, help me to sacrifice to you those things that keep me from you. Help me to see the world through your eyes.

Today, look at picture of you when you were young. It will bring back a lot of memories.

Happy birthday to my son today!

WELCOME TO SEPTEMBER

"When the Helper has come, whom I will send to you from the Father, the Spirit of truth, who proceeds from the Father, he will testify about me."
John 15:26

September 1*

"...says the Lord."
Jeremiah1:19a

☦ ☦ ☦

Three times in one chapter God says to Jeremiah the equivalent of, "I have spoken!" Three times he offers comfort to a worried and resistant young man and closes his words with, "says the Lord."

When God created the universe, He "spoke" it into being (Gen 1:3); when he came to Earth as the God-Man Messiah, John referred to Him as "the Word" (John 1:1); and when the author of Hebrews began his letter, he wrote that in these new days, God has "spoken" to us through His Son (Heb 1:2). When God speaks, universes literally spring from nothing, cosmic powers are overthrown, and human beings can pass from death to life.

When I was a music teacher, I would tell my students there was a difference between "hearing" and "listening". Hearing is a physiological function of the ear – sound waves pass through the ear canal and cause the ear to vibrate, and we "hear" a sound. Listening, however, is a function of the mind – it requires attention, intention, and thought. And when it comes to God, listening also involves the heart.

God's word has the power to transform us – if we will only listen to them (which means we put them into practice (Matt 7:24)). We know from the gospels there are many who "heard" Jesus' message, but not everyone "listened."

Father, give me a heart and mind to listen to your word, to find peace, comfort, encouragement, challenge, forgiveness, and acceptance in what you say. Team me to listen, for your words have power. Help me be like Peter, who proclaimed, "Lord, to whom would we go? You have the words of everlasting life." (John 6:68)

September 2

"Blessed are the peacemakers, for they will be called the children of God"
Matthew 5:9

†††

The MOST important way a person can be a peacemaker is to share with another how to have PEACE with the one who created them. Without the intervention of God, it is not possible to have peace with Him. The frightening thing is that a person can live their entire life never understanding that they are separated from God until they enter eternity. It is only then when their Creator confronts their behavior that they will come to understand God's holiness and their sinfulness. Without a Savior, they will suffer the consequences of a life that focused on self.

Father, motivate me to share Jesus with others so they too can experience peace with you. Lead and equip me to be a peacemaker.

Look through an old photo album today. Your memory will be exercised.

September 3

"The LORD is gracious, merciful, slow to anger, and of great loving kindness."
Psalms 145:8

☩ ☩ ☩

This verse is so very comforting. Words like gracious, compassionate, great in mercy are beautiful music to the ears of people – especially believers. But hidden in plain sight is something that should frighten people to their very core. Although slow to anger, the verse does not say He will not eventually be moved to anger. Most of the book of Revelation speaks of a time when the Lord will eventually manifest His anger for men and women who refuse to accept the sacrifice of His Son, Jesus. They choose other gods to worship and serve while mocking the death, burial, and resurrection of God's precious Son. If anyone is OUTSIDE of Jesus, they will suffer an ETERNITY of regret, pain, and sorrow, while believers in Christ will experience God's blessings. Choose wisely, it makes a difference.

Father, help me to NEVER take your grace, compassion, and mercy for granted. Keep the Cross of Jesus foremost in my mind knowing that it is foremost in Yours.

September 4

"The light of the righteous shines brightly, but the lamp of the wicked is snuffed out."
Proverbs 13:9

✝ ✝ ✝

The light referenced in this verse is spiritual light, a light that is obscured to unbelievers. They have been blinded to this light by the enemy and sin. They navigate the physical world but are oblivious to spiritual awareness, especially in regard to their estrangement from their Creator. Truthfully, only the Holy Spirit can bring forth the light of the Kingdom of God to a person, and it begins with the Gospel.

This is how we enter into that process; by sharing the Gospel with those in darkness. Yes, God and His Word are light but so are we. Jesus once told His listeners that those who believe in Him are the light of the world. He continued by telling them a light is not meant to be put under a bushel basket but rather on a lamp stand for all to see. Let us do what we are commissioned to do, let us share the Gospel by our words and our deeds.

September 5

"And he healed many who were sick with various diseases, and cast out many demons. He did not allow the demons to speak, because they knew him."
Mark 1:34

✝ ✝ ✝

In this verse we learn that demons recognized Jesus and were subject to His authority. Elsewhere in the Gospels we learn that the wind and restless waters of the Sea of Galilee recognized Him and were also subject to His authority. The irony of the Gospels is that God's greatest creation, Mankind, did not RECOGNIZE Him even though they were created in His image. Their obliviousness testifies to how significant the impact of sin is to humanity. No wonder Jesus tells a Jewish religious man (and all mankind) that he "must be born again." A brand NEW life is necessary to not only recognize Him but to also be of service to Him.

Father, be merciful to those who have yet to recognize Jesus. Draw them to His Cross through the Holy Spirit and the Gospel.

September 6

"But the path of the righteous is like a shining light, that shines brighter and brighter until the full day."
Proverbs 4:18

†††

There is coming a PERFECT Day for every born again believer. Ironically, it is the day we end our life's journey on planet earth and enter the heavenly kingdom of our great God where life is eternal. In that PERFECT Day we will see Jesus face to face and experience life without the trappings of sin.

We sing songs about that Day, read scripture, poetry, and books about it, but nothing will compare to the reality of the experience. It will be glorious! I am so ready. How about you?

September 7

"Cause me to hear your loving kindness in the morning, for I trust in you. Cause me to know the way in which I should walk, for I lift up my soul to you."
Psalms 143:8

†††

In this verse we see King David asking God to CAUSE him to not only HEAR about God's love, but also to KNOW God's plan for David, and the specific directions to accomplish that plan. To experience these things David proclaims that he LIFTS up his soul to God. It is a noble request, to be sure, but what does it mean to lift our soul to God? Our soul is our unique intellect, emotions, and mind; it is our very core given to us by God and it is eternal. It is who we are!

Imagine a little boy or girl lifting something they value up to their waiting father. As their eyes lock, nothing else is on the child's mind, their focus is EXCLUSIVELY on the father. The child has a genuine desire for the father to have the offering; it is their heart's ONLY desire. Is that an accurate depiction of us as we lift our soul to God? That is not a rhetorical question, but rather something to think about today. To whom or what am I sincerely lifting my soul?

Father, cause me to know the plan you have for my life. Cause my heart to reflect your heart to those you have set in my path.

September 8

"John came baptizing in the wilderness and preaching a baptism of repentance for forgiveness of sins."
Mark 1:4
(BUT)
"... Jesus came into Galilee, proclaiming the Good News of God, and saying, "The time is fulfilled, and the kingdom of God is near. Repent, and believe in the Good News."
Mark 1:14, 15

† † †

At first glance the difference in these verses may seem subtle but look again. John the Baptist calls for people to repent and in response to their repentance, baptizes them in the Jordon River. The picture is one of being washed clean. Jesus calls on people to turn from their sin but ALSO to believe in the Gospel. Earlier, John had told his followers that One was coming who would baptize them with the Holy Spirit. That One was Jesus. The implication being that the repentant man or woman COULD and WOULD be cleansed from the INSIDE, something water could never do.

After the resurrection of Jesus, baptism would be a witness to observers that the one being baptized had died to self (and sin) and, just like Jesus, was resurrected to a BRAND NEW life. As a reminder, "For God so loved the world that He gave His only begotten Son, that whoever believes in Him should not perish but have EVERLASTING life." That truth is the Gospel, and it remains a call from Heaven to ALL the people of earth to this very day.

September 9

"It shall happen, if you shall listen diligently to the voice of the LORD your God, to observe to do all his commandments which I command you this day, that the LORD your God will set you on high above all the nations of the earth: and all these blessings shall come on you, and overtake you, if you shall listen to the voice of the LORD your God."
Deuteronomy 28:1, 2

✝ ✝ ✝

Because we now live in a post-resurrection era, we can learn a valuable lesson as we consider these verses. The lesson is called Progressive Revelation. We must always temper any verse in the Bible with the WHOLE of the Bible. The most glaring example of this is the Mosaic Law with all its COMMANDMENTS and ceremonies being obsoleted and replaced by the GOSPEL. Progressive Revelation dictates that what was once truth can potentially be negated by a new truth as God continues to UNFOLD and REVEAL His plan for humanity. But be very careful, ONLY God can negate a previous truth in favor of a new truth, and He has established plenty of guardrails in the Bible to prevent us from IMAGINING not only His Will for mankind but also His expectations for how we are to live our lives. Some people cling to a single verse to justify their bad behavior while abandoning the TOTAL truth as revealed in the Bible. The responsibility for knowing ALL of scripture is ours, not God's. We must wrap OUR theology around Scripture and not wrap Scripture around OUR theology. How can we avoid being on the wrong side of God? Believe the Gospel, stay in the Word, the WHOLE Word, stay connected to God through abundant prayer and you will find the understanding you seek.

> "… If you remain in my word, then you are truly my disciples. You will know the truth, and the truth will make you free."
> Jesus of Nazareth, The Christ

September 10

> "And early in the morning, while it was still dark, he rose up and went out, and departed into a deserted place, and prayed there."
> Mark 1:35

✝ ✝ ✝

All through the Bible we see examples of prayer, teaching on prayer, and the results of prayer. There are hundreds and hundreds of verses that contain the words "pray" and "prayer" in scripture. I personally liken prayer as the soul of my relationship with my Heavenly Father. In this verse we see just one example of the prayer life of Jesus and this example is a doozy. Notice that Jesus STARTS His day long before daylight by seeking His Father's guidance and protection for the upcoming activities of the new day. Notice also that it is private and away from distractions and temptations. The Son of God is demonstrating His dependence on prayer for both the FELLOWSHIP and resources of His Father.

The Holy Spirit did not inspire Mark to write these words to add volume to his Gospel. Mark records this activity so we can understand how IMPORTANT and NECESSARY prayer was to Jesus, and consequently to US. Jesus did not just cruise through life disconnected from His Father; while separated from His Father, Jesus stayed connected to Him by intentional PRAYER. If anyone could have justified an anemic prayer life it would have been Jesus. After all, He was the Son of God, and by default His Father would always take care of Him. Instead, Jesus demonstrated His NEED to have a healthy prayer life. That should be a powerful and inspirational lesson for every born-again believer. Prayer may very well be the MOST important thing we can do while on planet earth.

September 11

"Thus Noah did. According to all that God commanded him, so he did."
Genesis 6:22

† † †

The story of Noah is well known throughout the world. His story is found in the book of Genesis, chapters six through ten. It is a compelling story that tragically ends in the death of all mankind except Noah and his family. Skeptics mock the story claiming it is only a fable dreamed up by the Jewish writers of the Old Testament. However, there is sufficient archeological evidence to support the account for those who choose to be objective, and Jesus spoke of Noah and the flood in the Gospels of both Matthew and Luke. In fact, He says that just before His return to earth the world will be just like it was immediately prior to the flood. If you wonder what that looked like here is what is written: "that the wickedness of man was great in the earth, and that every intent of the thoughts of his heart was only evil continually." No one but God the Father knows when this time will occur again, but it is a certainty.

The Ark that Noah built was the only way of escape from the flood, but no one believed Noah and consequently perished. Jesus is now the only "Ark" that will save us from the coming judgment of God. Let us make every effort to invite family, friends, and even enemies to join us in that Ark. The Christian is the Noah of today.

September 12

> "For this cause we also thank God without ceasing, that, when you received from us the word of the message of God, you accepted it not as a human word, but, as it is in truth, the word of God, which also works in you who believe."
>
> I Thessalonians 2:13

† † †

In his letter to the church in Thessalonica, the Apostle Paul reminds readers that the Word of God is WORKING in believers. How do words "work" in a person's life, some may ask? Jesus once said that the words He spoke "are spirit and they are life." Those spoken words have been recorded and herein lies the great

MYSTERY. Words printed on a page are just ink laid on top of paper, they have no special ability. However, when the HOLY SPIRIT is added to this equation the words really do come to life. The Holy Spirit uses the words to "speak" truth to the mind, soul, and spirit of a reader. The words become much more than information, they become a conduit for change, and that change is a renewing of the mind. It is part of the process of personal sanctification that occurs once a person has been born-again. When read, the Holy Spirit gives energy (faith) to the words, and that FAITH becomes power within the new creation that God creates when a person genuinely embraces the Gospel. The new creation takes root in the body, soul, and spirit, and dominates the old man by the power of the Holy Spirit.

My conclusion: since the coming of the Holy Spirit, billions of people have experienced the "work" of the Word of God in their lives while billions more have witnessed their transition. It is as real as gravity!

September 13

"Trouble and anguish have taken hold of me. Your commandments are my delight."
Psalms 119:143

✝ ✝ ✝

It seems paradoxical to be reading of trouble, anguish, and DELIGHT in the same sentence. Trouble and anguish; we have all visited that neighborhood from time to time, and it is a dark and foreboding place that challenges both body and soul. What "delights" is the Psalmist referring to in this verse?

Promises, yes, but not just the promises from a man or woman. The promises that the Psalmist found delight in were from the One who created the universe, who created him. The Psalmist could not understand that one day the Creator would send His Son to walk among His most prized creation, Man, and he could not understand that Jesus would one day experience trouble and anguish in the world that He created. What the Psalmist could understand was that God's promises can be trusted. He understood that, unlike men and women, God NEVER reneges on a promise, NEVER! So here is where the rubber meets the road. Do you and I have that same confidence in God's promises? Do we believe and trust Him in the midst of our troubles and anguishes? If so, we too can find DELIGHT in knowing that God is with us and that our ETERNITY will be free of any trouble or anguish. That is His promise!

September 14

"And he went out again by the seaside. All the crowd came to him, and he taught them."
Mark 2:13

Jesus continues this very day to teach those who have a desire to learn. The Bible reveals that the word of God became flesh and dwelt among us. The reference is to the earthly life of Jesus and although He is no longer here in the flesh, the word of God remains with us. The words are now ink on paper, but those words carry the same authority as when Jesus spoke to them while on earth. As a man, Jesus was physically limited to the location where He taught, but now the word of God, the Bible, can be found anywhere on the planet. When read, the Holy Spirit gives life to the words and ministers to the very soul of the reader. It genuinely is as if Jesus is present with the reader.

Would you like Jesus to teach you today? Find a quiet place, open the Bible, and enjoy His teaching. Oh, the things you will learn!

September 15

"And if a kingdom is divided against itself, that kingdom cannot stand. And if a house is divided against itself, that house will not be able to stand."
Mark 3:24, 25

The Kingdom of God has two distinct voices on planet earth. One is audible to the human ear while the other is audible to the human spirit. The Church, the body of Christ, is made up of born-again believers. They gather along with others who have not been born-again in various congregations of various denominations to worship God and advance the Gospel to others, and it is within this context that the first distinct voice is heard, the voices of men and women. But like all things that often migrate to the intellect and emotions of man, things can get out of alignment. Factions develop, emotions flare up, pride surfaces, errant doctrine is embraced, and suddenly the house (the denominational Church) is divided against itself. Sadly, the many, many denominations and splinter groups within those denominations witness to the active work of Satan to discredit Christ. Unbelievers often ridicule the denominational Church because of their inability to get along with one other, and their ridicule is not without merit.

The other distinct voice in the world is the Holy Spirit. He speaks to all but only those who have been born-again actually LISTEN, and more importantly, pay attention to what He says. He is ALWAYS in unity with God the Father and God the Son. They NEVER dispute one another, EVER! Herein, lies the dilemma of the born-again believer; where to collectively worship God and serve alongside others? That choice must be couched in prayer and "listening" to the Holy Spirit for His guidance. Regardless of where a born-again person worships God, it is important to remember that the HEAVENLY commissioned body of Christ (The Church) takes its direction exclusively from the WORD of God and the Holy Spirit. Pay close attention to the Holy Spirit and choose wisely because makes a difference.

September 16

> "Why do you set your eyes on that which is not? For it certainly sprouts wings like an eagle and flies in the sky."
> Proverbs 23:5

✝ ✝ ✝

There are many things to love in this life, but money is NOT one of them. God and people should be our first love along with the wonders of creation but too many people have elevated money to a god-like status, pursuing it with vigor their entire lives. Realistically thinking, it is better to have sufficient money than to be poor. The world in which we live demands some form of currency to purchase the essentials and niceties of life. But therein lies the dilemma; OUR determination of what is SUFFICIENT and ESSENTIAL.

In today's verse God warns the reader that money is not reliable, it is often fleeting and transient. By comparison, God IS reliable, He has planted His Holy Spirit in the hearts and consequently the lives of born again believers, and His promise is to NEVER forsake them. Perhaps it would be beneficial for each reader to privately and honestly consider their relationship with money. Creating a list of the five highest priorities in your life is a good place to start.

GIVE some of YOUR money away today. The ease or difficulty you experience in doing so will give you valuable insight into your relationship with money.

September 17

Jesus answered, "This voice hasn't come for my sake, but for your sakes. Now is the judgment of this world. Now the prince of this world will be cast out."
John 12:30, 31

†††

NOTE: THIS IS A MULTI DAY DEVOTION

Only the most ardent skeptic of the Bible can deny the existence of Satan and his ability to influence the affairs of Man. Various versions of the Bible lists over 80 direct references to Satan. Other veiled references include Lucifer, Devil, Abaddon, wicked one, evil one, dragon, (S)serpent, and other identifiers that appear in the pages of scripture. Jesus called Satan "the ruler of this world." Arguably, the most powerful reference is Jesus saying He witnessed Satan's expulsion from Heaven (Luke 10:18). Based exclusively on that testimony, denying the existence of Satan is akin to calling Jesus a liar. Additionally, the temptation of Jesus by Satan shortly after Jesus' baptism is a compelling account of Satan's ability to manifest in our physical world.

September 18 - AN EXTENSION FROM PREVIOUS

> Jesus answered, "This voice hasn't come for my sake, but for your sakes. Now is the judgment of this world. Now the prince of this world will be cast out."
> John 12:30, 31

† † †

Nonetheless, there are many questions and mysteries surrounding the one who desired to exalt his throne above the Most High (Isaiah 14:12-14). A common question people ask; "Why was Lucifer/Satan even created?" Believers are also likely to ask the following questions: What about the "war" in heaven (Revelation 12:7-9)? When did or when will that war occur? When will Satan be cast into the Lake of Fire (Revelation 20:10)? Specifically, what power does Satan have on planet earth and, more importantly, what power does he have in regard to Mankind (1 John 5:19; 2 Cor 4:4; Matt 28:18)? Does Satan still have direct access to the throne room of God (Job 1:6, 7)? These questions and others are legitimate and worthy of consideration and research. The answers, however, may be inconclusive. Not every Biblical question is answerable (Deut 29:29), however, careful consideration of the scriptures may bring clarity, albeit limited, to the reader. The reader is challenged to come to his/her own conclusions about these questions. There is sufficient Biblical and extra-Biblical material available to adequately research and develop a personal understanding or, at least, an opinion of these issues.

September 19 - AN EXTENSION FROM PREVIOUS

> Jesus answered, "This voice hasn't come for my sake, but for your sakes. Now is the judgment of this world. Now the prince of this world will be cast out."
> John 12:30, 31

✝ ✝ ✝

I offer the following comments in regard to the present day status of Satan relative to believers. Does Satan continue to have a "kingdom" on earth? Yes, and his subjects are people who reject the God of Abraham, Isaac, Jacob, and, critically important, reject the risen Jesus. Jesus prays for His Father's kingdom to come to earth (Matt 6:10), and it has come. He proclaims that where He and His followers are, there also is the kingdom of God (Mathew 12:28; Luke 10:8-11). However, even the most naïve among us can readily glean from current events, both personal and worldwide, that the kingdom of God does not prevail in this world, but it can rule in our hearts. Sadly, it is the fallen and dark nature of Man that prevails. The kingdom of God does exist by the power of the Holy Spirit working through the Church, and it continues to grow but is significantly hindered and outnumbered by those living in the kingdom of Satan. Wars, famine, murder, pride, greed, lust of the eyes and flesh are the hallmarks of the kingdom of Satan. "Me first", is the mantra of that kingdom. Every possible abomination towards God is practiced daily in every society on earth; some horrifically displayed on the world stage while others are covert and secret, known only to God and the perpetrators (Proverbs 15:3).

September 20 - AN EXTENSION FROM PREVIOUS

Jesus answered, "This voice hasn't come for my sake, but for your sakes. Now is the judgment of this world. Now the prince of this world will be cast out."
John 12:30, 31

Thankfully, born again believers have the absolute assurance of the Holy Scriptures in regard to all things spiritual and temporal (John 17:17). Neither Satan nor his minions will ever be able to defeat God or separate believers from His love (John 10:28-30; Romans 8:38, 39; 1 John 4:4). Satan is not omniscient, omnipotent, or omnipresent; he is created and subject to the limitations God places upon him (Job 1:7-13). God provides ample advice to believers on how to have victory over Satan and his schemes (Ephesians 6:10, 13-17; Romans 13:12; James 4:7, 8; 1 Peter 5:8, 9).

September 21

"Do not weary yourself to be rich. In your wisdom, show restraint. Why do you set your eyes on that which is not? For it certainly sprouts wings like an eagle and flies in the sky."
Proverbs 23:4,5
(AND)
"For the love of money is a root of all kinds of evil. Some have been led astray from the faith in their greed, and have pierced themselves through with many sorrows."
1 Timothy 6:10

In his classic work The Odyssey, the Greek poet Homer writes about Sirens, half woman and half bird creatures that sing so beautifully that sailors who listened to their seductive songs lost their senses. Consequently, their ships would sink after crashing into the rocky shoals.

Of course, this account is mythological, but the lure of riches is not. It continues to this very day. Many a man or woman has lost their soul in the pursuit of the Siren call of money. It promises freedom but has the potential to enslave. Jesus once warned His listeners that "No one can serve two masters, for either he will hate the one and love the other; or else he will be devoted to one and despise the other. You cannot serve both God and Mammon (Matthew 6:24)." It is true, only one will prevail, and His reference was to God and money. Be careful, be aware, and pay attention to what Jesus says about our relationship with money.

Remember, money is amoral, it is neither good nor bad, but it can be used for either. It is our responsibility to establish correct priorities to the issues of our lives, including money, and God gives ample council in His Word in this regard.

If you are able, spend time with a friend today. Your visit will be beneficial to both you and your friend.

September 22

"I am a stranger on the earth. Do not hide your commandments from me."
Psalms 119:19

† † †

Have you ever been somewhere, and you instinctively knew that you really did not belong there? You were uncomfortable, feeling out of place while trying to fit in. It was not like the people were unfriendly or disagreeable, but you knew that somehow you were a round peg trying to fit into a square hole.

I remember attending a business convention in Denver, Colorado. It had been a long three days of meetings, events, dinners, and fun with business associates. I woke up early Sunday morning and decided to go for a walk and collect my thoughts while I anticipated returning home that afternoon. The hotel was not far from the football stadium and there was a game scheduled for that day. As I was walking near the stadium, I noticed in a parking lot there were a number of RV campers and a small group of people having coffee together. On one of the campers had a prominent Cross fixed to the vehicle. I walked over and asked one of the men if he owned the camper. He said he did indeed own it and the people with him were all believers having a time of prayer and coffee. He offered me a cup of coffee and I joined the little group explaining that I, too, was a believer who was visiting Denver for a convention. I felt so at "home" for the first time in days. There was no upscale hotel grandeur, but I had a glorious time talking about Jesus with others who believed the same. I remember thinking that this is how I would feel when I finally entered heaven, my true HOME.

The Apostle Paul echoes this thought in his letter to the Church in Philippi. "For our citizenship is in heaven, from which we also eagerly wait for the Savior, the Lord Jesus Christ."

September 23

"Wisdom is before the face of one who has understanding, but the eyes of a fool wander everywhere."
Proverbs 17:24

✝ ✝ ✝

I am not sure what the Psalmist was thinking when he wrote this verse, but I do know what I am thinking when I read it. When I am reading the Bible, "WISDOM" is in my sight. I need not look to anything else to understand who created the world, how it was created, who created me and how, why the world is the way it is, why I am the way I am, and where I will spend eternity. Most of all, I know how to be reconciled to my Creator!

While other eyes are searching the ends of the earth for wisdom, I have found it, and it did not come from any man or woman. It came from my Creator. It came by revelation from the Holy Spirit as my eyes feasted on the words of the Bible, and it cannot be explained, only experienced. Ask your Creator to give you wisdom as you focus your eyes on His Holy Book.

September 24*

"I revealed your name to the people whom you have given me out of the world. They were yours, and you have given them to me. They have kept your word."
John 17:6

✝ ✝ ✝

Do you notice what Jesus says about you and me? He says we are gifts to Him from the Father! Often, we consider Jesus the gift God gave to us - it's why we give gifts on Christmas. And He is. But have you ever considered you are also God's gift to His Son?

As parents we give good gifts to our children. We give gifts to friends and loved ones. And when we give gifts, we give gifts which have value and meaning. If this is true for us, how much more is it true of God? Didn't Jesus use this same argument about God when He talked of how God cares for us more than the birds of the air?

God gave you as a gift to His Son, and in so doing He has filled you with His Spirit and is transforming you into His likeness. Perhaps this is why Paul can so confidently write, "He who began a good work in you will complete it!" You are a gift to His Son, and He wants you to be perfect.

September 25*

My heart said to you, "I have sought your face. Your face, LORD, I will seek."
Psalm 27:8

✝ ✝ ✝

God wants to talk with me. He desires it, He initiates it, and He invites me in. This suggests that when we don't hear Him, it could be because we're not listening rather than He is not talking.

Notice the preposition here...The translation is "with." God wants to talk with us, not "to" us. Either is it for us to talk "to" Him; rather, God invites us to talk "with" Him. "With" is an abiding word - a together word - a word where both are involved. Think of the differences between going for a walk to a friend and going for a walk with a friend.

God wants us to talk with Him; He wants to listen to us, yes, and He wants us to listen to Him! You see, in conversations (and relationships), whenever someone talks another must listen. Notice the first phrase of the verse: "My heart has heard you..."

Prayer is a back-and-forth conversation. It involves listening and speaking. Which one are you better at? Which one do you engage in more? So often for me it's the talking. I have much to say to God (or at least I think I do.) I'm like the little kid who runs into the room to tell his parents something then runs out before bothering to listen for a response

"Lord, teach me to pray" includes "Lord, teach me to listen."

September 26*

"My heart has trusted in him, and I am helped. Therefore my heart greatly rejoices. With my song I will thank him."
Psalm 28:7b

† † †

Have you ever been someplace – perhaps a restaurant or office – and heard and announcement along the lines of, "Hey everybody – it's _____'s birthday! Let's all sing!" And what generally happens? People start singing "Happy Birthday to ____" – even when they don't know the person. Why is that? Is it to meet some hidden cultural rule? Is it because they don't want to be the only person NOT singing? My guess is that while both these statements contain some truth, a deeper reason is we all value life and understand that another birthday means someone has overcome another year's worth of challenges. We celebrate the victories, the perseverance, and, yes, we celebrate the value of the individual.

Have you ever been someplace – perhaps a church service or Bible study – and someone says, "Hey everyone, let's sing a song!" And they start singing a well-known song most people in the room probably know, yet when you looked around the room there are some (many?) people (perhaps even you) just standing and watching? Why is that? Why is it we will sing a joyous version of "Happy Birthday" to a complete stranger, or a rousing rendition of "Take me out to the ballgame" during a 7 inning stretch, yet when invited to sing a song of adoration to the King of Kings and Lord of Lords – the very creator of the universe and the one who sustains our life – we shrink back?

The psalmist wrote that he "bursts forth" in song. Why? He was thankful because of all God had done to help him – which means he sees and knows what God had done to help him.

When we struggle to praise God – either on Sunday morning or during the week – I believe it's rarely because of external factors such as not knowing the words or unfamiliarity with the music. I have found that, more often than not, it's because we haven't walked closely with God. Praise and worship, you see, is a response to God – to who He is and what He's done. And you can't respond to what you don't know.

September 27*

"I will extol you, LORD, for you have raised me up,"
Ps 30:1a

✝ ✝ ✝

So often when I read Psalms of God delivering someone from their enemies I think, "But that doesn't apply to me. No one is trying to kill or harm me!" I picture David hiding in a cave while Saul's men search for him, or someone going into battlefield against a larger, stronger foe (Goliath, perhaps?). But this vision belies a very basic fact: I do have an enemy trying to kill me – and that enemy is Satan. The Apostle Peter even compared Satan to a lion "looking for someone to devour." (1 Pet 5:8) To fall into complacency regarding the truth of a mortal enemy is to lower my guard and make me susceptible to fail.

At the same time, God has already delivered me from what Satan wants for me: eternal death and damnation. Through Jesus' work on the cross, I have been rescued!. Just like David, I can praise God for saving me from my enemy. More than David, I can praise him because my rescue – my salvation – is secure and complete for all eternity, whereas David's was temporary, only until the next time. Even though my enemy looks to devour me, I stand already in victory over him through the finished work of Christ on the cross, and so when I fight, I fight from victory, not for victory. And for that, I can (and should) offer praise and thanksgiving to God – I can "exalt [the Lord] for [He] has rescued me."

When I feel myself struggling to praise, I try to go back and remind myself of all God has done for and is doing in me. By seeing what I have been saved from and recognizing the depth of my sin and the power of my enemy, I see even more clearly the overwhelming power, glory, and grace of God. In seeing that, my only natural response is to bow down in praise and surrender all I am and have to Him.

September 28*

> "For the word of the LORD is right. All his work is done in faithfulness."
> Psalms 33:4b

✝ ✝ ✝

Do I trust God with everything He does believing that all His work is done in faithfulness? While I want to say "Yes," because that's the "Christian" response, so often I think the answer is probably something different. Too often I think I know better than He does... I think I know better how to spend my money, how to allot my time, how to treat other people.... And I love to question Him when He allows things to happen outside of what I want.

Trust Him with everything He does – even when "everything" involves someone getting cancer, or getting in a car wreck, experiencing the loss of a child, or getting laid off? Trust him with everything – even what "everything" means a friend betrays you? How do I trust Him when He allows those things to happen?

The short answer is that if I don't trust Him in those situations, I really don't trust Him at all. We like to think of trust as something one has or doesn't have – like a glass which is either full or empty. But the truth is that we are always trusting – the question is not, "Do you trust?" the question is really, "In whom (or what) do you trust?" When I say I don't trust a person, what I'm saying is that I trust someone (or something) else more. The person who says, "I don't trust what you're saying about _____" is really saying, "I trust my own words more than yours."

So, if I'm not going to trust the one who gave His own Son to save me, who raised Him back to life, who can I trust? Is there anyone more deserving than Him? After all, as bad as my life may seem at times (and, let's be honest, the vast majority of my "problems" are really first-world concerns), they are nothing compared to what God has done for me.

So maybe I need to focus on trusting Him more and me less.

September 29*

"I will bless the LORD at all times."
Psalms 34:1a

✝ ✝ ✝

It's easy to praise God when life is going well, but what about when things are hard? Why is it so hard to praise Him then? Could it be because I focus more on the gift than the giver – the "stuff" of life rather than the source of life? To say I can't praise God at all times is to say there is something I value more than Him at that moment.

This doesn't mean I'm happy at all times, it is simply means I need to recognize who God is and who I am in relation to Him. Job said God gives and takes away, "blessed be the name of the Lord" (Job 1:21). I've learned that when I struggle to praise, I need to ask what it is that's in the way – what situation – and then I need to surrender that to Him because it's coming between us.

Again, easy to say, yet harder to do. Though necessary. I can only praise God at "all times" when He is truly all above all else in my life.

September 30*

"The law of his God is in his heart. None of his steps shall slide."
Psalms 37:31

†††

We don't like to submit to authorities outside ourselves. It's a human problem, and it's also a cultural one. We believe (or want to believe) that we know best – perhaps even know everything worth knowing. We want to set our own standards and decide for ourselves what is right and wrong, often based on what we think or feel at any given point in time.

Yet scripture tells us that there is a law out there higher than us – God's law. His ways may not be our ways, but that doesn't mean they don't exist. And, by definition of Him being God, His ways are better. God has established an order based on His creation and design, and when we go against that order we stumble and slip.

So often in our culture we look at things as they are and assume that is how it should be but if we have a foundational understanding that we live in a fallen world where sin distorts (and ruins) everything, we can see that just because something is does not necessarily mean it is as it should be. Only in God's order (His law), will we find how things are designed to be.

God has established a way of living – of being – and when we live contrary to that we "slip." Only in Him, as He has revealed through His word, will we find truth for living. This means we need to be spending time anchoring ourselves in His word by reading, studying, memorizing, and applying it. When we choose to follow what we see in His word, we will experience life as He designed it.

WELCOME TO OCTOBER

"I have told you these things, that in me you may have peace. In the world you have oppression; but cheer up. I have overcome the world."
John 16:33

October 1

"Cast your burden on the LORD, and he will sustain you. He will never allow the righteous to be moved."
Psalms 55:22

✝ ✝ ✝

Some burdens in our lives cannot be changed, we simply do not have the ability to do so. It is those burdens we can give to The Father who has promised to sustain us in and through the burden. Other burdens, however, are those that we have the ability to change. His Holy Spirit will give us the wisdom and the desire to make the changes. Pray that God will reveal the difference to you.

Read one page of a dictionary today. You will increase in knowledge.

October 2

"Cause me to hear your loving kindness in the morning, for I trust in you. Cause me to know the way in which I should walk, for I lift up my soul to you."
Psalms 143:8

†††

Is this my attitude when I pray or read the Bible? Do I really want God to "cause" (compel) me to hear (actually listen) and direct my attitude and understanding of life? I certainly would like to think so, but I do not know if I am really there every time I pray or read the Bible. In fact, after reading that sentence, I can say with authority that I am not. There are many times when I am not one hundred percent focused on what I am praying or reading. My mind is multi-tasking when it should be omni-tasking. I suspect I am not alone in this. I need to do better and perhaps you do, too. God loves when we are honest about our relationship with Him. He wants us to know what He already knows.

Father, I genuinely do want you to CAUSE me to know the way in which I should walk this day and always. Please CAUSE me to develop a prayer and Bible study practice that shuts out distractions from You.

October 3

"Like a city that is broken down and without walls is a man whose spirit is without restraint."
Proverbs 25:28

When this was written, walls were critical for the safety of those living in a city. Enemies would move across the countryside pillaging towns and cities. The first line of defense against these marauders was high walls with watchmen to alert the men of the city if an enemy force was spotted. Strong walls could mean the difference between life and death. Those who read this verse in the centuries before Christ would have a keen understanding of its meaning in regard to physical safety.

The verse, however, is an analogy of an individual's personal integrity. A healthy spiritual life, one connected to Jesus via the Holy Spirit, provides protection from enemies that threaten a person's moral and spiritual well-being. Pride, lust, greed, unbelief, are but a few of the enemies that attack a believer, and unlike the enemies that attack our body, these attack our soul and can be as DEADLY as the sword. It is incumbent that we keep reinforcing the "walls" of our spirit with faith, prayer, Bible reading, and focusing on the kingdom of God and not the kingdom of the world. The enemies are real, but our God is greater than any enemy. TRUST Him!

October 4

> "The horse is prepared for the day of battle; but victory is with the LORD."
> Proverbs 21:31

† † †

I love this verse. But why, what does it reveal? LOTS! The first part instructs an unnamed soldier to prepare his horse for the upcoming battle. I believe this to be an allegory for born again believers to live their lives according to the principles that God has revealed in His Holy Word. FAITH in Jesus is preparation for eternity, and it is at the very moment we enter eternity that God will overcome death on our behalf. He will DELIVER us from the torments of hell because of what Jesus has accomplished on the Cross. He alone has won the battle for our souls, yet we have prepared ourselves to enjoy the victory.

Does this verse teach a partnership with God? Only in the sense that our part of the partnership is believing God and although critically necessary, the truth is that we have nothing to contribute other than our FAITH in the Gospel. But here is where we are humbled by a reminder from scripture that even our faith is a GIFT from God (Ephesians 2:8, 9). Is your "horse" ready for the day of battle?

October 5

"Every way of a man is right in his own eyes, but the LORD weighs the hearts."
Proverbs 21:2

☩ ☩ ☩

I remember having a discussion with a man who was stubborn in his belief that because God has created us with intellect, we have the ability and responsibility to chart our OWN way in life. He was unrelenting in his belief that we have the right to decide what is right and wrong. Ironically, the man was a prisoner behind bars with whom I was sharing the Gospel.

Albeit misguided, he did have a few things right. God has indeed given us intellect and He has indeed given us the ability to choose how we will live our lives. It is called free will. But that does not mean we will use our intellect WISELY or that we will choose CORRECTLY how to live, nor does it mean we have the right to decide what is right and wrong. I know that using a criminal behind bars as an example is extreme but how many times have you and I had similar thoughts? How many times have we been stubborn about our life choices while ignoring the counsel of God in favor of OUR own understanding and desire? We can be masterful at justifying our bad behavior, truly masterful!

Is there something that is "right" in my eyes but conflicts with God's word? How about you? In the mid 1970's there was a Broadway play called "Your arms are too short to box with God." Think about it! Our hearts may be calling out to us this very moment to repent. To be sure, God is!

Write a letter to God today as if it was a letter to the love of your life. It will be good for your soul.

October 6

"And he said, "Whoever has ears to hear, let him hear."
Mark 4:9

† † †

This is not the only time Jesus directs people in this regard. This phrase is recorded several times in the Gospels and at first read this saying seems a bit redundant. Of course, people with ears hear, but when I consider all the things I will HEAR today, I begin to understand what Jesus meant. Today I will hear so many things; cars and trucks, water running, people talking in a store, a TV or radio in the background, birds singing, a phone ringing, and so much more. Yes, I am going to hear a lot of things today, but most will be just noise. When the day is done, I will only remember a very small portion of all that I heard.

So, what will I remember? I will remember the things I actually LISTENED to. It may seem like semantics, but it is not. Hearing and listening are two very different things. Hearing is automatic, like a plane being on autopilot, but listening is intentional, and God wants us to listen to Him. He wants us to give Him our undivided attention while in prayer and while reading His Words in the Bible. I do not think I am alone when I confess that my mind often wanders while doing both, and when it does, I pray Jesus will remind me how vital it is for me to truly LISTEN. Remember, listening is for our benefit, not His.

Memorize just ONE verse in the Bible today.

October 7

"Your hands have made me and formed me. Give me understanding, that I may learn your commandments."
Psalms 119:73
(AND)
"For you formed my in most being. You knit me together in my mother's womb."
Psalms 139:13

✝ ✝ ✝

Some argue, in an effort to legitimize and justify abortion, that life begins at physical birth. But in these verses King David proclaims that his life began at conception, and furthermore, that the Lord was active in the process from the very beginning. The only way he could have known this was for the One who created him to have revealed it to him by His Holy Spirit.

Although Adam's body was fully grown when it was created, it was still necessary for God to breathe life into his nostrils for Adam to have LIFE (Genesis 2:7). At that moment, Adam received his soul and spirit but without God, neither a body nor soul would have been created. Rather than necessitating the need for God to personally create a body and breathe life to every future human, God gifted Adam and subsequently Eve with a "seed" that replicated the process. To be sure, some of the dynamics are now different but the MOMENT of LIFE remains the same. Mysteriously, God is still present at the conception of every child in the womb. That is why Jesus teaches us to pray "Our Father" when we pray.

Father, thank you that You have known me from the moment of my conception. Help me to cherish the sanctity of life and to celebrate the gift of life, especially eternal life.

October 8

> "One thing I have asked of the LORD, that I will seek after, that I may dwell in the house of the LORD all the days of my life, to see the LORD's beauty, and to inquire in his temple."
> Psalms 27:4

† † †

When the Psalmist penned these words, they referenced a house of the Lord that had been built for a dwelling place of the Lord, a temple. There was a special area in that temple that was only accessed once a year by the High Priest of Israel. It was during that encounter that the High Priest would offer a sacrifice for himself and the whole nation. Other than that one yearly occasion, the Holy of Holy was off limits. It was a perfect visualization that a Holy God could and would not be in the presence of sin (mankind).

That all changed when Jesus was resurrected from the dead. The curtain that separated the Holy of Holy from other parts of the temple was torn in two from the top down. That God initiated action symbolized that, going forward, God would be with His people WHEREVER they were by virtue of His Holy Spirit dwelling in the "new" temple, the body of the BELIEVER. Sin, the thing that separated man from God had been dealt with on the Cross of Jesus.

The Son of God had taken the punishment that all mankind deserved upon Himself, and those who believe this will be reconciled to their Creator. That is the Gospel.

Are you still separated from your Creator? Like so many others, you can enjoy the presence of God in your life by believing that Jesus died for YOUR sin and was resurrected from the dead to make intercession for you.

October 9

"And he did not speak to them without a parable; but privately to his own disciples he explained everything."
Mark 4:34

Do you find the things you read in the Bible confusing? Do you find them inexplicable? Some are, they are secrets that belong only to the Lord (Deuteronomy 29:29). Nonetheless, everything you need to understand about God's will for mankind can be found in the Bible. God does not want us to be clueless when it comes to Him. He has revealed Himself to mankind in many ways; the creation, the nation of Israel, the Holy Scriptures, and the Holy Spirit. Through creation He demonstrates His power and creativity, through Israel He gives witness to His faithfulness to His promises, through scripture He reveals Himself, past, present, and future. The Holy Spirit, however, is the most INTMATE and PERSONAL revelation of Himself to mankind. When these resources are working in concert, they give the BELIEVER clarity of God.

Read the verse again. Take careful notice that clarity was only given to the DISCIPLES of Jesus. Discipleship is the key that unlocks understanding the things of God.

October 10

"The LORD will give strength to his people. The LORD will bless his people with peace."
Psalms 29:11

† † †

A skeptic would point to this scripture as "proof" that the faith of a Christian is in vain. They would ridicule these promises as unfulfilled and characterize them as foolishness or wishful thinking. They forget important details that give validity to this verse. First, this was originally aimed at the people of Israel during a time when they were obligated to the Mosaic Law. That Law was conditional, bilateral – if the people obeyed God's commandments, then He would bless the nation with peace and prosperity. A reading, even a casual reading of the Old Testament reveals that Israel did in fact enjoy strength and peace when they kept their commitment to the covenant THEY made with God. The truth of the verse prevailed.

"But what about now?" they scoff. They fail to realize the second principle. The resurrection of Jesus ushered in a NEW covenant that is unilateral. The OLD covenant has been retired. Man can do nothing to avail himself of the benefits of the new covenant other than to BELIEVE that God so loved the world that He gave His only begotten Son, that whoever believes in Him will not perish but have everlasting life. The people of God are now those who believe in Jesus. Look at the verse again, it is still true. Believers have PEACE with God and an internal STRENGTH to overcome sin, and that strength eclipses physical strength. Yes, it is a peace that passes all UNDERSTANDING and a strength that is not understandable unless a person has experienced that strength. This verse remains as true and relevant today as the day in which it was written. The scoffers are wrong. Pray that God will draw them to the Cross of Jesus so they too can enjoy peace and strength.

October 11

> "who delivered us out of the power of darkness, and transferred us into the kingdom of the Son of his love; ... yet now he has reconciled in the body of his flesh through death, to present you holy and without blemish and blameless before him"
> Colossians 1:13, 22

✝ ✝ ✝

What is of first importance - over everything - is Jesus. Not what we do or do not do, but Jesus. And when we know Him, love Him, and serve Him, He will change our hearts and give us the strength to overcome temptations and sin.

This is the good news of the gospel - that because God has rescued us, we now live and reign with Him, having already been cleansed by the blood of Jesus. Eternal life doesn't start some day in the future after we die – eternal life started the day we became children of God.

October 12

> After Being Born Again, Who Am I and What is My Purpose?
> II Corinthians 5:16-21

✝ ✝ ✝

NOTE: THIS IS A MULTI DAY DEVOTION

"Therefore we know no one after the flesh from now on. Even though we have known Christ after the flesh, yet now we no longer know him in this way. Therefore if anyone is in Christ, he is a new creation. The old things have passed away. Look, new things have come. But all things are of God, who reconciled us to himself through Jesus Christ, and gave to us the ministry of reconciliation; namely, that God was in Christ reconciling the world to himself, not counting their trespasses against them, and having committed to us the word of reconciliation. We are therefore ambassadors on behalf of Christ, as though God were making his appeal through us. We implore you on behalf of Christ, be reconciled to God. For him who knew no sin he made to be sin on our behalf; so that in him we might become the righteousness of God.

According to verse 16, I am not to regard myself, or any other person from a human point of view. What does this mean? I suggest the reader prayerfully consider the first 15 verses of the chapter and from those verses come to an understanding of how to intellectually embrace verse 16. Nonetheless, I am sure the meaning is subjective to as many who would choose to comment on verse 16, but to me it means that every human being on this planet needs forgiveness of sin regardless of their appearance (see verse 12), reputation, or position in the world. I am not allowed to evaluate a person by worldly standards including creed, social economics, race, success or lack thereof, gender, age, profession, trade, skill, morality, or any other criteria. My now prioritized view of humanity is one dimensional; all need a Savior, and that Savior is none other than Jesus of Nazareth.

Furthermore, without the Savior a person is destined to spend eternity separated from God. That is a dismal and frightening future.

October 13 - AN EXTENSION FROM PREVIOUS

1Corinthians 5:16-21

After Being Born Again, Who Am I and What is My Purpose?

"Therefore we know no one after the flesh from now on. Even though we have known Christ after the flesh, yet now we no longer know him in this way. Therefore if anyone is in Christ, he is a new creation. The old things have passed away. Look, new things have come. But all things are of God, who reconciled us to himself through Jesus Christ, and gave to us the ministry of reconciliation; namely, that God was in Christ reconciling the world to himself, not counting their trespasses against them, and having committed to us the word of reconciliation. We are therefore ambassadors on behalf of Christ, as though God were making his appeal through us. We implore you on behalf of Christ, be reconciled to God. For him who knew no sin he made to be sin on our behalf; so that in him we might become the righteousness of God.

† † †

But it also means something very personal to me. It means this world is no longer my home, and I must embrace the reality of a heavenly home focusing my attention on the principles of that kingdom while simultaneously living in this world. It means God no longer views me as separated from Him but rather as a son, and as a son I must act accordingly. It means my past, although still my past, has been traded up for my present and future reality. It demands I see myself as God now sees me, as a priest and king cleansed of sin –

Rev 1:5, 6 - 5. and from Jesus Christ, the faithful witness, the firstborn from the dead, and the ruler over the kings of the earth. To Him who loved us and washed us from our sins in His own blood, 6. and has made us kings and priests to His God and Father, to Him be glory and dominion forever and ever. Amen. - It means the radical nature of salvation has replaced my earthly and earthy nature. Yes, I am still on planet earth but now consider my time here to be a journey to my real home, my permanent residence. My home, from which I am now absent, is not anchored to earth and this cosmos. It means the Holy Spirit and God's Word that contain His promises are changing my perspective about life; my mind is being renewed; life is no longer limited to my time on earth. My inclinations are now toward the spiritual and not the carnal. I am being changed into the likeness of Christ.

October 14- AN EXTENSION FROM PREVIOUS

1Corinthians 5:16-21

After Being Born Again, Who Am I and What is My Purpose?

"Therefore we know no one after the flesh from now on. Even though we have known Christ after the flesh, yet now we no longer know him in this way. Therefore if anyone is in Christ, he is a new creation. The old things have passed away. Look, new things have come. But all things are of God, who reconciled us to himself through Jesus Christ, and gave to us the ministry of reconciliation; namely, that God was in Christ reconciling the world to himself, not counting their trespasses against them, and having committed to us the word of reconciliation. We are therefore ambassadors on behalf of Christ, as though God were making his appeal through us. We implore you on behalf of Christ, be reconciled to God. For him who knew no sin he made to be sin on our behalf; so that in him we might become the righteousness of God.

✝ ✝ ✝

Verse 17 is a declaration and reminder that I am now a new creation. What it does not say is that someday I will become a new creation; according to the verse the event has already occurred. I have not been given just a second, third, or beyond that chance. I have been given a brand new life. I am not recycled or even repurposed. I am brand new, as if fresh from my mother's womb. It is now incumbent on me to resist carrying the old into the new. New and old wines are not compatible. It is alike to what John the Baptist once told his followers, "I must decrease and He must increase." Unlike John, however, who was referring to Jesus' presence in this world, and the growing awareness of the citizens of Israel to His presence, the increase of Jesus in my life now becomes very personal, very individual. His increase is in my life, and I am to live out His presence in me for the benefit of others. I do this by the power of the Holy Spirit who now resides in me.

October 15 - AN EXTENSION FROM PREVIOUS

1Corinthians 5:16-21

After Being Born Again, Who Am I and What is My Purpose?

"Therefore we know no one after the flesh from now on. Even though we have known Christ after the flesh, yet now we no longer know him in this way. Therefore if anyone is in Christ, he is a new creation. The old things have passed away. Look, new things have come. But all things are of God, who reconciled us to himself through Jesus Christ, and gave to us the ministry of reconciliation; namely, that God was in Christ reconciling the world to himself, not counting their trespasses against them, and having committed to us the word of reconciliation. We are therefore ambassadors on behalf of Christ, as though God were making his appeal through us. We implore you on behalf of Christ, be reconciled to God. For him who knew no sin he made to be sin on our behalf; so that in him we might become the righteousness of God.

Verse 18 and 19 define what is the purpose of the new creation, indeed, my purpose. The fact that I have been reconciled to God, by God, inspires me to share the good news of reconciliation with others. Actually, the Holy Spirit compels me to fulfill my purpose. Exactly how that unfolds is according to the spiritual gift or gifts He has given me in regard to kingdom living. One thing is for certain, however, sharing God's gospel and grace is now His Will for each individual and also the collective of new creations, which is the Church, the body of Christ. Whether by personal evangelism or supporting the evangelistic efforts of others, new creations have a responsibility to do so with vigor. Verse 19 states that God has entrusted the message of reconciliation to the Church. That trust also includes giving me His Holy Spirit to equip me for my God given assignment. When someone entrusts something to another it is with full confidence that the specific purpose will be accomplished. It is no different with God entrusting the ministry of reconciliation to the Church, to me. He has full confidence and expectation that I will be faithful to that call.

October 16 - AN EXTENSION FROM PREVIOUS

1Corinthians 5:16-21

After Being Born Again, Who Am I and What is My Purpose?

"Therefore we know no one after the flesh from now on. Even though we have known Christ after the flesh, yet now we no longer know him in this way. Therefore if anyone is in Christ, he is a new creation. The old things have passed away. Look, new things have come. But all things are of God, who reconciled us to himself through Jesus Christ, and gave to us the ministry of reconciliation; namely, that God was in Christ reconciling the world to himself, not counting their trespasses against them, and having committed to us the word of reconciliation. We are therefore ambassadors on behalf of Christ, as though God were making his appeal through us. We implore you on behalf of Christ, be reconciled to God. For him who knew no sin he made to be sin on our behalf; so that in him we might become the righteousness of God.

†††

Verse 20 unequivocally states that I am now an ambassador for Christ since God is making His appeal for reconciliation not only through me, but also through all born again believers. The role of an earthly ambassador is to represent his/her country to a different land or culture that may not be familiar with the ambassador's homeland. The ambassador shares the virtues and advantages of the homeland to all those who will listen. The ambassador offers the resources of the homeland to meet the needs of the host country, and the ambassador ultimately has the power and authority to offer citizenship to his/her homeland to others. With those thoughts as a backdrop, I also can offer citizenship in the kingdom of God to those who are without the forgiveness of the Cross of Jesus. As an ambassador of the kingdom of God, I have and enjoy the full support and resources of that kingdom as I make an appeal for reconciliation to those in need.

October 17 – AN EXTENSION FROM PREVIOUS

1Corinthians 5:16-21

After Being Born Again, Who Am I and What is My Purpose?

"Therefore we know no one after the flesh from now on. Even though we have known Christ after the flesh, yet now we no longer know him in this way. Therefore if anyone is in Christ, he is a new creation. The old things have passed away. Look, new things have come. But all things are of God, who reconciled us to himself through Jesus Christ, and gave to us the ministry of reconciliation; namely, that God was in Christ reconciling the world to himself, not counting their trespasses against them, and having committed to us the word of reconciliation. We are therefore ambassadors on behalf of Christ, as though God were making his appeal through us. We implore you on behalf of Christ, be reconciled to God. For him who knew no sin he made to be sin on our behalf; so that in him we might become the righteousness of God.

††††

Verse 21 reveals my status before God. Of the verses listed, this one is the most difficult for me to fully embrace. Like aging Abraham struggling to believe that he would become the father of many nations while still childless, I too struggle to believe that in Jesus, I, and all born again believers have become the righteousness of God. My inclination is to focus on me and not on the finished work of Jesus. What I see while gazing in the mirror is not the righteousness of God but rather a flawed and sinful man. It is what I see because I am viewing myself through human eyes. It is then that I have a choice of whom to believe. It is at that moment I must trust in the Lord with all my heart and lean not on my own understanding. It is then, with great humility and gratitude, that I accept that status because God has declared it as His reality. It is here that the Word of God trumps my human understanding of such a lofty reality. It is here that I cling with gratitude for and to my God given and inspired faith. In the final analysis, it is not what I think but rather what God declares that establishes reality. All else is fleeting; all else is vanity.

October 18*

"Let love be without hypocrisy. Abhor that which is evil. Cling to that which is good."
Romans 12:9

It's fall as I write this, and for the past month my wife has had a sign on the wall which reads, "The trees are about to show us how beautiful it is to let things go." Every time I see it, I ask God what it is I'm holding on to that distracts, so I can start the process of letting go.

And every time I see it, I'm reminded of Paul's words to "cling to what is good." Other translations use the words, "hold on to" or "hold fast to." Scripture calls us to "lay aside every weight and the sin which so easily entangles us" (Heb 12:1) and "hold fast to what is good." And while it's easy to get caught up in consumerism of our society – to try to "keep up with the Joneses" – it's more than physical things we need to let go off. Beyond unforgiveness, anger, and bitterness, I'm challenged often to examine my thoughts and beliefs and consider what I'm holding on to that might be holding me back. What about the books I read, the shows or movies I watch, or the music I listen to? I was recently talking with some of my discipleship guys about the media we consume, and someone shared that a question they ask regularly is, "Does this song (book, movie, etc.) draw me and make me more like Jesus, or does it push me away?" I think that's a good question to ask of many "things" in our lives.

Teach me your ways, Lord, so I can hold on to them. Mold my heart to learn your voice and hold on to your words and show me what I must let go of so that I can cling to what is good.

October 19

"Two things I have asked of you; do not deny me before I die: Remove far from me falsehood and lies. Give me neither poverty nor riches. Feed me with the food that is needful for me; lest I be full, deny you, and say, 'Who is the LORD?' or lest I be poor, and steal, and so dishonor the name of my God."
Proverbs 30:7, 9

✝ ✝ ✝

No comment is necessary. Read the verse again. It is dripping with wisdom.

October 20

"And he will wipe away every tear from their eyes, and death will be no more, nor will there be mourning, nor crying, nor pain, anymore, for the first things have passed away."
Revelation 21:4

† † †

One day, one glorious day, the promise of this verse will be fulfilled. Until then we can live our lives in the shadow and hope of the promise. Until then we can live a life of LOVE that transcends the pain and sorrow of a fallen world. God has given us His love to experience so we can pass it on to others.

May you continue to have a keen awareness of His presence. May your heart be filled with heavenly thoughts.

Look for an opportunity to help a stranger today, and after doing so, tell them that God loves them.

October 21

"Streams of tears run down my eyes, because they do not observe your Law."
Psalms 119:136

† † †

Have you ever been so distraught over the behavior of a loved one that you wept in anguish? Your heart was breaking because you realized the consequences of their actions. It happens more often than we might think, especially with parents. Perhaps you have wept because people have been captured by a wicked enemy and their outcome looks hopeless. As far back as history records, wars have been started over such issues with countless men and women dying in battles to set others free from their captors. Countries maintain standing armies to defend against enemies that could potentially take away their freedom while civilian police guard the freedoms of people in their jurisdiction. This very day, someone somewhere will die defending freedom, maybe even the very moment you read this.

In this verse the Psalmist cries for people who do not listen to their Creator. He cries because unless they repent and turn towards God, something far worse than loss of freedom in this life will occur. They will be separated from their Creator for eternity and experience eternal suffering in a place called Hell. People like this are all around us, family, friends, acquaintances, and strangers. If we would go to war and risk our lives to free people from cruel enemies on earth, should we not go to war with the one responsible for these things – Satan? Our weapons? The Gospel, prayer, the Holy Spirit, God's Word, righteousness, truth, our own salvation, and faith that we are doing the will of God.

October 22

"Evening, morning, and at noon, I will cry out in distress. He will hear my voice."
Psalms 55:17
(AND)
"My eyes stay open through the night watches, that I might meditate on your word."
Psalms 119:148

✝ ✝ ✝

Have you ever been mocked for your faith? Someone once openly criticized me for being ONE-DIMENSIONAL, claiming I was always talking about Jesus, always relating life events to the Bible. To this person I was clearly an offense. I wonder how this person would have related to King David, a man who REALLY was one-dimensional. Read again the above verses that he authored, and you will understand his unmistakable priority in life.

To be clear, I am NOT that man. My thoughts, words, and actions too often contradict the claim levied against me. Also, to be clear, I wish I were that man, however, like many others, the things of this world are far less important to me than they once were. They are now in my rear view mirror rather than my windshield. In the final years of my life, I pray this person's criticism was actually prophetic, but until then, although unjustified, I will view it as a compliment. If you have experienced something similar remember the words of Jesus, "BLESSED are you when they revile and persecute you and say all kinds of evil against you falsely for My sake."

Father, help me to pray for those who mock my faith.

October 23

"Come now, and let us reason together," says the LORD: "Though your sins are like scarlet, they shall be as white as snow. Though they are red like crimson, they shall be as wool." Isaiah 1:18

† † †

How many times does God invite us to REASON together with Him? The skeptic ignores the majesty of the creation, preferring to explain it away through absurd hypotheses. Nonetheless, night and day creation "reasons" with mankind that there is a Creator. The skeptic does all in his or her power to discredit the Bible, pointing out translation errors or questioning its canonization process. The fact that the scriptures survive to this very day is God "reasoning" with mankind. The incredible endurance of Israel stands as a witness to God's ability and willingness to keep His promises; once again, God "reasoning" with us.

The greatest of all is when Jesus, the Son of God, became flesh and dwelt among us, "reasoning" with any and all who would LISTEN to Him; His ministry on earth culminating in His resurrection from death. Still, billions of people refuse the "reasoning" of their Creator. It is truly the most significant fundamental flaw of the human heart.

Father, have mercy on those who reject your reasoning and continue to draw them to the Cross of Jesus.

October 24

> "And he could do no mighty work there, except that he laid his hands on a few sick people, and healed them. And he was amazed because of their unbelief."
> Mark 6:5, 6

† † †

The "He" in this verse is Jesus and it reveals a unique and remarkable time in the earthly ministry of Jesus. It is hard to imagine but the One who commanded the wind and waves, walked on water, turned water into wine, raised people from the dead, opened blind eyes and deaf ears, healed the sick and lame, and overpowered demons could NOT do many works in His hometown. And why? Because of UNBELIEF and it is the same reason some people will enjoy eternity in heaven and others suffer eternal torment in hell.

The perfect description of Free Will is this, a double edged sword. One side saves while the other kills, but it is not indiscriminate, it is intentional. We wield the sword of our will by deliberate CHOICE, choosing where to place our belief or unbelief. Someone once said that if a person goes to hell, he or she will jump over a big CROSS to get there. God will not force anyone to love Him, to believe Him, to trust Him, but He does invite us to do those things, and in doing so we will enjoy all the blessings that God has to offer. Read the verse again and be sure it is not referring to YOU. The consequences for unbelief are eternal.

If you are able, take a walk in the woods today. Look closely and listen intently. The forest is an amazing place.

October 25

> "And he could do no mighty work there, except that he laid his hands on a few sick people, and healed them. And he was amazed because of their unbelief."
> Mark 8:36

† † †

It may be hard to imagine but MY soul really is worth more than the entire world. That is what Jesus says in this verse and I believe Him. So, when I see people clamoring after more and more money and things, it troubles my heart, and when I see drug addicts sleeping in the streets, my heart is broken because they do not know how valuable they are. When I see prisoners behind bars, starving men, women, and children in third world nations, people being demoralized by repressive governments, babies being aborted, and all the other injustices in this world, my heart GRIEVES.

Jesus spoke of the dignity and value of the individual. He did so because EVERY human being is created in the image of God (Genesis 1:26). Perhaps like me, you occasionally lose sight of that when frustrated with others. Our frustration and anger hide THEIR value because we are thinking only of OUR value. I do understand there are wicked people in this world, those who have given themselves over to God's enemy, Satan. I do not dispute this, but hopelessly wicked people are far and few between. Perhaps in God's eyes that person does not exist, after all, Jesus died for everyone and although not everyone will come to Jesus for forgiveness, that does not negate the worth of their soul.

Father, burden my heart with a desire for ALL people to be saved and move me to pray for their souls.

October 26

"Let your speech always be with grace, seasoned with salt, that you may know how you ought to answer each one."
Colossians 4:6

† † †

Most people struggle with managing their tongue. I know I do. Words that have nothing to do with grace often seem to "magically" fall from my lips to someone's ears. Of course, there is nothing "magical" about those times. Those words come from the heart of the old man who continues to fight for a prominent place in my life. Vulgar words, hateful words, demeaning and discouraging words are stealthily lurking for an opportunity to be expressed. The first twelve verses of chapter three in the book of James provide a vivid picture of the tongue, and it is not flattering.

Thankfully, the NEW man can now have precedent over the old when I yield my tongue to the Holy Spirit. My tongue can now express the grace of God to listeners, especially when it speaks the Gospel. When I share the words of Jesus, my words are SEASONED with the salt of truth and wisdom. Those words bring the seasoning of HOPE and LOVE to a listening ear. This verse teaches me to rely on the Holy Spirit when speaking because He knows what others need to hear.

Father, guard my tongue and lips to speak only grace.

October 27

"The name of the LORD is a strong tower; the righteous run into it and are safe."
(BUT)
"The rich man's wealth is his strong city, like an unscalable wall in his own imagination."
Proverbs 18:10, 11

There is certainly an abundance of imagery in these two verses. They do, however, paint vivid contrasting pictures. In verse ten the Lord is described as a strong tower capable of protecting all those who are inside but notice who is actually inside the tower – the RIGHTEOUS. Notice something else; those inside choose to be there. It is where they sought and received safety. But who exactly are the righteous? After all, the Bible declares that "none are righteous, no not one" (Romans 3:10). It is here, right here, that we enter into the grand ballroom of FAITH, and that faith has an object - JESUS. It is here that we cross the bridge that takes us from the physical world to the Kingdom of God. It is here that our self-righteousness is replaced by the righteousness of Christ, a holy righteousness that is imputed to us by God when we genuinely believe the Gospel.

But beware! The world offers a substitute for righteousness – the strong city of WEALTH. It calls to men and women to trust in the "high wall" of MONEY for happiness, peace, good health, fine food and clothing, friends, esteem, wisdom, and security. But just like fools' gold proves worthless when assayed, so will earthy wealth prove worthless at the Judgement Seat of Christ. Only the righteousness of Christ will keep us safe from an eternity separated from our Creator.

Father, help my heart to trust in true wealth that is found at the Cross of Jesus.

October 28

"Come to me, all you who labor and are heavily burdened, and I will give you rest."
Matthew 11:28

✝ ✝ ✝

Because of what Jesus accomplished on the Cross, we no longer need to labor trying to please God, always wondering when our labors will be sufficient. The truth is OUR labors will never be sufficient. Only Jesus has lived a perfectly SINLESS life and has accomplished what we could never accomplish. We need only to trust in Him for sufficiency. Because of Him we can now enjoy an intimate and very PERSONAL relationship with our Creator.

Pray you will see and hear beautiful things today. If you struggle to find something beautiful in the world, just look in the mirror.

October 29

"So they went out and proclaimed that all should repent."
Mark 6:12

✝ ✝ ✝

Have you ever told someone that they need to repent, or perhaps someone has said that to you. How did that go? My guess is that it did not go well. But why? It is because the human heart is often fiercely prideful, easily offended, and openly opposed to criticism; it wants to be the captain of the ship, not a crew member. That desire to be captain is both the best and worst part of our soul. God commanded Man, both male and female, to have dominion over all the earth (Genesis 1:27) and that desire is still innate in the heart of Man. The problem is that it is now out of alignment, corrupted by sin. What was meant as a way for Man to maintain order on planet earth has now morphed into disorder. Yes, God gave Man authority but never relinquished His authority over Man, and in the beginning it worked well. Tragically, Satan tempted Man to have an authority that Man was never meant to have - authority to disobey a commandment of God, and when that happened Man was separated from God. Death occurred, both spiritually and physically.

Is there a path back to God? Thankfully God has provided a way to be reconciled to Him. God sent His Son Jesus to pay the penalty for our willful disobedience. It was the ONLY way God could reconcile now sinful Man. Without the death, burial, and resurrection of Jesus we would still be hopelessly separated from our Creator. Just like God asked the first couple to believe that if they disobeyed His commandment they would surely die, He now asks mankind to believe in the Gospel. When we truly believe that Jesus died for our personal sins and believe that God raised Him back to life, we will be reunited with our Creator. Pray for the many who have yet to be reconciled to their creator.

October 30 - The Holy Spirit - My Observation

NOTE: THIS IS A MULTI DAY DEVOTION

There can be no doubt that when Jesus was present on earth surely the Kingdom of God was present. The Bible declares it (Matthew 1:22, 23). His ministry connected Heaven to earth and by virtue of the incarnation, earth to Heaven. God stepped into the finite, time and space, and there He experienced His creation through the body of Jesus. In the beginning, prior to the fall of Man as chronicled in Genesis chapter three, God regularly visited Adam and Eve in the Garden of Eden. Their fellowship was sweet, innocent, and unencumbered by any disobedience or lack of devotion from His greatest creation, Adam and Eve. It was an idyllic time. The account of God creating Adam from soil and breathing life into his nostrils is precious in the sight of believers. Sadly, following the fall of Man, future visits were mostly veiled until His incarnation. Prior to the incarnation, God briefly manifested His presence through various theophany appearances. After the death and resurrection of Jesus and His return to Heaven, the void of His physical presence on earth seemingly returned.

Fortunately, prior to His death Jesus revealed that He would send the HOLY SPIRIT to minister to believers during His physical absence from earth (John 14:25, 26). Jesus promised the Holy Spirit would INDWELL believers thereby creating a tangible linchpin between Heaven and earth, the physical body of a believer indwelt by the Holy Spirit, and so it is till this very day. The Holy Spirit is that linchpin. The ministry of the Holy Spirit is varied, providing both a PERSONAL and CORPORATE (Church) connection to Heaven. Scripture reveals that our life is HIDDEN in Christ in God, and we have been raised with Christ (Colossians 3:1-4). All this has been accomplished by the power of the Holy Spirit.

October 31 - AN EXTENSION FROM PREVIOUS - The Holy Spirit - My Observation

I have listed are six distinct aspects of the ministry of the Holy Spirit to and through believers...

1. It is important for believer to be aware that The Holy Spirit is ACTIVE in a believer's life. Although, at times, covert, His activities recognizable only in the Spirit world, His activity is also overt. According to Scripture, He is the believer's HELPER (John 14:26). He indwells and SEALS believers until the day of redemption, and that indwelling is proof that a believer's adoption by God is irreversible. He GUARDS and GUARANTEES a believer's salvation (Ephesians 1:13; 4:30). The Holy Spirit ASSISTS believers in prayer (Jude 1:20) and INTERCEDES for believers in accordance with the will of God (Romans 8:26, 27).

2. The Holy Spirit REGENERATES and renews believers (Titus 3:5). At the moment of salvation, He BAPTIZES believers into the Body of Christ (Romans 6:3). Believers receive the new birth by the power of the Spirit (John 3:5-8). He COMFORTS believers when necessary (1 Thessalonians 1:6). He fills believers with all joy and peace as they trust the Lord, causing them to overflow with hope (Romans 15:13).

WELCOME TO NOVEMBER

"Sanctify them in the truth. Your word is truth."
John 17:17

November 1 - AN EXTENSION FROM PREVIOUS - The Holy Spirit - My Observation

3. SANCTIFICATION is the work of the Holy Spirit in our lives. He gives believers the power to war against the desires of the flesh and LEADS the believer into righteousness (Galatians 5:16-18 - Psalms 23:3) The works of the believer's flesh lessen while the FRUIT of the Spirit becomes prevalent and obvious in their lives. Because of His presence believers are commanded to be FILLED with the Spirit" (Ephesians 5:18), meaning we are to YIELD to the Spirit's FULL control.

4. The Holy Spirit is a gift-giver (1 Corinthians 12:4). Believers have been given individual gift(s) by the Holy Spirit as He determines in His wisdom (1 Corinthians 12:11). . We do not APPROPRIATE spiritual gifts; we RECEIVE them.

November 2 - AN EXTENSION FROM PREVIOUS - The Holy Spirit - My Observation

5. The Holy Spirit works among UNBELIEVERS. Jesus promised that He would send the Holy Spirit to convict the WORLD concerning sin and righteousness and judgment (John 16:8). He TESTIFIES of Christ (John 15:26), POINTING people to the Lord. Currently, the Holy Spirit is RESTRAINING sin and CAPPING the

mystery of lawlessness in the world. This action prevents the rise of the Antichrist until the appointed time (2 Thessalonians 2:6-10).

6. A critical role of The Holy Spirit is to GIVE believers wisdom by which they we can UNDERSTAND God (1 Corinthians 2:10-11). Since believers have been GIVEN the gift of God's Spirit, they can COMPREHEND the thoughts of God, as revealed in Scripture. He helps us UNDERSTAND. This is wisdom from God, rather than wisdom from man. No amount of human knowledge can ever replace the Holy Spirit's teaching (1 Corinthians 2:12, 13).

It is in the resource and truth of the Holy Spirit where believers discover their potential to do great things, exceptional things, amazing things, and, yes, Godly things.

November 3

> "For the word of God is living, and active, and sharper than any two-edged sword, and piercing even to the dividing of soul and spirit, of both joints and marrow, and is able to discern the thoughts and intentions of the heart."
> Hebrews 4:12

Do you believe this to be TRUE? How you HONESTLY answer this question could very well give you an accurate snapshot of your faith. Think of your faith as an object in a cabinet where you display your most treasured items. In those cabinets we always put the MOST valuable item on the eye level shelf so it is the first anyone will see. Sure, items on the lower shelves are still valuable, but they have less priority than those on the prized shelf. Now imagine God looking into that display cabinet. Is the Bible on the eye level shelf or is it placed elsewhere?

Faith in Jesus and belief that the BIBLE can be believed and trusted can be two different things. There are people who readily confess Jesus as their Savior but have serious doubts about the accuracy of the Bible. Consequently, they spend little time or energy studying scripture. I know that believers come in all shapes, sizes, colors, ages and maturity, and for those reasons I tend to avoid judging others. I think that is a task better left for God. What I do know is that Jesus once said if we CONTINUE in His word, we shall know the truth and the truth will make us free. I also know that His once spoken words have now become written words that are recorded in the Bible.

I encourage you to look at the verse again. Do YOU believe that the word of God is LIVING? Do YOU believe that it genuinely has the POWER described in the verse? The truth is that only you and the Holy Spirit know the answer to that question.

November 4

"I tell you, among those who are born of women there is none greater than John, yet he who is least in the kingdom of God is greater than he."
Luke 7:28

This is a BIG piece of information! Jesus is telling the world that there is no greater prophet than John the Baptist. Think of all the hero prophets of the Old Testament, Elijah, Elisha, and all the others that are memorialized in scripture. Was Jesus using hyperbole when He spoke these word? I do not think so; I think He was speaking plainly. Imagine how you would feel if Jesus called you the greatest prophet to have ever lived. As I write this, I am trying to imagine how I would feel and all I can think of is humility. Clearly John was anointed with the GIFT of the Holy Spirit and because it was a gift, John could not boast. In fact, at one point in his ministry he told his disciples that Jesus must INCREASE while he must DECREASE. That sure sounds like humility to me.

But here is what really fascinates me; what Jesus says about those who are in the Kingdom of God. That Kingdom is both broad and narrow. In the broadest sense God owns heaven and earth and everything ever created. In a narrow sense, men and women are free to relinquish their souls to Satan and consequently are not part of the Kingdom of God. They are the one stand-alone in all creation. Ironically, they have been given this authority by their Creator; ONLY men and women have the ability of choosing to be in another kingdom. Now look at the verse again. Even the least in the Kingdom of God are GREATER than John the Baptist, according to Jesus. Those who are born-again have surrendered their lives to King Jesus and are in the kingdom of God. That truth brings me to my knees in gratitude to my God and Savior, Jesus the Christ! How about you?

November 5

"You are good, and do good. Teach me your statutes."
Psalms 119:68

† † †

This is such a simple declaration that it is easy to miss its profound truth. Once someone in a crowd addressed Jesus as "good teacher." He responded by saying that "no one is good but One, that is, God." Are there people we know that we consider good? Of course there are, but the criteria we use is comparing one man to another man or one woman to another woman. When we compare ourselves or others to a Holy God, Jesus is right, NONE can be declared good.

It is in this truth that God's LOVE for mankind becomes obvious. Without love, God would have no motive for sending His Son to become a sacrifice for those that are not "good" and frequently oppose His will. God wants to have fellowship with His best creation and the sacrifice of Jesus allows Him to do so. Love, God's love is the one catalyst that will stand the test of time and thankfully, when we are born again, God puts that same love in our hearts by virtue of the Holy Spirit.

Father, help me to love others just like you love me.

November 6

> He said, "That which proceeds out of the person, that defiles the person. For from within, out of a person's heart, proceed evil thoughts, adulteries, sexual sins, murders, thefts, covetings, wickedness, deceit, lustful desires, an evil eye, blasphemy, pride, and foolishness. All these evil things come from within, and defile the person."
> Mark 7:20-23

✝ ✝ ✝

Oh my, that is quite a list! The scary thing is that the things on the list seem all too familiar to me. How about you? Do you recognize any of them? I cannot say with a clear conscience that I have not done or thought about each of these things at some time in my life. Yes, it is shameful to admit, but truthful. What makes that truth so incredible is even so, God loves me. Even so, God wanted me to be reunited with Him. But not just me, every man, woman, and child were on His mind when He sent Jesus to provide a way to be reconciled to Him, and not just in this life but for all eternity.

To this very day when I see Jesus on the Cross my heart breaks because I know that I did my part to put Him there. But also, to this very day my heart is filled with gratitude and joy that God loved me and sent Jesus to rescue me. To this very day I am in awe of His Grace. To this very day I surrender myself to Him. How about you?

November 7

"The LORD's faithful love does not cease; his compassion does not fail. They are new every morning; great is your faithfulness." Lamentations 3:22, 23

What a wonderful promise. God's compassion toward us will never fail. Each new day brings NEW mercies and compassion to us, sufficient to sustain us that day.

Have you ever gone to sleep at night TOTALLY exhausted physically? It was all you could do to find a safe place to lie down, and sleep came almost immediately. But oddly enough, when you awakened the next morning, you felt refreshed and energized, and you were able to negotiate that day with vigor. Now think of those times when you were spiritually and emotionally exhausted, unable to focus on your relationship with others, leave alone your relationship with God. But fear not! Just like your body rebuilds and refreshes during sleep, the LORD will refresh and rebuild your spirit daily. He brings forgiveness, hope, joy, love, and peace to us EACH new day, and He brings these blessings to us by the Holy Spirit who lives in every born again believer. He NEVER wearies in His compassion and mercy toward us.

Father, thank you for providing ALL I will need to live successfully each new day of my life. May I be a blessing to others as you have been a blessing to me.

November 8

"He who has pity on the poor lends to the LORD; he will reward him."
Proverbs 19:17
(AND)
"Whoever stops his ears at the cry of the poor, he will also cry out, but shall not be heard."
Proverbs 21:13

† † †

Jesus said the poor will always be with us and, of course, He was right. I see them everywhere, on street corners, parking lots, television, and sometimes in my own neighborhood. I confess that at times I am irritated by the entitled attitude that some display and often pretend that I just do not see them, but that does nothing to solve the problem of poverty.

Admittedly, poverty and homelessness are often a result of poor life choices while for others it is an issue of unfavorable circumstances. Nonetheless, there is always something I can do in regard to people experiencing poverty - PRAY. Like it or not, Jesus died for EVERYONE, there are no exceptions. To think otherwise is an affront to Jesus' sacrifice. Because I belong to Jesus, I have a responsibility to extend God's love to everyone, but I know that some will reject that love. What I also know is that no donation or prayer for the poor or homeless goes unnoticed by God. I encourage you to read the first verse again and come to your own conclusion. To whom would you rather lend, God or man?

November 9

> "He began to teach them that the Son of Man must suffer many things, and be rejected by the elders, the chief priests, and the scribes, and be killed, and after three days rise again."
> Mark 8:31

† † †

How do you think YOU would have reacted if you were one of Jesus' disciples and heard this from Him? I most likely would have reacted in disbelief or disregard, much like they did. Peter was much more proactive in his reaction. He actually corrected Jesus, or as the Bible says, REBUKED Him. I understand Peter's reluctance to accept this teaching of Jesus. Peter, and the others, saw Jesus as the Messiah that would overthrow Roman rule over Israel and set up a new government; once again Israel would be "king of the hill." The disciples had given up everything to follow Him and His talk of being killed by His enemies was unacceptable.

Jesus in turn rebukes Peter saying, "Get behind Me, Satan! For you are not mindful of the things of God, but the things of men." That is a strong rebuke to be sure. This story reveals important truths. The FIRST is that Jesus became human to become a sacrifice for our sinful nature; He knew exactly how and why He would die. SECONDLY, Satan opposed that mission and used a man to express that opposition. ADDITONALLY, the things of God and the things of men are in opposition to one another. King Solomon once wrote, "There is nothing new under the sun." What was true in times past is still true today. It is incumbent on every believer to know the

DIFFERENCE between the things of God and the things of man. Fortunately, God has provided ways for us to distinguish between the two – the BIBLE and the HOLY SPIRIT.

Father, keep me from being a mouthpiece of Satan. Teach me YOUR things!

November 10

"He said to them, "But who do you say that I am?"
Mark 8:29

Does this question that Jesus asks His disciples remind you that every individual is accountable for their OWN belief about Jesus? If not, it should. We can often be influenced by public opinion or peer pressure, and that influence or pressure can lead us to do and say things that oppose the will of God. On Judgement Day it will not matter what others believe or say about Jesus – it will ONLY matter who YOU believe Him to be. While it may be true on earth that the majority rules, I can assure you it is not true in heaven.

We have probably all been there at some point in our lives, following a crowd that was headed in the wrong direction. Perhaps a philosophy, an opinion about a person, a way of life, a political persuasion, or maybe something else may come to mind. History is full of examples of the masses following bad leaders or bad philosophies. I suspect if you are reading this devotion that your answer to the question Jesus asks will be the same as Peter's answer, "You are the Christ." If not, I remind you that on Judgement Day the majority will NOT rule in the courtroom of God.

Father, thank you that you have revealed who Jesus is to me.

November 11

"Do not say, "I will do to him as he has done to me; I will render to the man according to his work.""
Proverbs 24:29

† † †

Retribution is an ingrained trait in the human heart. Songs have been sung and novels written about men and women who plotted and achieved revenge on an adversary. Even if we avoid the action, we often fantasize about getting even with someone who caused us pain or embarrassment. All this is rooted in pride, a fundamental flaw of the human heart.

Those living in the Kingdom of God are called to a different standard. The bedrock of Christianity is FORGIVENESS. God is first to demonstrate this standard by sending His Son Jesus to die for our sins thereby providing forgiveness to those who believe in His death, burial, and resurrection. But then the focus on forgiveness is redirected to us. Just like we are forgiven of our sins, we are called to forgive others who sin against us. We pray it every time we pray the Lord's Prayer, "Forgive us our trespasses as we forgive those who trespass against us." On our own, we cannot forgive the small "trespasses" leave alone the most grievous ones. Nonetheless, it honors God when we do so because in doing so, we reflect His character and will for our lives.

Father, give me desire and power to forgive others as you have forgiven me.

November 12

"If you stop listening to instruction, my son, you will stray from the words of knowledge."
Proverbs 19:27

Can you remember a time when you were daydreaming in a class? Perhaps you have been guilty of this during a business meeting or even a church service. I suspect we could all raise our hands as an admission of guilt. In regard to school, do you remember then being quizzed on the material and NOT knowing the answer; it happened to me all too frequently and perhaps also to you.

The same thing can happen to us in regard to how we live our lives when we stop LISTENING to the instruction of the Holy Spirit. He will use our conscience, our prayers, and our reading of the Bible to KEEP us from straying. But there is another who wants to lead us, Satan. He will dull our conscience, keep us from praying, and challenge the authenticity and authority of the Bible and before we know it, we have ceased listening to instruction. Beyond that, lurking in the human heart is pride and a host of other ungodly traits that compete for our attention. Sadly, falling prey to the bad influencers is easier than we think. No wonder the Holy Spirit inspires the Apostle Paul to write, "Do not quench the Spirit." This was Godly advice for the church in Thessalonica in the first century, and Godly advice for us today.

Father, give the discipline and desire to keep listening to You.

November 13

"It is better to take refuge in the LORD, than to put confidence in man. It is better to take refuge in the LORD, than to put confidence in princes."
Psalms 118:8, 9

† † †

Have you ever been disappointed by a friend, a confidant, or a government? Now ask the same question of yourself. Have you been the one disappointing others? It happens because friends and confidants are human, and governments are made up of humans. It happens because WE are human. Jesus once remarked, "The spirit is willing, but the flesh is weak."

There is One, however, that we can trust to NEVER break a promise or commitment to us – The LORD, our Creator. In this life we WILL have troubles and disappointments because we live in a fallen world where Satan has significant sway on mankind. We live in a world where "ME FIRST" is often the clarion call. A simple truth is that we may not see all the promises of God fleshed out in THIS lifetime, but ETERNITY awaits us and in eternity EVERY promise of God will be fulfilled. Until then, Jesus promises to NEVER leave us or FORSAKE us!

Father, I trust you above ALL others.

November 14

He said to all, "If anyone desires to come after me, let him deny himself, take up his cross daily, and follow me."
Luke 9:23

† † †

I remember the first time I read this verse. Deny myself? How do I do that? Take up MY cross daily? What cross is He talking about? That was forty-five years ago. I am a different man than I was back then, much different. I am not a reformed man, I am a brand NEW man, born again by the Holy Spirit of God. I cannot say that I breezed through the decades, but I cannot say I stumbled through them either. There were times, however, that I struggled, not with my faith but rather with my behavior. Being saved was only the BEGINNING; desiring and committing to FOLLOW Him was how I learned what Jesus meant when He spoke these words.

Perhaps I could offer my explanation of this verse, but I think it is better for a person to LEARN the meaning by embracing the last part – FOLLOW ME. The Gospels detail His teaching, His actions, His life, His death, His resurrection, and how He expects us to relate to Him. Those details, however, are only knowledge. It is in OUR FOLLOWING Him that we learn about self-denial and our PERSONAL cross. It is in our WALKING in His footsteps that the Holy Spirit brings reality to this verse, and that reality brings understanding. There is significant difference between head knowledge and the experiential knowledge of self-denial and a personal cross. I pray every reader knows the latter.

Father, help me to be faithful in following Jesus.

November 15

"For in him all the fullness of Deity dwells in bodily form, and in him you are made full, who is the head of all principality and power"
Colossians 2:9, 10

† † †

The Him in this verse is Jesus. It is comforting to know that in Him I am complete, I have been restored to right relationship with the One who created me. I no longer have to wonder about an afterlife and where I will spend eternity. It is settled because of Him.

Let us pray for the many people in this world who do not have that assurance and confidence. They strive to please THEIR god while all the time wondering if their efforts are sufficient. They live in fear that hell awaits them, or worse, they do not believe that there is a hell. Let us pray for the multitude who believe that this life is ALL there is. Please join me in praying that the One and Only true God will open their hearts and minds to the truth.

November 16

> "If we say that we have no sin, we deceive ourselves, and the truth is not in us. If we confess our sins, he is faithful and righteous to forgive us the sins, and to cleanse us from all unrighteousness."
> I John 1:8, 9

The promise here is not only for forgiveness but also for CLEANSING. Just like dirt soils our body, sin soils our soul. There is something refreshing about putting on clothing that has been washed and brightened with soap and bleach. This verse is a reminder that our soul has been cleansed by the forgiveness that God offers the repentant sinner. A "clean" soul is refreshed, allowing us to continue in life free from guilt. Satan will heap guilt on our soul, but our guilt has been absolved by God's forgiveness. Remember, we have not sinned against Satan but rather against a holy God, and if God forgives our offense, He also forgets our offense. We need to do the same.

Take a friend to lunch today and tell them how much they mean to you.

November 17

"As for man, his days are like grass. As a flower of the field, so he flourishes. For the wind passes over it, and it is gone, and its place remembers it no more."
Psalms 103:15, 16

Only in my seventh decade of life have I understood the truth of this verse. When I was a young man, I had no thoughts of death. Even in Vietnam I always thought of myself as invincible. My, how my perspective has changed! I am now keenly aware of my mortality. As I look back at my life, I am astounded by how I am now in the winter of my life, realizing that I have rounded third base and headed for home plate. I am certain I have had many challenges, disappointments, and tribulation in my life but, truthfully, I can only remember a few. The things I once anguished over are not even a memory.

This verse testifies to the brevity of life and is a vivid reminder that I should live each day as if it were my last because one day it really will be my last day. The irony is that my perspective now is more on eternity than the present. That perspective prompts me to reflect the love God gives me to any and all in my life. Whatever your age, I urge you to do the same.

Father, help me to remember that my time on planet earth is brief and to act accordingly.

November 18

"Like a city that is broken down and without walls is a man whose spirit is without restraint."
Proverbs 25:28

† † †

When this was written, walls were critical for the safety of those living in a city. Enemies would move across the countryside pillaging towns and cities. The first line of defense against these marauders was high walls with watchmen to alert the men of the city if an enemy force was spotted. Strong walls could mean the difference between life and death. Those who read this verse in the centuries before Christ would have a keen understanding of its meaning in regard to physical safety.

The verse, however, is now an analogy of an individual's personal integrity. A healthy spiritual life, one connected to Jesus via the Holy Spirit, provides protection from enemies that threaten a person's moral and spiritual well-being. Pride, lust, greed, unbelief, are but a few of the enemies that attack a believer, and unlike the enemies that attack our body, these attack our soul and can be as DEADLY as the sword. It is incumbent that we keep reinforcing the "walls" of our spirit with faith, prayer, Bible reading, and focusing on the kingdom of God and not the kingdom of the world. The enemies are real, but our God is greater than any enemy. TRUST Him!

If you have a living parent, call or visit them today. Remember the fifth commandment.

November 19

"Praise the LORD, my soul, and all that is within me, praise his holy name."
Psalms 103:1

† † †

The word "praise" the Lord in this verse could also be rendered "bless" the Lord. How can we bless God? How is that even possible? If we think of blessing as ADDING something to His life, we are thinking incorrectly. Just the opposite is true, He adds to OUR lives. Although we cannot add anything to His life, we can WORSHIP Him. We can PRAISE Him. We can CHOOSE Him over the world. We can tell others of His MAGNIFICENCE. We can BELIEVE His promises that are revealed in the Bible. Even though we are doing these things, these things are all focused on Him and NOT us.

Our desire to bless God comes from the heart, not the head. It is borne out of LOVE, a love that is put there by the Holy Spirit of God. For that we can take no credit, it is a GIFT from God to every born again believer. Can we bless God? Unequivocally, YES!

Have you laughed today? Not just a smile but a real laugh. Try it, you will not be disappointed.

November 20

"Praise the LORD, my soul, and all that is within me, praise his holy name."
Psalms 19:1, 2

There is something humbling about staring at a night sky. Most of us have done it many times. It makes us feel small, even tiny. The Psalmist had another understanding when he penned this verse. He saw the heavens as a continual declaration by God of His glory, His handiwork. It is hard to disagree with the Psalmist when we sit quietly and stare at the night sky on a clear night.

Someone once noted that the two most prominent bodies in the sky are the sun and moon. These could very well be a testimony of God about our relationship with Him. The moon does not have any ability to PRODUCE light, it only REFLECTS the light of the sun. It is a great illustration of the role of believers or even the Church in the world. We are to be like the moon reflecting God's "light" to a spiritually dark world.

So, what do I do with this understanding? Here is the honest reality in my life; sometimes I am a "full" moon and sometimes a "partial" or even a "new" moon, however, I am so grateful that God's light to me is ALWAYS full because He IS the light!

Father, help me to be a spiritual light to those around me.

November 21

"But many who are first will be last; and the last first."
Mark 10:31

✝ ✝ ✝

To be sure, this statement by Jesus is a paradox. To gain understanding the reader must view it through the lens of two kingdoms, the Kingdom of God and the Kingdom of the World. What is held in high esteem in one is not necessarily true of the other. "Me first" is a primary tenant of the world but it is despised in God's kingdom. Money is held in high regard by the world but has no eternal value in God's kingdom. Death is to be feared in the world while it does not even exist in God's kingdom.

So, who was Jesus referring to in the verse? In His time, He was most likely referring to the many Jewish religious leaders and pious people that exalted themselves while rendering judgement on the masses. They were critical of any and all who did not live up to the letter of the Mosaic Law. Although they considered themselves to be upstanding citizens of the Kingdom of God, Jesus often rebuked them for their hypocrisy. In contemporary time, the same can be said for the wealthy and ultra successful that look down on people that have not attained their status. They are those who contribute their wealth and success to themselves with no regard for God. As a matter of principle, it could be ANYONE who exalts him/herself above others. The TRUTH is that God hates PRIDE!

Father, forgive my pride and maintain a spirit of humility in me.

November 22

> "So I will obey your Law continually, forever and ever. I will walk in liberty, for I have sought your precepts."
> Psalms 119:44, 45

This claim by King David at first glance appears to be an oxymoron. How can KEEPING God's laws allow one to walk in LIBERTY, one may ask? The better question would be this; in keeping His laws, what am I liberated FROM? The simplest answer is ironically the most profound. Adhering to God's advice for living keeps us from sin and the burden of guilt, and who among us does not want that? Sin is destructive in so many ways. It skews human relationships, it can cause loss of life, ours or others, it can destroy the well-being of others, it can lead to poor health, it can sabotage our career, it can cause depression, it can cause us to deceive loved ones and others, it can even cause wars, but most of all, it can prevent us from having an INTIMATE relationship with the Lord God, our Creator. Yes, it really does have all this potential and more!

King David was right, nonetheless, at times he FAILED in the very thing he knew to be true. If we are honest, we see that same failure in our own lives, and that reality of failure is the reason we need a Savior. We need someone to save us when we do falter and fail. Thankfully, God has provided that Savior – His Son, Jesus. When we confess our failures, when we trust Him for forgiveness, we too can walk "at liberty." If you have never done so, ask Jesus to be the Lord of your life. You will never regret doing so.

Wave to a stranger today. They just might wave back.

November 23

> The disciples were amazed at his words. But Jesus answered again and said to them, "Children, how hard it is for those who trust in riches to enter the kingdom of God."
> Mark 10:4, 5
> (AND)
> Jesus, looking at them, said, "With humans it is impossible, but not with God, for all things are possible with God."
> Mark 10:27

The word IMPOSSIBLE is such an all-encompassing word. It leaves NO room for an alternative. The word POSSIBLE, however, is pregnant with options. Jesus is emphatic in His answer to His disciples when they questioned Him about who can be saved if wealth might be a stumbling block to salvation. In Jesus' time, wealth was looked upon as a sign that God was blessing a Jewish person of wealth because of their faithfulness. Jesus warned them that, in fact, it would be extremely DIFFICULT for those who TRUSTED in their wealth to enter the Kingdom of God. Money may be an important commodity on earth, but it literally has no VALUE in heaven.

Money is amoral, neither good or bad; it can USED for good or evil but is particularly egregious when a person TRUSTS or LOVES it above all else. Believers are called to trust in the Lord with all their heart, not in money or lack thereof. It is not immoral or unspiritual to have money, even a lot of money. Just be certain to have a proper perspective on its accumulation and usage. MOST importantly, remember Jesus' words about ALL things being possible with God.

November 24

"Listen, sons, to a father's instruction. Pay attention and know understanding; for I give you sound learning. Do not forsake my law."
Proverbs 4:1, 2

✝ ✝ ✝

We all live our lives guided by personal doctrine. We have a lot of different names for doctrine; belief, instinct, peer pressure, societal norms, following my heart, institutional mandates, culture, political persuasion, following the crowd, and more. Nonetheless, these are all doctrine.

There is only ONE doctrine of which God approves. Trust God with all your heart and lean not on your own understanding. That verse sums up everything that is between the covers of the Bible. The

Bible reveals how it has worked in the past, how it works presently, and how it will work in the future, with plenty of examples of those who chose to ignore good doctrine and follow after another. It is ALL there, hiding in plain sight for those who have a genuine desire to live a life directed by GOOD doctrine. Remember, the very fact there is GOOD doctrine reveals the truth that the opposite exists. Choose wisely, it really does make a difference both in this life and eternity.

November 25

"Truly I tell you, whoever will not receive the kingdom of God like a little child, he will in no way enter into it."
Mark 10:15

†††

Children, especially little children, are not hampered by prejudices and unbelief. They believe without reluctance until taught otherwise. Little children are rarely skeptical. If it feels good, looks good, or tastes good, a little child will fearlessly engage. In a perfect world this trait would lend itself to happiness. In a world compromised by sin, the consequences of such naivety could be disastrous and is the reason parents remain vigilant over their little children.

Nonetheless, this is the attitude Jesus says is NECESSARY to receive and enter the Kingdom of God. Yes, adults bring their "baggage" of sin, guilt, and fear to the Cross of Jesus, but not their UNBELIEF. SIN is forgiven by faith in the Gospel and the repentant sinner is instructed to leave their baggage of guilt and fear behind. Sadly, adults often instead drag it into the Kingdom, but fear not. The Holy Spirit will teach the believer to jettison that baggage. And if, per chance, the believer drags those bags to the finish line of this life, those bags will CERTAINLY be left behind as they enter eternity.

Jesus said He came to bring ABUNDANT life to people. Do not COMPROMISE that abundant life by dragging around unnecessary guilt and fear.

November 26

"James and John, the sons of Zebedee, came near to him, and said to him, "Teacher, we want you to do for us whatever we will ask."
Mark 10:35

✝ ✝ ✝

Sadly, I know there have been times in my life that although I may not have said those exact words, it was certainly what I meant. I wanted what I wanted and wanted God to do it for me. Making demands of God is NEVER a good idea. Although the brothers were not officially praying to God, they were asking the Messiah and the Son of God to grant their asking. In reality, it was a De facto prayer to God. If you choose to read further in the chapter, you will discover that their request sparked resentment among the other disciples. I suspect they, too, wanted those seats.

Most certainly God hears ALL our prayers. He wants us to express our wants and needs to Him, but just like Jesus says NO to the brothers, He often says the same to us. Why? Because we ask to elevate ourselves and not the principles of the Kingdom of God. The benchmark in that Kingdom is LOVE for God and OTHERS. The brothers were expressing love for themselves, they wanted to lead, not serve. This verse is a good primer on what not to pray. Is God able to field such prayers? Of course, but it is far better to pray for others than for selfish desires that reflect the principles of the Kingdom of the World.

Father, help my heart to desire to be a servant to both You and others.

November 27

"The LORD is my strength and song. He has become my salvation."
Psalms 118:14

† † †

If I were to ask one-hundred people what THEIR strength and salvation was, I suspect most would not say what the Psalmist does in this verse. They would likely point to some PERSONAL attribute or skill for strength, and some would not even recognize the need for salvation. Prior to being saved, I know that would have been my response. Even after being born again, we often maintain a high regard for OUR personal abilities and strength.

It is true that we have all been uniquely GIFTED with abilities and strengths, but the operative word is GIFTED. The Bible reveals that God has gifted us with personal abilities that are meant to enhance the body of Christ, the CHURCH. That should in no way demean individual efforts and accomplishments because many are worth celebrating, while all the while proclaiming our dependence on the Holy Spirit to optimize those GIFTS. I encourage the reader to assess their gifts and thank God for them.

Father, help me to use my GIFTS to further your Kingdom.

November 28

"and to know Christ's love which surpasses knowledge, that you may be filled with all the fullness of God."
Ephesians 3:19

☩ ☩ ☩

How can we KNOW something that surpasses KNOWLEDGE? It seems like the two should be synonymous. The best way for me to reconcile this question is by distinguishing the difference between knowing ABOUT someone and ACTUALLY knowing them. I can know all ABOUT a person through autobiographies, biographies, documentaries, and testimonies from friends and acquaintances, however, that is just information, and as valuable as information may be, it still lacks personal intimacy. It is intimacy that allows me to actually KNOW a person. It is intimacy that lends itself to understanding the personality, hopes, dreams, and nuances of another person.

That is my pursuit, to not only know ABOUT Jesus but to KNOW Him personally! How about you? Read the verse again and consider the possibility of being filled to the brim with God!

Father, help me to know Jesus personally and intimately.

November 29

"Now to him who is able to keep you from stumbling, and to present you faultless before the presence of his glory in great joy, to the only God our Savior, through Jesus Christ our Lord, be glory and majesty, dominion and power, both now and forever. Amen."
Jude 1:24, 25

✝ ✝ ✝

There are many benedictions in the Bible, but this is one of my favorites. Those are promises from God proclaimed by Jude through inspiration of the Holy Spirit, and I believe that they are made to ALL believers. But here is the thing; I do not deserve the blessings and I pray I never feel as if I do. Why? Because then I would negate the mystery and miracle of the Grace of God! I would have exchanged humility for pride, the Gospel for works.

Yes, we are all called to engage in good works, not for the purpose of salvation but rather as a response to being saved (Ephesians 2:10). We engage in good works because we ARE saved, not to be saved. Every born again person laid aside their good and bad works at the Cross of Jesus, choosing His sacrifice above all else. May God forbid that I should EVER see myself as deserving of His Grace. Like the Apostle Paul, may I see myself as the chief of sinners, undeserving of God's unconditional forgiveness. That is the reality of my life, a sinner saved by Grace who has been adopted His family. What a splendid reality!

Sing your favorite hymn today with vigor and sincerity.

November 30

"Therefore do not be foolish, but understand what the will of the Lord is."
Ephesians 5:17

How many times have we all wondered what was God's will for a particular situation? Perhaps a job, perhaps a relationship, a health issue, a temptation, a call to serve, and many more questions have caused us uncertainty. That pesky thing called "free will" can be both a blessing and a curse. When we choose wisely it is a blessing, choosing otherwise is a curse. Free will was never meant to encourage us to disregard the will of God. It was meant for us to CHOOSE His will over any other because in doing so we bring honor to God.

But how can we know God's will? The first place to start is to ask Him. Next, look to the Bible for a principle or example chronicled in His word. Asking other trusted believers for their opinion is an additional resource but understand that we will be held responsible for our choice, not others. Finally, sometimes, as difficult as it may be, it is necessary to wait for understanding. That waiting may very well be the perfect will of God. Remember, God has given us a plethora of resources, His Holy Spirit, prayer, the Bible, the Church, a sound mind, and brothers and sisters in Christ to bring clarity to any dilemma. The Apostle Paul, inspired by the Holy Spirit, tells his followers that he does not want them to be ignorant about an important issue. That continues to be God's will for our lives.

WELCOME TO DECEMBER

He said to them, "Do not be amazed. You seek Jesus, the Nazarene, who has been crucified. He has risen. He is not here. Look, the place where they put him."
Mark 16:6

December 1

"And there is salvation in no one else, for there is no other name under heaven that is given among people by which we must be saved."
Acts 4:12

† † †

These words were spoken by the Apostle Peter after he was filled with the Holy Spirit of God to the rulers of the people and elders of Israel. As you might imagine, his words were rejected. If YOU have ever spoken these words to others, I suspect you may have also experienced a similar reaction. When we speak these words, we are often labeled as intolerant, closed minded, bigoted, or worse because we reference exclusivity. But that is exactly what it is, an EXCLUSIVE way to salvation and that exclusivity was not created by man but rather by our Creator.

Although exclusive, it is NOT secret. It is hinged to the very public crucifixion and RESURRECTION of Jesus. It has been proclaimed by men and women for two millenniums to people groups all over the world. It has been proclaimed in print and on radio and television since their inception. It is now proclaimed via the internet. Any hour of any day the Gospel is being proclaimed somewhere. But why? Because God loves men and women and wants them to be saved from the coming judgement. Instead of celebrating having been given THE way back to their Creator, countless men and women continue to search for that way while some proclaim there is NO Creator. Sadly, this very hour people are entering eternity without a Savior and will suffer ETERNAL consequences. That, dear reader, is not the will of God. Let us do all we can to proclaim the message that Peter once preached. I know God is!

Today, tell someone, anyone, that God loves them.

December 2

"When a wicked man dies, hope perishes, and expectation of power comes to nothing."
Proverbs 11:7

✝ ✝ ✝

It is impossible to know what every wicked man is expecting at the time of his death. The same is true for the hopes of the unjust. Some think that their death is the end of their existence, that there is no afterlife. Some think their non-Christian belief system will be verified in death. Others think that their good deeds will certainly outweigh their bad ones and consequently God will allow them entrance into His home, heaven. Others may be thinking nothing at all.

Born again believers have a unified expectation and hope (confidence) that there is a heaven and hell, and everyone will spend eternity in one or the other, and furthermore, that THEY will spend eternity in heaven. Why? Because Jesus said so. His authority and claims were all proven true at His resurrection. It was God's most perfect testimony to the deity of Jesus and the truth of the words He spoke.

Father, I pray You will draw ALL to the Cross of Jesus. Leave no one behind.

December 3*

"In my Father's house are many rooms. If it weren't so, I would have told you; for I go to prepare a place for you. And if I go and prepare a place for you, I will come again, and will receive you to myself; that where I am, you may be there also."
John 14:2, 3

† † †

There's a saying that people often share, something along the lines of "I'm still here on Earth because I haven't finished the work God gave me to do." And while I am thinking there is some truth to that, these verses say that Jesus doesn't take us home until He is finished doing the work…. The work of preparing the place He has for us - and, according to Philippians, I think one could argue it is also the work He is doing in us (Phil 1:6). What is that work? At its most basic, it is to make us more like to Him – to purify us into His likeness. Paul told the church in Ephesus that he continually prays for them, asking specifically for God to grant them "that the God of our Lord Jesus Christ, the Father of glory, may give to you a spirit of wisdom and revelation in the knowledge of him (Eph 1:17).

So, when it comes to life here on Earth, we have an idea of what Jesus is doing – what He is preparing. He's working in us – He gave himself up for us – so that we could be presented back to Him "not having spot or wrinkle...instead, [we] but that it should be holy and without blemish"(Eph 5:27). At the same time, I wonder what He's doing in His Father's house – what is he getting ready?

Here's what I do know: it must be pretty amazing! He created this world in six days: he's been working on the next one for thousands of years.

December 4*

"Sanctify them in the truth. Your word is truth."
John 17:17

† † †

These words are straight from the mouth of Jesus, and they were spoken as a prayer for us. Jesus wants us to be holy – He prayed for us to be holy in his last hours before His crucifixion. But how does this come about? He proclaims it in the second half of the verse: We are made holy (sanctified) through The Word. If ever there was a Bible verse which reinforced the necessity of reading, studying, memorizing, and learning The Word, this is it. Jesus literally prayed in the garden, before His trial and death, that we would be taught The Word. In a very real sense, Jesus literally prayed that you and I would read the Bible. That word, according to Jesus, is truth – and it sanctifies us.

But what makes The Word so powerful? Well, if we see The Bible as simply words on a page, they have no power – no life – no transforming potential. But remember that Jesus himself is called both "the Word" (chapter 1) and "the truth" (chapter 14); the author of Hebrews tells us that God speaks to us "through His Son" (Heb 1:2). Want to draw close to God? Draw close to His Son Jesus. Want to know Jesus? Read The Word. All scripture points to Jesus (John 5:39).

The more we read and study the Word, the more we allow it to penetrate into our hearts and transform us, the more like Jesus we become.

December 5*

> "But even though we, or an angel from heaven, should proclaim to you a 'good news' other than that which we preached to you, let him be cursed. As we have said before, so I now say again: if anyone preaches to you a 'good news' other than that which you received, let him be cursed."
> Galatians 1:8, 9

† † †

Paul makes it clear that there is ONE gospel of Jesus, and any other "gospel", no matter how close, is still A WRONG (or false) gospel! Read that statement again and let it sink in.... One either believes (and preaches) the gospel of Jesus or they do not; there is no "close to the gospel." Anything – everything – other than the Jesus of the scriptures is not just "a little off" – it's completely wrong. We live in a world where we like to "give grace" when someone is "close enough," or they "try really hard." But when it comes to our relationship with God, there is no "you're close enough" and there is not "well, you had good intentions." There is only Jesus.

Paul identifies the gospel multiple times throughout his letter to the Galatians: that Jesus died for our sins and was raised from the dead, and when we believe that we are transformed and no longer under the curse of sin! This truly is Good News!

December 6*

These things I have written to you who believe in the name of the Son of God, that you may know that you have everlasting life.
1 John 5:13

Whereas in his gospel John wrote so that we could come to eternal life through Jesus, in this book he writes to assure His readers that they have that life. Apparently first century believers struggled as much with their salvation as people today do. I hear so many people talk about whether they know they are saved or not. John's readers apparently had the same concern – so much so that he wrote so that they could be confident in their salvation.

And in his letter, John told his readers how to be confident in their salvation. On one hand, it's looking at how we live our lives, for "he who says he remains in him ought himself also to walk just like he walked" (1 John 2:6). If you met someone who told you they were a Chicago Cubs follower (or an Atlanta Braves or New York Giants or LA Lakers... pick the team), how might you know? Wouldn't it show in how they lived? For example, if they couldn't tell you any of the players on the team, or they didn't know their current win/loss record, or they didn't even understand the game itself, you'd probably start to wonder whether they really followed the team. The same is true in our spiritual lives – Jesus told us we can know a tree by its fruit. When you look at your own life (when I look at mine), do I see evidence that I follow Jesus in how I talk and behave? When I was growing up my mom used to have a sign hanging in our kitchen which read, "If you were accused of being a Christian, would there be enough evidence to prove it?" Good question.

But even when we live like Jesus lived, at some point I think all of us will have feelings of doubt? It's in these moments we need to remember that we trust not in ourselves but in God, who is greater than all - including our doubt. We're going to make mistakes – we're human – and when we make those mistakes (when we sin), we will feel the conviction (guilt) of the Holy Spirit drawing us back to God. John addresses this struggle, and he tells us that "because if our heart condemns us, God is greater than our heart, and knows all things" (1 John 3:20). Our salvation is not dependent upon us – if it was it would not last because we are weak and feeble; thank God it depends on Him – the all-powerful, eternal God. If our faith is in ourselves, it is not authentic. But if it is in God, He will not fail.

December 7

"The entrance of your words gives light. It gives understanding to the simple."
Psalms 119:130

✝ ✝ ✝

Have you ever been in a dark space? It could be a room, basement, garage, hallway or any other space. The darker the space, the harder it was to navigate. You would feel your way along often bumping into unseen objects, but then suddenly a light was turned on and everything became visible. Even though you had previously occupied the space, you were UNAWARE of ALL the contents because of the darkness.

That scenario can easily be applied to our spiritual life. The Bible, God's word brings light to the spiritual darkness of our lives, and just like we become aware of physical things that are not seen in darkness, so too, we become aware of spiritual realities as the light of the Bible provides awareness. It is both refreshing and remarkable to SEE spiritual truth, the things that God holds in high regard.

Father, thank you for bringing light to my once spiritual darkness.

December 8*

"And this is love, that we should walk according to his commandments..."
2 John 1:6

☦ ☦ ☦

If "love means doing what God has commanded" then it is hard – nay, impossible - to do God's will if we don't know His commands. It has always struck me that to the early church, they could only learn God's commands (at least the NT ones) based off the direct teaching of the apostles or from letters such as these. But we have the written word in the scriptures themselves - it is to my shame if these early believers had a better understanding of God's commands when they didn't even have access to the word like I do.

I remember hearing a story from a missionary who served in the old USSR. He told me of a conversation he had had with someone in that country about some of the differences between living under Communism and living here in The States. When this missionary told the man that here in The States, "We don't have to wait hours and hours to get a loaf of bread or a gallon of milk, " the man replied "Wow! The Christians there must really know the word so well!" In his mind, he assumed that American Christians would spend their "free time" studying the Word (since that's what he would have done).

When I was in graduate school, I would spend hours and hours reading my assignments every week – literally hundreds of pages of articles and books – just to prepare for my next class. And more often than I'd like to admit – more often than I can even count – I would fall asleep at night having never read my Bible. Until one day the Spirit challenged me – He simply said, "Why is it, Tom, you can find time to read your studies for hours but to spend 15 minutes with me seems too much to ask?" He was pointing to a problem in my priorities – it wasn't lack of time (skill), it was lack of will. Something I confessed and repented of. Do I still struggle to make time? Yes, of course – I'm human after all – but its far less than it used to be.

December 9*

> "Do not be anxious about anything, but in everything, by prayer and petition with thanksgiving, let your requests be made known to God. And the peace of God, which surpasses all understanding, will guard your hearts and your minds in Christ Jesus."
> Philippians 4:6, 7

†††

It strikes me that "you will experience God's peace" comes after the word, "then." Standard grammar rules would suggest this means there is a conditional aspect of peace. But what is that condition? It's found in the preceding verse: do not worry but rather "Tell God what you need and thank him for all He has done." It's in the act of submitting our requests to God and thanking Him when we find His peace.

When we hold on to worry, we do not allow ourselves to experience His peace. To release worry means we must submit to His authority, leadership, and goodness. It means we trust Him in every situation, knowing He is working for our good and His glory. In short, we are focusing on Him and not us.

Only when we focus on Him in full dependence do we open ourselves to receiving the peace He offers. "Come to me all you who are heavy laden, " Jesus said, "and I will give you rest." Notice that the first word in that invitation is to "come".

December 10*

> "Everyone therefore who hears these words of mine, and does them, will be compared to a wise man, who built his house on a rock." ... "And everyone who hears these words of mine, and does not do them will be like a foolish man, who built his house on the sand."
> Matthew 7:24, 26

✝ ✝ ✝

When I was younger, I thought the difference between the wise and the foolish person in this passage was knowledge of God's Word. But it is not knowledge – it is action. Notice what Jesus says: both people – the wise and the foolish person – hears Jesus' words. They both have knowledge. The difference though is that the wise person "follows it" whereas the foolish "doesn't obey."

And while God is often compared to a "strong rock" throughout scripture, and Jesus is the "rock that makes men stumble," in this verse "the rock" is not Jesus – it is the person who does what Jesus commands. Maybe this is one reason why Peter is "the rock" – because he learned to do what Jesus commanded.

To know God's word is not enough, neither is only intellectual ascent to the belief in God – James says that "even the demons" do that, and their destiny is eternal damnation and punishment. Building on a rock and building on sand are two matters of choice, not matters of knowledge. "But wisdom is justified by her actions." (Matthew 11:19b).

Choose to be one who builds on a rock rather than one who builds on sand. It really is YOUR choice.

December 11

"Therefore, you should pray this way: 'Our Father in heaven, revered be your name."
Matthew 6:9

☩ ☩ ☩

There have been many excellent earthly fathers in the history of the world. However, the Greatest Of All Times father is the Heavenly Father. All others pale in comparison. To be sure, honor your earthly father, it is the fifth of the Ten Commandments, but remember what Jesus said was the greatest commandment; "You shall love God with all your heart, with all your soul, with all your mind, with all your strength."

Thank you, Heavenly Father, that you have given me the mercy and grace to become a child of yours. Thank you also for my earthly Father.

December 12

"Now these were more noble than those in Thessalonica, in that they received the word with all readiness of the mind, examining the Scriptures daily to see whether these things were so. Many

of them therefore believed; also of the prominent Greek women, and not a few men."
Acts 17:11, 12

✝✝✝

Luke, the author of Acts, points out multiple times how people "searched the scriptures, " and in the scriptures they found confirmation of Jesus. Yet, given the time frame of the stories he is sharing, "The Bible" as we know it did not exist. "The scriptures" here referred to the Old Testament.

This raises the challenge for me: when I read the Old Testament, how much do I look for Jesus? I have spoken with so many Christians over the years who do not read the Old Testament because, "it doesn't apply to me." Perhaps I have even thought that at times. Oftentimes I have viewed the Old Testament as a collection of great moral stories, or of prophecies that were eventually fulfilled so I did not need to read them. But notice what Luke points out: that the Old Testament scriptures are all about Jesus.

Several years ago, two things really changed my view on the Old Testament and helped me approach it with a different spirit. One was listening to a pastor preach through some Old Testament passages and he would begin his messages by saying, "This story we are going to study today is our story. This is our family – the family of God. Yes, they lived thousands of years ago before Jesus, but through Jesus we are members of the same family. And, so, this is our story."

The second was starting to ask the question when I read, "Where does Jesus show up in this passage? What does it teach me about Him?" He is there – sometimes I have to look a little harder than others – but Jesus is there. The early church saw it, and we can, too.

December 13

Jesus said to them, "Is not this because you are mistaken, not knowing the Scriptures, nor the power of God?"
Mark 12:24

† † †

Is not this also the reason why we have the potential of being mistaken about our understanding of God and how He relates to us? Think about it, those whom He is addressing are the learned men of Israel, spiritual leaders who crafted doctrine. They boasted of knowing the scriptures, yet Jesus says otherwise. Beyond that, Jesus says they did not understand the power of God.

Solomon once said that "there is nothing new under the sun" and how true that statement is to this very day. Individuals and Christian denominations are often far apart on their "knowing" the scriptures or the power of God. But why this great diversity? It is because we too often shape scripture around OUR priorities rather than shaping OUR priorities around scripture, hence the denominational and individual differences. The ONLY solution for this is a TOTAL surrender to the teaching of the Holy Spirit. This means stripping out prejudices, pre-conclusions, denominational doctrine, pride, emotions, what we WANT scripture to mean, and ANYTHING else that could skew the intended truth of scripture. This approach could be likened to seeing only black and white rather than shades of grey. Listen and learn from the Holy Spirit of God. He WANTS us to know the truth, the whole truth, and NOTHING but the truth.

Christmas is only a few weeks away. Consider the miraculous birth of the Savior today. It is never too early or too late to consider that glorious day!

Happy birthday to my son today.

December 14

"Your promises have been thoroughly tested, and your servant loves them."
Psalms 119:140

I contend that the word of God is pure. Pure! Now there is a word to contemplate. It can be difficult to find purity in the world today. The air we breathe is often polluted, the water we drink often contains chemicals, many foods are tainted with additives. Who among us can claim to have purity of thought and speech? Sadly, we have become so accustomed to impurity that we are no longer offended by it and even see it as an improvement on the original.

In this verse the Psalmist understands the purity of God's word, and if the concept of purity holds true, WE also can TRUST it for all things temporal and eternal. It is neither polluted nor tainted but is pure TRUTH. Let us be refreshed minute by minute, hour by hour, and day by day as we read and contemplate the purity of God's word, the Bible.

Father, help me to embrace the purity of your word daily.

December 15

"The thief only comes to steal, kill, and destroy. I came that they may have life, and may have it abundantly."
John 10:10

†††

"Yes, Virginia, there really is a Santa Claus." That was a reply written to a young girl reader by newspaper editor many years ago. It is famous. Unlike Santa Claus, however, Satan is real, and his goal is to keep us from believing God. He really does come to steal, kill, and destroy. He knows he cannot successfully attack God the Father, but he can attack one created in God's image, and so we have become ground zero for his attacks. They are often subtle, just enough truth to disguise the lies. Satan knows he will spend eternity in hell and wants to take as many with him as he possibly can. The good news is that we are safe if we are "in" Christ. Our souls have been locked in a God guarded lock box until our eventual transition to heaven. Knowing the truth as it is presented in the Bible is our best defense for falling prey to the lies of the enemy. Study the Bible as if your life depended on it because it does.

If you cannot dance today, watch others. Dancing always brings a smile.

December 16

> "Truly, truly, I tell you, he who hears my word, and believes him who sent me, has everlasting life, and does not come into judgment, but has passed out of death into life."
> John 5:24

†††

Have you ever doubted your salvation, wondered if you are genuinely saved? It can happen to even the most ardent believer. Guilt, Satan attacking the mind, people challenging the Gospel, a nagging sinful habit we wrestle with, depression, death of a friend or loved one, sickness, and so much more can cause a believer to question their personal salvation. Perhaps the doubt was just a fleeting moment or perhaps the doubt is chronic. Perhaps the very fact that you have doubted adds to the uncertainty.

What do you think Jesus would say if He suddenly appeared and stood before you? What if His only response was the above verse? What if you protested by listing one reason on top of another as justification for your doubt? Again, what if His ONLY response to your protestation was the above words? Would that be enough to calm your troubled mind? I suspect they would suffice.

So, here is the conclusion: Jesus is alive and although not physically on earth, He is present by virtue of the Holy Spirit. It is why the Church (every born again believer) is called the body of Christ. Jesus does not have to add to His words, they truly are sufficient. They convey certainty and assurance. Memorize this verse or read it frequently. Your doubts will vaporize!

Pray for someone you do not like. Forgive someone who has wronged you. In doing so you will be conforming to the image of Christ.

December 17

"Are you so foolish? Having begun in the Spirit, are you now completed in the flesh?"
Galatians 3:3

✝ ✝ ✝

Unfortunately, this potentially can be an attitude of a believer today. It happens when a person is saved by grace but over time begins to assimilate his or her own BEHAVIOR into the salvation equation. He or she loses the initial joy of receiving underserved forgiveness (GRACE) and consequently the preeminence of Jesus in their relationship with God. They become judgmental of the behavior of others and prideful of their own. Perhaps you have encountered this person, they seem to be in every Church. Perhaps we have even been this person.

Is a believer's behavior important? Of course it is, none should ever DISPUTE that. The Holy Spirit not only inspires personal righteousness but also directs the believer into a path of righteousness. The born again heart is now bent toward righteousness, not sin. However, righteous behavior is NOT the bridge to salvation. It is only FAITH in the sacrifice of Jesus that CONTINUALLY cleanses the child of God. That is the righteousness that saves. BELIEVING God is the faith that endeared Abraham to God, and it will do likewise for the believer. It was Abraham's faith that God reckoned to him as righteousness, not his works.

Happy Birthday to my son today!

December 18*

"that you no longer should live the rest of your time in the flesh for human desires, but for the will of God."
1 Peter 4:2

† † †

Anxiety – it is a difficult thing. Having spent my professional life working in schools (particularly middle schools), I am well acquainted with working with those who suffer from anxiety. A friend of mine has a daughter who for several years suffered greatly with anxiety - often becoming physically sick during anxiety attacks.

Only after much therapy and support was she able to learn to control her anxiety in a healthy way.

Surely Peter isn't talking here about that NEGATIVE version of anxiety - for just one chapter later Peter commends his readers to, "cast your anxieties on [Jesus], for he cares for you."

No, I think this use of "be anxious" is synonymous to "be excited." Peter here is telling us that we should be excited to do the will of God. Would you describe your feelings toward following God - of obeying His law, of acting as He commands us to act - as one of "excitement"? Would I describe myself that way? So often we (I?) see obedience to God as something to be endured, but Peter tells us here it is something for which we can be excited!

But how? Let's read the phrase in context: "Forasmuch then as Christ suffered in the flesh, arm yourselves also with the same mind; for he who has suffered in the flesh has ceased from sin; that you no longer should live the rest of your time in the flesh for human desires, but for the will of God"(1 Peter 4:1, 2). We become anxious (excited) to do God's will when we have the same attitude as Jesus.

And what was His attitude? While Peter describes it extensively in the previous chapters, let's look to Paul for a succinct version: "Have this in your attitude, which was also in Christ Jesus, who, existing in the form of God, did not consider equality with God a thing to be grasped, but emptied himself, taking the form of a servant, being made in the likeness of men. And being found in human form, he humbled himself, becoming obedient to death, yes, the death of the cross."(Phil 2:5-8)

Jesus was a humble, obedient servant. Are you? Am I?

December 19

"Then he answered and spoke to me, saying, "This is the word of the LORD to Zerubbabel, saying, 'Not by might, nor by power, but by my Spirit,' says the LORD of hosts."
Zechariah 4:6

☦ ☦ ☦

Zerubbabel, a Jewish man, was in charge of rebuilding the Temple in Jerusalem when the Jews were allowed to return to Israel after seventy years of captivity. It most assuredly seemed like a daunting task if you take the time to read the whole story. Besides the total dilapidation of the infrastructure, the people living in the area were openly hostile towards the returning Jews. If ever a person needed assurance from God, Zerubbabel was one.

Two things become apparent to me when I read the verse. FIRST, although Jewish MEN would rebuild the Temple under Zerubbabel's leadership, GOD would provide the resources, protection, and strength to accomplish the build. Yes, the builders needed to proceed with the THEIR work, but it was God's Spirit that would be the real resource. Their part was to DO what they were called to DO and trust God for success; so easy to say yet so hard to do. SECOND, this promise is for EVERY believer who is called by God to accomplish God's will in their lives. Perhaps His will for us may seem monumental or perhaps mundane. Nonetheless, God's call is personal to each of us. I encourage you to read the declaration of God again. It is for you, me, and EVERY born again believer.

December 20

"For in those days there will be oppression, such as there has not been the like from the beginning of the creation which God created until now, and never will be."
Mark 13:19

†††

Tribulation is a word that we seldom if ever use. It is used to describe grievous or severe trouble. Even so, Jesus in this verse warns any and all who will listen that there is tribulation on our horizon. Yes, the world has experienced extremely difficult times in the past including world wars, famine and plagues, however, according to Jesus past calamities will pale in comparison to what He references in this verse. Read the verse again. It scares me and should scare everyone else.

There is coming a time of judgement on mankind. It will be the final battle between good and evil and although good will prevail, the cost in human carnage is impossible to calculate. The Bible book of Revelation chapters six through nineteen paints an ominous picture of upcoming events. Jesus is warning the world but much of the world is not listening. Billions of people refuse to accept the teaching of Jesus while following false teachers and worshiping false gods, but there is a day coming when all will be held accountable for their rejection of Jesus, the Son of the living God.

Thankfully, God continues to offer a way to escape from the coming tribulation. That "way" is not complicated or secretive, it does not discriminate or restrict but is available to ALL people everywhere. The way is none other than Jesus the Christ, and when a person surrenders their life to Him, believes and trusts Him for forgiveness and salvation, they will be delivered from the coming tribulation.

Father, use every believer to show others the glory of Jesus.

December 21

> Now when Jesus was born in Bethlehem of Judea in the days of Herod the king, look, Magi from the east came to Jerusalem, saying, "Where is he who is born King of the Jews? For we saw his star in the east, and have come to worship him."
> Matthew 2:1, 2

✝ ✝ ✝

The purpose of the mysterious wise men has always been a curiosity to me. Of course, they were not mysterious or unknown to God. Still, who were these men and where specifically were they from? What were their names and why were they given revelation of a unique star while it went unnoticed by everyone else? What did they tell their people when they left their homeland or when they returned? Did they tell them anything? Did they somehow know the God of Abraham, Isaac, and Jacob? Much has been written about them, but it is mostly speculative, yet they are very much a part of the Christmas story.

In the end I guess none of those details really matter. If they did God would have provided them. What we do know is that God can and does reveal Himself and His will to whomever He chooses. That includes a family member, a neighbor, an enemy, friend, acquaintance, stranger, literally anyone. Let us keep that in mind the next time we are hesitant to share the Gospel with someone God has put in our path.

While the purpose of the wise men remains veiled, the need for us to share the Gospel remains obvious. Let us "Go tell it on the mountain, over the hills, and everywhere that Jesus Christ is born."

December 22

And Jesus said to them, "Render to Caesar the things that are Caesar's, and to God the things that are God's."
Mark 12:17

This was a response from Jesus when asked whether or not a Jew should pay taxes to the Roman government. It is in His answer that Jesus reveals two kingdoms, the kingdom of God and the kingdom of the world. It is both easy and natural for us to connect to the physical world. We do it through sight, sound, smell, touch, and hearing, but that is not what Jesus is referring to in this verse. He is referring to the GOVERNMENTS of this world and their various ideologies, all of which are crafted and directed by men and women. These governments provide human services, at least they are supposed to. Some are good at doing so while others fail miserably. Nonetheless, a citizen of a government has an obligation to that world authority. That obligation is what Jesus refers to as the "things" which belong to Caesar. Certainly, money minted by a government is but one of those things.

The "things" that belong to God are different. Why, because Jesus says they are. I could offer my opinion as to what those things are, but I will defer to the Holy Spirit to reveal to each reader the "things" of God. It is like being transported back to the very time when Jesus spoke these words. He did not elaborate then, and I will not elaborate now. Ask God to reveal these "things" to you and then give them to Him. It will be a beneficial spiritual exercise.

Hint: these "things" are revealed in the Bible.

December 23

> "For to us a child is born. To us a son is given; and the government will be on his shoulders. His name will be called Wonderful, Counselor, Mighty God, Everlasting Father, Prince of Peace."
> Isaiah 9:6

†††

It is good to remember the promise and revelation of Christmas. Jesus is that child that is referenced in this passage, and although hard to understand, He was ALL those things named in this verse. Give Jesus the best gift you can give, YOUR heart.

I am glad to be alive today. It is a new day that will bring opportunities to serve and honor Him. There are lots of people who struggle during the Christmas season for so many different reasons. Let us share the love of God with them to ease their pain.

Wishing every reader a blessed Christmas celebration.

December 24

Last night I sat quietly contemplating the incarnation. Like the crucifixion, the incarnation has greater implications than I can fully fathom, ETERNAL implications. Our Creator living among us in the same form He fashioned us; occupying the Throne in heaven and the body of an earthly baby simultaneously; being omnipotent and helpless simultaneously? It all breaks my brain! Words are not enough to explain this one-of-a-kind miracle. Perhaps that is why there were angels, a virgin girl giving birth, a unique star in the sky, wise men traveling from who knows where, dozens of prophetic messages, some hundreds of years prior to the event itself. What I do know for certain is that if it had never happened, I would still be separated from my Creator because of sin, and for that I am forever grateful. Do YOU feel the same?

December 25

"And she gave birth to her firstborn son, and wrapped him with pieces of cloth, and placed him in a feeding trough, because there was no guest room available for them."
Luke 2:7

It sounds like a dilemma for Joseph and Mary, and so it was. Mary giving birth to God's Son in a stable, meanwhile nearby, people are sleeping secure in a local inn while worldly kings and princes slept in palaces all over the world. At that very moment babies were being born worldwide in secure, familiar, and comfortable environments, often surrounded by family and friends. What was God thinking? Certainly not about even the mundane, leave alone grandeur. This humble beginning would end with God's Son crucified on a Roman cross. This is an exceptional but puzzling beginning and end to the life story of the King of Kings.

Fortunately, God tells us that His WAYS are not our ways. That is painfully clear in the story of Jesus on planet earth. There is never any record of Him owning anything except His clothes, yet EVERYTHING belonged to Him. He NEVER sinned against God, yet He was crucified as a sinner. He NEVER lied, yet He was condemned by Jewish authorities as being a liar, claiming to be the

Son of God. If ever the dichotomy of God and man was unabashedly demonstrated, it was in the earthly life of Jesus.

Today we celebrate His birth and celebrate we should. The Lamb of God who takes away the sin of the world has been born. Rejoice and worship the King. MERRY CHRISTMAS, DEAR READER!

December 26

"Heaven and earth will pass away, but my words will not pass away."
Mark 13:31

† † †

It is difficult to imagine that something we have in our possession today will last FOREVER. In fact, according to this verse it will even out last heaven and earth which, according to this verse, WILL one day pass away. If you are wondering what this could be, look now at your Bible. Yes, the actual BOOK may eventually pass away but the WORDS in the book are eternal, and if something we have with us today is eternal, that something must be exceedingly important.

So here is a question that needs answering. What do you and I consider the MOST important thing in our lives? Now ask what do we think God considers the most important thing in our lives? Do the two answers coincide? If not, would we be able to justify the difference to God?

Think about this. If God did not exist, neither would we, in fact, NOTHING would exist. BUT He does exist and so do we. However, WITHOUT the words recorded in the Bible, how would we know anything definitive about our Creator? How would we know why we need a Savior or who is that needed Savior? Perhaps this would be a good time to think again about what the most important thing in our lives is.

The gifts have all been opened and the parties are now just a memory. In conclusion, it was never about the gifts or the parties. It was and continues to be about the birth of a Savior.

December 27

"Direct me in the path of your commandments, for I delight in them."
Psalms 119:35

Elsewhere in the Bible the Psalmist says that he is led into the PATH of righteousness. Jesus talks about entering through a narrow gate that leads to life. Solomon writes about the various TIMES that we experience in our lives. The point is that our earthly life is a JOURNEY that starts at birth and ends at physical death. But where are we going on that journey? Do we just live day to day knowing that someday our life will end, much like treading water, staying afloat but never going anywhere? Does our journey in this life have a destination? Are we meant to pass over some invisible bridge and enter eternity? And then what?

Jesus told a man being crucified next to Him that the man would be in Paradise that very day. Obviously, this would occur AFTER his physical death. Jesus also warns of an AWFUL place where some people will spend eternity. Yes, we are all on a journey that will lead to one or the other. Think about it: did you ever decide to go on a trip without a destination in mind? But that is exactly what billions of people are doing this very moment. They are living life without ever considering where their journey in this life will culminate.

We can tell them about eternity and how to enter heaven by sharing the Gospel with them. Some will listen and believe the Gospel while others will reject it. Rejoice with those who accept and pray for those who reject; it is what Jesus would do.

December 28

Pilate said to him, "What is truth?"
John 18:38

✝ ✝ ✝

Unfortunately, TRUTH can be elusive because it has been skewed by men and women fashioning THE truth into what they WANT it to be - THEIR truth. We see it often, heck, we may even be guilty of doing so ourselves. Little "white" lies, situational truth, personal truth, half-truths, cultural truth, enlightened truth, and more are all an assault on truth. Is it any wonder why Pilate was skeptical when he uttered the words in today's verse? Pilate's question could be interpreted as him saying "Jesus, there is NO truth."

From the very beginning, ever since Eve questioned God's warning to Adam in regard to eating the fruit of the Tree of the Knowledge of Good and Evil, truth has been assailed. In an effort to maintain a clear path to knowing the truth, God has given us the Bible. Nothing else compares to it but how many of us devote the energy and concentration to it as we do to other things in our lives? What would the world, my world, look like if I spent as much time in the Bible as I do watching television, reading a book, or spending time on my computer?

Had Pilate been with Jesus the previous night he would have heard Jesus declare that "I am the way, the TRUTH, and the life ..." The good news for us is that we can be with Jesus, THE TRUTH, every time we read His Words in the Bible. Enjoy your time with Him today!

December 29

Do not seek revenge yourselves, beloved, but leave room for the wrath. For it is written, "Vengeance belongs to me; I will repay, says the Lord."
Romans 12:19

The fact that revenge is such a natural response is why God cautions us to avoid it. It seems that "getting even" is part of sinful man's spiritual DNA. Wars between countries have been started with the goal of getting even, and on a smaller scale people have killed one another for this same reason. Murder is not the only manifestation of revenge. Character assassination, gossip, hindrance of advancement, monetary punishment, withholding favor, and more are weapons of revenge. Songs and books have been written about it as well as countless movies made both glorifying and vilifying it. At some point, ALL of us have either crafted or executed a revenge plan and it is all hinged to PRIDE.

Revenge has NO place in the Kingdom of God and that Kingdom is where every born again believer has been catapulted into citizenship. Do not misunderstand, justice, including punishment, will be accomplished, but not by us. Read the verse again, especially the last part. The Lord promises to avenge injustice, but on His time, not ours. Sadly, there will most likely be another occasion when WE will be tempted to avenge an offense against us, but God wants us to leave it alone, turn the other cheek and forgive our offender. This is exactly what God did for each of us. Revenge is easy but according to this verse it is NOT for the believer.

Ask the Holy Spirit to reveal to you any bitterness or unforgiveness you may have against another person. If any are found, exercise forgiveness.

December 30

"As for you, you meant evil against me, but God turned it into good in order to bring about this present result, to save the lives of many people."
Genesis 50:20

The story of Joseph, a son of Jacob, is an amazing story of jealousy, treachery, hardship, faithfulness, patience, and grace. It can be found in Genesis chapters 37 through 50. The verse above is Joseph speaking to his brothers about their betrayal. He references his brothers selling him to slave traders and telling his father that he was killed by a wild animal. It is both an ugly yet beautiful story about the life of Joseph and the sovereignty of God.

Perhaps we can all relate to this story. As we look back at our lives, perhaps we see what was once a dilemma or even a crisis that eventually morphed into a blessing. Perhaps it was a relationship, a career, a child, a friend, a health issue or something else that changed the trajectory of our lives. Perhaps it was God saying NO to a heartfelt prayer or the closing of a "door" we desperately wanted to go through. It is difficult to understand but the reality is that God really does know the future and can keep us from the pitfalls that await us. Beyond that, He has a master plan, and He may use US to accomplish a tiny or large portion of that plan. We are, after all, His servants.

Father, when I am disappointed, when I struggle to see good in my life, remind me that I am not only your servant but also your child.

December 31

"Therefore if anyone is in Christ, he is a new creation. The old things have passed away. Look, new things have come."
II Corinthians 5:17

As we wave goodbye to this year and say hello to the next, we often consider how we might do things differently to improve our lives. There is probably not a person alive that at some point did not want a do-over of a bad decision, a bad relationship, or a bad choice of whatever. If we could only have a second chance, we are sure we would do better. That may or may not be true, but we cling to that thought. The problem is that unless we change how we prioritize our lives and what we believe, we are destined to repeat our misfires over and over again.

God promises us something infinitely better than a second chance. He promises us a brand-new life! A life that prioritizes others before ourselves, a life that is fulfilled by a personal and intimate relationship with our Creator, a life that is eternal, and a life that has unexplained peace even in the midst of chaos or tragedy, a quiet joy even in sorrow. How can we get this brand-new life? Notice the verse. "In Christ" is how, but how do we get that status? It is a choice we make to surrender our lives to our Creator and believe that He has made provision for a relationship through the sacrifice of His Son, Jesus. It is trusting in the truths for life that God has revealed in the Bible.

If you are tired of second chances, ask the One who created you to give you a brand-new life. It will be like walking from a dark room into the light of day.

Wishing each reader a blessed New Year! May you have a keen awareness of His presence.

THE END

ABOUT THE AUTHOR

An autobiography, hmmm, where does one begin to tell the story of their life? I suspect that is why biographies are much more interesting than autobiographies because most people just do not like to talk about themselves. Nonetheless, I do want you to get to know me; so here we go...

Born in the mid-forties in Chicago and raised primarily in a blue-collar suburb, I am most assuredly a Midwesterner in my heart. There is something about the Midwest and particularly the upper Midwest and the Great Lakes that is both romantic and gritty to me. Although most have disappeared, I have remembrance of an abundance of large and small factories, steel mills, tool and die shops, mom and pop stores, and rough and tumble neighborhood baseball and football games. I remember men going to work with lunch boxes and moms being home when children came home from school. Cub and Boy Scouts, camping, fishing, canoeing, and summer camps were my early passions. School? I never liked school and never pretended to either.

What does my life resume look like? Listed in no particular order, although some are vitally more important than others, my experiences include the following: Husband, father, grandfather, great-grandfather, brother, son, best and worst friend, non-Christian, Christian, lost, saved, loved by some, hated by others, enlisted soldier, Viet Nam veteran, truck driver, student, day laborer, poodle groomer, factory worker, entrepreneur, business owner, salesman, boss, employee, employer, migrant farm worker (one day only), tornado survivor, prison and jail chaplain, author, good and bad neighbor, vagabond, corporate President and officer, handyman, hospital patient, political activist, campaign manager, dog lover and owner, Chicago Cubs and Bears fan, lover, hater, and everything in between. I'm sure there is more, so much more but by now you realize I am just like you. Perhaps your life resume is not as long as mine but that is only because I have probably lived longer than you. In the end, it will most likely look similar to mine.

Why have I written the Tree book series, short stories, and a devotional? I write because I love to, words are precious to me. When I look at a dictionary I see the greatest book ever written by man. All the words are there and all any one of us has to do is put them together in the right order. That is why I write. I keep searching for the right order.

ENOCH

RECOGNIZING THE EXTRAORDINARY

The following story is taken from the historical archives of Man that have been compiled by the tree community since the beginning of time. Although I was not an eyewitness to this encounter, those that were eyewitnesses were specific in their chronicling of the event.

In every generation of every society there are men and women who shape the direction and destiny of that generation. Sometimes they stand alone while at other times they work in concert, and although their influence may move a generation against the will of their Creator, there has always been a remnant of those whose hearts reflect the heart and will of the One who created them. Identifying these individuals is a matter of comparing their behavior in regard to good and evil. That comparison must be based on certainty because any uncertainty, as it relates to truth, ushers in unbelief and hostility against what is true, and frequently errors on the side of evil. I am keenly aware of this principle because my earliest ancestor is the Tree of the Knowledge of Good and Evil, a name and distinction given to him by the Creator of all things. The knowledge my ancestor was gifted with is resident in his posterity so although I am now separated by time and space, I have the identical knowledge and insight he possessed in discerning good from evil. That knowledge is fact based, like the certainty that the sun will be on the morning horizon whether hidden from view by clouds or unhindered in its appearance. It is a certainty that is without emotion, rooted in what my forefather saw and heard in the Paradise, and it is undeniable. He was a witness to it all.

The tree community is without emotion but not without understanding. Emotions are unique gifts given to humans, and to a lesser degree, the animal kingdom. The emotions of the animal kingdom, however, are most likened to instincts, without reason or control and are directed toward self-preservation and procreation, not necessarily unique attributes provided by a Creator to complete and enhance the human experience. It is most surely Man alone who stands on the highest pedestal of creation, all else being created for him and her.

Recognizing an individual destined to profoundly influence a generation is decidedly more complicated than behavior alone, however. The real measure is the authenticity of the intentions of one's heart; it is the motivation of a heart pursuing good for a worthy outcome that determines holiness and kinship with the Holy Creator of this world. Although manifested in the body, it is most assuredly birthed and nourished in the soul. It is light overcoming darkness that is stubbornly resident in the now corrupted human heart, and although the tree community lacks a window to the human soul, we are not without insight. Our continual chronicling of human behavior since the beginning of time provides us with reliable historical markers that alert us to pay particular attention to individuals that demonstrate the potential for extraordinary excellence in following the earliest intentions of their Creator.

In the history of Man, one of the earliest contenders for distinction is a man named Enoch. After Adam and Eve were expelled from the Garden of Eden because of disobedience, the world became a complicated and dangerous place. Gone were the days of bliss and peace that my original ancestor detailed in the historical record. As I observe the complexity of mankind now, it is difficult for me to imagine the reported simplicity and purity of the now sequestered Paradise. What I observe daily are people engaged in lives that rarely resemble purity and tranquility, and certainly not simplicity. There is war within the human and animal community. Animals feed upon one another, as do some in the bird community, and it is often a matter of survival for the weakest species. Tragically, that is frequently true in the human community as well. Brute strength is too often the tool of control of one over another, the weaker being subject to the whims and demands of the more powerful. After the rebellion of Adam, universal harmony is now only a concept and not a reality in the present world.

It is most certainly the human community that is the most perplexing to trees. After the expulsion of the first couple from the Paradise, the appearance of the Creator became less and less frequent. Prior to the tragic fall of Man, the Creator would appear daily in the Paradise to spend time with His most precious creation, Adam. My ancestor once noted that the Creator and Adam were of a common heart and it was obvious to him that they both genuinely delighted in their daily visitations. There were no barriers between the two. He reported that they would spend hours walking and discussing issues that were too lofty for the rest of creation, and it was not until the creation of Eve that there was any diversion of Adam's attention. Even so, at His appearance, both Adam and Eve would focus exclusively on their Creator. It was only after an uninvited stranger entered the Paradise that Eve's attention began to divide.

The Creator, at times, did appear to Cain and Abel, as well as some of the other earliest descendants of Adam and Eve, but mostly it is now a human representing and modeling the Creator's will for life that is substituting for His appearance. It is in this modeling that tension and contention occur within the human community. Those that have little or no regard for their Creator are openly antagonistic toward those who seek to follow Him, and that antagonism often leads to hostility. Those who have denied the authority of the Creator have claimed that same authority for themselves. They have reasoned that their strength and craftiness is sufficient to place others under their authority. Licentiousness passes from one generation to another and as the population of the world grows, so does living without any perceived accountability to a Creator. Lust after the flesh, greed, self-promotion, murder, dishonesty, and a host of other distasteful traits have been introduced and embraced by many in the human community. Nevertheless, as the world appears to fall deeper and deeper into lawlessness there are men and women who choose to follow the One who created everything, including humans. The following is the story of one such individual.

Enoch first came to our attention when the Creator surprisingly appeared and spent time with him. The Creator's appearance was, by this time, a rare phenomenon and prompted the tree community to pay special attention to this man. Enoch came from good stock. We traced his lineage back to a favored son of Adam named Seth. Seth had a heart for the Creator and listened well to the teachings of Adam in regard to life choices between good and evil. Thousands of years passed after Seth died but his posterity demonstrated similar devotion to good versus evil. When Enoch was sixty-five years of age he fathered a son named Methuselah. It was after the birth of Methuselah that the Creator first appeared to Enoch. It happened as Enoch sat on a grassy hill not far from his family's settlement. He sat cross-legged peering over the lush valley where his family farmed both grain and livestock. He often came to that place seeking solitude and to enjoy the stillness at the end of the day. While there, he spoke quietly to the world around him. He told his friends and family that it was his time to talk with his God, and it was on one such occasion that a stranger suddenly appeared before him.

"Hello, stranger. I did not see you come up the hillside nor did I hear your footsteps. Forgive me; I was deep in thought. If you have come in peace you are most welcome to stay with us as long as necessary. Do you have a name?" asked Enoch, as he considered the man standing before him.

"What were those deep thoughts you were having, Enoch?" replied the stranger, his eyebrows lifted high. At the mention of his name, Enoch appeared startled. There was an extended pause in the conversation as Enoch looked intently and suspiciously at the stranger. There was a puzzled look on his face.

"Why do I have the feeling you already know the answer to that question, and how is it that you know my name? I know all those living in this valley and the surrounding area and you are not from here. Furthermore, I am not familiar with the colors of your robes. What tribe do you come from? You do not resemble any particular family living nearby and yet you somehow resemble them all. Have we made acquaintance before? Who are you, stranger?" asked Enoch with a tone of authority in his voice.

"I am only here for a short time, Enoch, so please tell me what were you thinking about? What were those deep thoughts?" said the stranger again as he moved closer to Enoch. There was a friendly and disarming smile on his face that appeared to put Enoch at ease.

"If you must know, I was thinking about some of the mysteries of life. I was wondering where the sun goes when, even now, it is moving toward the horizon and will soon disappear. What happens to it and how does it know when to return? I was thinking about the breeze that cools my face; where has it come from and where it is going? I was wondering how many other men and women it touched today and what were the circumstances in their lives. I was considering how far it is to the moon and stars that will soon be visible and I was also wondering how they hang in the sky with no support, " replied Enoch in a contemplative voice. "Do you know the answers to these questions, stranger?" finishes Enoch with a good-hearted chuckle.

"Those are hard questions, Enoch. Why do you ask them? Do you suppose someone has the answers to such questions? Who would have understanding about such things as you are considering? Is there such a man?" asked the stranger. He was now sitting next to Enoch, and both were looking toward the valley. The air was calm as hues of red appeared on the horizon in the direction of the setting sun. There was a long pause as Enoch considered his answer.

"If you think those are hard questions, I have many more equally difficult, but these are very private thoughts, perhaps not meant to be answered; certainly not today. If there is such a man, one that has the answers, I do not know of him. It will be dark soon and I must go, stranger. Would you like to come with me? It is obvious that you have no provisions. Do you need shelter and food for this night?" inquired Enoch.

"No. I have no need of anything. Tell me, Enoch, how is Methuselah, your son?" replied the stranger. The mention of Methuselah again startled Enoch and he quickly stood, as did the stranger. They were now looking directly at one another and Enoch again appeared puzzled as he once again considered the stranger.

"Should I fear you?" eventually asked Enoch in a quiet voice. The question does not fit his demeanor, however. Neither his voice nor his countenance indicates fear.

"No, I mean you no harm," replied the stranger in an equally quiet voice, shaking his head slightly from side to side.

"Will I see you again?" asked Enoch, his brow now furrowed. There was hope in his voice.

"Yes. You will see me again," answered the stranger. There was a small smile on his face as he turned and walked the opposite direction from Enoch's home. Enoch watched as the stranger disappeared over the hillside and then turned and began his walk home. "Who was that man?" he whispered to himself.

It was a restless night for Enoch. He told his wife about his brief encounter with the stranger but she had no insight to offer as to his identity. She awoke in the middle of the night to find her husband outside the home staring into the night sky.

"Are you still troubled by the stranger you met today? Tell me more about him, my husband. Tell me again what he looked like?" said his wife after joining him. She brought two wraps with her, one for her and another for her husband. It was a clear, crisp night with a full moon accompanied by brightly shining stars.

"No, it is not trouble that I feel but my soul is restless because of him, and it is not just that he knew my name, but there was something about the way he looked at me. It was as if he knew me better than you know me or even better than I know myself. When I asked him if I should fear him, I somehow already knew the answer because I was at peace while in his presence. As for his appearance, it was not like other men. When I looked into his eyes it was as if I was looking into the deepest recesses of my own heart. There was an inexplicable softness about his physical appearance and perhaps it is just my imagination, but he looked to have a subtle glow surrounding him. This was no ordinary man, dear wife, and strangely enough, I both fear and hope I will never see him again," explained Enoch while massaging his temples with both hands.

"Enoch, you are different from the other men in the valley. There is none like you who yearn for good will and righteousness that you say your God desires and even demands. I have seen you weep at the injustice and distress of this life, and I have seen you reach out to men and women who are bent on mischief, calling them to be accountable to your God. I have seen you help the widow in need and I have heard you praying to your unseen God. Perhaps he has answered you, husband. Perhaps he has sent an emissary from where he lives to encourage you. I do not know if you will ever see this stranger again, but oddly, I suspect you are somehow being watched by him and others like him," said Enoch's wife. There is kindness and compassion in her voice.

"It is hard to explain but there has always been a burning within me. It is like a flame that, at times, flickers and other times explodes in fury. I feel like I do not belong here, like I am out of place in this world. Do you remember when we travelled to the river and how the people who lived there were so different from us? Do you remember how uncomfortable you were, how you were anxious to leave that place? Well, that is how I feel all the time. Yes, it is true that I weep for what my eyes see, the violence, the lustful living, the many people who are trodden down by wicked men and women. But my sorrow is equally great for those who give no regard to the One who created them. I realize that no matter how desperately I try; I cannot right the wrongs. There are few who seek after the things that will please my God. Instead, most mock the concept of a Creator and clamor after the things that please them. This world is becoming more reckless and I do not see a solution for its ills. Fear grows within me that my God will not allow this to go on forever and my fear is for mankind. I am sorry for this kind of talk. I do not want to frighten you. Come, let us return to bed for it will soon be dawn, " replied Enoch. Without further discussion the two return to their bedchamber. Enoch was right; a new day in the history of Man was about to begin.

Several days passed after Enoch's encounter with the mysterious stranger. It was on the third day after that encounter that the stranger again appeared to Enoch. Just like before, Enoch was perched on the highest hill overlooking the valley. This time the stranger came into view while walking toward Enoch. A broad smile appeared on Enoch's face as he stands and waves to the stranger. He then runs toward the stranger and it is not long before he is standing in front of him.

"I have been thinking about you since we first met and was hoping that I would see you again. I am not sure why, but I feel you have the answers to the questions that have haunted me ever since I came of age. This may sound curious to you but I feel I somehow know you and you somehow know me, and I am not referring to our last meeting; I feel as if I have always known you. You must tell me your name, " blurted out Enoch. His words were overflowing with anticipation.

"Patience, Enoch, patience. We have all the time we need for answers to your questions. You are correct about knowing me and about me knowing you. It is true but not in a way you can completely understand. I knew you when you were but a seed in your father Jared and when he was a seed in Mahalalel, his father. In truth, I knew you before the world in which you now live was created, and yes, you have known me since you came of age. I have been revealing myself to your spirit and your spirit has been revealing that to your heart. Because your understanding is restricted by time and space, I know you find this revelation puzzling, but do not let that restriction keep you from believing what I say to you is truth. Do you believe me, Enoch?" said the stranger in a calm voice. "Do you believe that what I say is truth?" He and Enoch were locked in a stare. There was a long pause as Enoch continued to focus on the eyes of the stranger.

"Yes, I do believe you, but there is something I must ask you. Are you, " there is an extremely long pause that occurs before Enoch finishes his question, "are you the Creator?" asked Enoch quietly with his head now bowed. He closed his eyes, held his breath, and bit his lower lip while awaiting an answer from the stranger. Without hesitation, the stranger replied.

"I am." At that confirmation Enoch prostrated himself before the stranger. "Enoch, stand up and come close but do not touch me. Do not be afraid to do as I ask. Yes, I am the Creator but I am cloaked in a form that protects you from fully seeing my glory. Without that protection you would surely die. I know your thoughts and I know the intentions of your heart, there is nothing hidden from me. I want you to know that you are unique to this generation, " continued the Creator. At these words, Enoch rose and stood before his God.

"My heart grieves for the people of this world," lamented Enoch while shaking his head from side to side. "My ancestors warned of the consequences that would come upon mankind if they rejected your authority. The people have not only done this but they have rejected your very existence. In their imagination, they have claimed to be their own gods, and some have even created objects to worship from the common elements of this world. I fear that there is reprisal coming from you that is inevitable. My heart also grieves for you. You deserve recognition, respect, and obedience from the men and women of this world. You are our Creator and you deserve our love and devotion, but because we fail to do so, I fear the consequences of our actions," said Enoch. His voice was soft but it did not waiver.

"You are right in your assumption; there is great catastrophe that lies ahead for mankind. What you do not understand, what you cannot understand at this moment is that the coming catastrophe will save mankind. There is an evil coming to this world that you cannot possibly comprehend, Enoch. It will seek to compromise the very fabric of Man, but I will rescue Adam's posterity from this evil. It is a certainty but neither you, your wife, nor your son Methuselah will experience this coming catastrophe," said the Creator.

"Why have you revealed yourself to me? Why me?" inquired Enoch. Tears were now streaming down his face.

"I have come to you because it is my desire to walk with you. Enoch, listen very carefully to what I am about to say. I created Adam in my image for a particular reason. It is Adam and his entire posterity that have authority to fellowship with me. Just like Methuselah came from your seed, likewise, Adam came from me. He is distinct in all of creation in that regard and because every person in the world comes from Adam's seed, every person is connected to me and has the potential for fellowship, but precious few have the desire to do so. None are excluded except by their own choice. In the beginning I visited Adam daily and later included Eve in those visitations. When they both chose to disobey me, the intimacy we enjoyed was severed. I was no longer the single most important aspect of their lives. Self-serving interests had corrupted their spirits and self-serving interests are contrary to my character. There will come a day when the intimacy will be restored, but for now a disconnect prevails. Would you like to walk these hills with me, Enoch? Would you like to spend time with me? We will talk about the secrets of life that you so often consider, and I will answer your questions about such matters, and at the conclusion of our walk, you will come with me, " replied the Creator.

"Where will we go? You are not a man of this world, " asked Enoch.

"Do you trust me, Enoch?" replied the Creator.

"Yes, " said Enoch, without hesitation. At that reply, the two began their walk. Several hours passed as the Creator and Enoch strolled the lush green hillsides and just as the Creator promised, He answered all Enoch's questions. Beyond that, Enoch was given the ability to understand that which the Creator shared with him. As the sun slowly disappeared below the horizon the Creator's prediction about Enoch was realized; both He and Enoch disappeared and Enoch no longer was a resident of this world.

His disappearance ushered in the end of the story of one of the earliest notables in the chronicles of Man. There was never another exactly like him. Although not privy to the conversations between the Creator and Enoch, his family that remained in that valley spoke of righteous Enoch and his mysterious disappearance for generations to come. The tree community has had many discussions as to what the Creator meant when He referred to a catastrophe that would come upon mankind. Many years later we experienced the reality of that prediction along with a man named Noah and his family. The event predicted by the Creator was indeed catastrophic, more catastrophic than Enoch could have possibly imagined.

THE END

www.ingramcontent.com/pod-product-compliance
Lightning Source LLC
LaVergne TN
LVHW031605060526
838201LV00063B/4730